ANGELICA

ANGELICA

For Love and Country in a Time of Revolution

MOLLY BEER

W. W. NORTON & COMPANY

Independent Publishers Since 1923

For information about permission to reproduce selections from this book, write to
Permissions, W. W. Norton & Company, Inc., 500 Fifth Avenue, New York, NY 10110

For information about special discounts for bulk purchases, please contact
W. W. Norton Special Sales at specialsales@wwnorton.com or 800-233-4830

Manufacturing by Lake Book Manufacturing
Book design by Chris Welch
Production manager: Lauren Abbate

ISBN 978-1-324-05021-6

W. W. Norton & Company, Inc.
500 Fifth Avenue, New York, NY 10110
www.wwnorton.com

W. W. Norton & Company Ltd.
15 Carlisle Street, London W1D 3BS

1 2 3 4 5 6 7 8 9 0

For my sister

CONTENTS

AUTHOR'S NOTE

I grew up in Angelica, New York, a village with a population of 1,300 people in northernmost Appalachia. As a little girl, I rode the Angelica Central School bus past Angelica Schuyler Church's beautiful Villa Belvidere to recite the Pledge of Allegiance and learn what "We the People" meant. What I already knew, from local lore, was that Angelica Church was a leading member of the generation that fought the War for Independence and carried out the American Revolution, through the years of forming a constitutional government and a more-or-less-united democratic republic. I was always disappointed that my social studies textbooks neglected to mention her.

The American historian Mary Ritter Beard once wrote that "Women have been a force in making all the history that has been made." Obvious as this is to a child—children's worlds are ruled by women—written history still obfuscates women's presence and involvement. Women's work and words have been unseen or unheard or unvalued, appropriated by or attributed to others, or excised from the telling as unimportant or superfluous. Women perpetrate this erasure themselves. Traditional women's work is best when it is invisible—sewing all those invisible stitches, hiding the sweat, striving for that illusion of "effortlessness." The skirt is designed to conceal the work of walking.

To be clear, I did not write this book to celebrate Angelica Church, or to judge her, but to see her. In seeing her, I saw other women, too, and

I saw the men I'd seen before more clearly—less like two-dimensional shadow puppets and more like the messy, anxious, self-important, needy humans we all are. The American Revolution was and continues to be a movement carried out by the many—not marching in lockstep under a general (if that's ever really true either), but raucous and dynamic, full of pushing and pulling and cajoling and arguing and trusting that all that discord, friction, and difference will generate still more liberty and justice for all.

The nation's first figureheads whose faces jangle in our pockets represent armies, parties, and electorates: They are idealized models, but not the mold. Likewise, Angelica was an iconic woman of her revolutionary generation, which she mirrored and manifested. Certainly, she was not like all women, but, like all women, all people, she was multifaceted, fallible, and often inscrutable, likely even to herself. In her own lifetime, living in so many places, Angelica meant different things to different people, and the roles she played shifted with the seasons of her life. Observing her life, her words and actions, through the prism of a quarter millennium of ideas and events further colors and shades her significance. And this book is only one telling of that life, filtered through me, another messy, anxious human existing in a particular historical moment, and now through you, whoever and wherever you are.

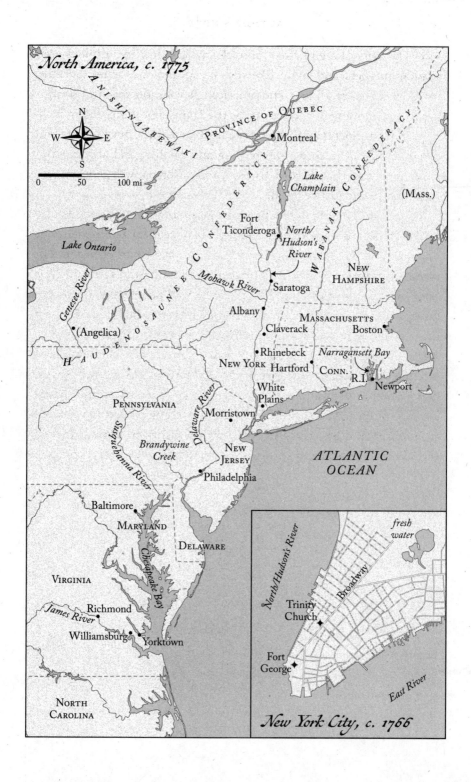

North America, c. 1775

ANISHINAABEWAKI

PROVINCE OF QUEBEC

Montreal

N
W E
S

0   50   100 mi

Lake Ontario

Genesee River

HAUDENOSAUNEE CONFEDERACY

(Angelica)

Mohawk River

Lake Champlain

WABANAKI CONFEDERACY

Fort Ticonderoga

North/Hudson's River

Saratoga

NEW HAMPSHIRE

(MASS.)

Albany

MASSACHUSETTS

Claverack

Boston

Rhinebeck

Narragansett Bay

NEW YORK

Hartford

CONN.

R.I.

Newport

White Plains

PENNSYLVANIA

Delaware River

Morristown

ATLANTIC OCEAN

Susquehanna River

Brandywine Creek

NEW JERSEY

Philadelphia

Baltimore

MARYLAND

DELAWARE

VIRGINIA

Chesapeake Bay

James River

Richmond

Williamsburg

Yorktown

NORTH CAROLINA

fresh water

North/Hudson's River

Broadway

Trinity Church

Fort George

East River

New York City, c. 1766

Part 1

COLONY OF NEW YORK

There is something independent and agreeable
in living where one was born.

—Angelica Church

CHAPTER 1

Engeltje

1755–1756

After the ceremony and before witnesses in the parlor of the bride's manor house, the groom opened the leather-bound wedding-gift Bible and dipped a quill in ink. *"In hett Jaar 1755 September den 7 en. ben Ick Philip Johannis Schuyler,"* he scratched out on the blank page. *"In den Houwelycke Stadt Getreden mett Catharina Van Rensselaer."* Under the English laws of the Royal Province of New York, one man and one woman became two parts of one person: a head and a body.

Law is written by and for men, however. For Catharina van Rensselaer, now Schuyler, it was not laws that structured her rights and roles, but duty: Duty to this tall, sunburned New York Dutchman, and duty to the baby she was just beginning to perceive in the cradle of her pelvis. Still, certifying that union—a proper exchange of vows before witnesses—was so important to her that her betrothed, the militia captain Philip Schuyler, had been summoned home from the war's front just as the advancing French threatened to reach the Noort Rivier and gain water access to their home, their country.

Philip and Catharina were colonists. A century earlier, their ancestors had transplanted their families upon the banks of a river that had been claimed by the Republic of the United Netherlands after the hired explorer Henry Hudson sailed up it seeking his elusive Northwest Passage in 1609. Where Henry Hudson's *Halve Maen* had been forced to come about, subsequent Dutch ventures established a trading post and began exchanging metal wares for beaver pelts with the Mohawk and Mahican nations. Then the Dutch began to buy land as well, and settlers came. Dutch and Walloon settlers and indentured servants—two hundred by 1652—were followed by enslaved Africans who aided the hard labor of building farms and a town. Over several lifetimes, and the transition from Dutch to British rule, settlers had subdued, cultivated, and husbanded land they held by occasional force and constant diplomacy toward the people and peoples they neighbored. They hunted deer and beaver, farmed imported sheep and hogs, and eradicated wolves and rattlesnakes. They rooted out what they deemed weeds and planted wheat and cabbages in rows. With each expanding generation, they built more houses and barns, roads and windmills, wharves and churches, spreading over the land like a neat patchwork quilt. While men broke and cleared the land—of rocks and trees and other men—and marked their boundaries, women planted. Not just vegetables, but people. If anyone thought to question this ordering of the natural world, the church reinforced its righteousness: *"Maakt recht in de wildernis"* the domine of the Dutch Reformed Church reminded those who could not or preferred not to read their Bibles. Make right in the wilderness. Literally interpreted, this meant right angles, straight rows, and social order: property and propriety.

After a hundred years of this process, the Dutch colonists' interwoven family roots were deeply established along both sides of the broad Noort Rivier, from New Amsterdam, now New York, all the way to Beverwijck, now Albany, which was as far as oceangoing ships could sail. And they were still expanding, along with each new bride's waistline.

These settlers were not unique to conceive of country as a web of kinship. Even the empires of Europe were mapped first by genealogy and second by geography. The affairs of Europe were all matters of blood and marriage. Now, as King George II of Britain considered an alliance with his sister's son, King Frederick II of Prussia, Austria's Archduchess Maria Theresa, pregnant with her fifteenth child, and her husband, the Holy Roman Emperor, were contracting an alliance with

King Louis XV of France, whose army was—at that moment of Catharina and Philip's wedding—a mere fifty miles north.

On their wedding night, Philip and Catharina tossed cookies and a few coins from the bedroom window to the neighbors banging pots outside, before drawing closed the curtains on their bed. But as they began to explore the terrain of one another's bodies—not for the first time—a nimble army of French, Canadian, Wabanaki, and Wyandot soldiers crossed the pivotal divide, "the carrying place," between the waters of Lake Champlain that drained northward into the Saint Lawrence River near Montreal, and those of the Noort Rivier that flowed south to the town of New York. By the time the newlyweds arose the next morning, British, American, and Mohawk soldiers were in position to meet this invasion. And by the end of Philip and Catharina's first day of matrimony, the blood of those several nations ran in all directions.

After the wedding, the bride moved across the river into the groom's family home within the palisades of Albany and Philip returned to the war. The Schuylers' old Dutch house on Jonckerstraet had been built by Philip's grandfather about the time the British seized New Netherland, nearly a century earlier. By local standards, the house was large—six of its rooms had fireplaces—but it was sometimes crowded. When Catharina, the newest Mrs. Schuyler, moved in, she joined two others: Philip's widowed mother, Cornelia van Cortlandt Schuyler, who owned the house, and his widowed sister, Geertruy Schuyler Schuyler (her late husband was a cousin). With Philip and his brothers busy at war, these three women headed the household of children and servants—most of them enslaved, perhaps a few of them indentured. Overall, the house was not unlike her own home, across the mile-wide river, but every household is its own country, and a newcomer had to learn its ways.

As for work, the three Mrs. Schuylers and all who lived with them had plenty. As in the Netherlands, the houses of the Albany Dutch families were more than residences, with storerooms on the topmost floor for the share of the harvest that came as rent from farms and orchards outside of town. Also typical for Dutch women, Catharina's mother-in-law was a businesswoman, a merchant, so one of the ground-floor rooms likely served as her shop, where customers could call to see her collection of imported goods—perhaps cloth or lace, copper kettles, or silver tea services.

Catharina's most critical labor as a colonist—producing new colonists—came on in February. Delivering a first child would not be easy. It would test her body and mind. As it was for men who went to war or to sea, strength and courage were no guarantees of survival. She was used to risk. For all who lived in or around Albany in the Royal Province of New York in 1756, ordinary life possessed perpetual mortal risk. Between the unforgiving seasons and the perils of traveling by water, foot, or horse, between each wave of war or pox, survival required grit, muscle, luck, and friends.

As word spread of the birth underway, neighbors and relatives began trudging over the crusted snow of Jonckerstraet, cradling baskets of pastries—waffles, crullers, sweet *olie-koecken* fresh from an oil pot—to contribute to the day. Once inside, the visitors stamped the snow from their clogs or deerskin boots and paused to allow their snow blindness to clear. The house was dim; its windows—grids of lead and watery glass etched with frost—were shuttered and draped against winter drafts and dangerous vapors. The air was thickened with steam from pots of simmering meat broth and caudle wine—steeping with cloves and mace—and tinged with smoke from wood fire and candle tallow. Once they could see, the women—whose work it was to wash the dead, dress a bride, and deliver children—climbed the stairs to the birth chamber.

In this room, the fire had been stoked to an unusual intensity. A pallet had been prepared on the floor, near the fire, where the laboring woman could be made as comfortable as possible, without the risk of ruining a good mattress with the sweat, blood, and effluvia of birth. Perhaps the Schuylers owned their own birth chair, with handles to grip and stirrups to brace against. If they did not, the midwife may have lugged one in with her.

But all of that would come later.

During the early contractions, the room would have been festive. Probably one of the enslaved maids poured wine for the attendants and fortifying caudle for Catharina, and, as the wine took effect, the stories began (in Dutch, of course), making the younger women redden or laugh as they laid out clean linens and the midwife's supplies—oils, unction, and silk thread. As with a funeral, however, stories and laughter and free-flowing wine served a ceremonial purpose.

One colonial pamphleteer advised pregnant women that "preparation for Death is that Most Reasonable and Most Seasonable thing to which you must now Apply your self." In his recent pamphlet *The Increase of Mankind*, the Philadelphia printer Benjamin Franklin calculated that a child born in the colonies was as likely to die as to reach the age of ten. This information was obvious to the women of the Schuyler household. Catharina's mother-in-law, Cornelia Schuyler, had given birth to nine children. She lost two infants before Philip was born, then, the summer he was eight, she buried two more children and their father in quick succession. Catharina's sister-in-law, Geertruy, had lost a son. In that year alone, her own Dutch Reformed Church had buried as many children as it had buried adults of any age. Children died of measles and scarlatina and smallpox. They died of infections, parasites, and the flux. Others died of the duress of being born. As for mothers' lives, nine Februarys earlier, Catharina had watched her own mother take three excruciating weeks to die after giving birth for the seventh time.

Guiding a woman's mind from dread and memory was the work of the women who gathered in the birth chamber, just as it was the work of a midwife, with her ambergris, quilts of gillyflower, and seeds of angelica, to see to her physical progress. If it occurred to the Schuyler women to want a childbirth practitioner with more science and certification rather than merely "a person that keeps her Wits together, without suffering them to be scattered by fear," there were no alternatives. There was no trained doctor in Albany in 1756. There was not even a medical school in all of British North America. General hospitals, and male and female noncombatants to staff them, were part of the British strategy for equipping its military in the colonies, but they had yet to cross the Atlantic.

As for midwifery, most medical interventions centered around "humorial theory," which involved balancing body fluids—the blood, bile, and phlegm—but in Europe, obstetrics had been altered by the invention of forceps, not always for the better. Most manuals on childbirth composed by experts did not go far beyond fumes of pellitory and melilot, violets, and mugwort chopped finely and boiled in good white wine, or "sallet oyl." But an experienced midwife could turn a breeched baby, or, if a baby would not emerge, some were bold enough to dismantle the fetus and extract the body piecemeal from the mother, before both were lost. In case of such calamity, a midwife had dispensation to perform an emergency baptism, anointing whatever part of the living child she could access.

Fortunately, no hooks were necessary to extricate Catharina's baby. The infant's skull cleared her pelvic bone and the baby slid, glistening, into the hands of family and kinship and was immediately swaddled in a legacy of explorers and conquerors, of pilgrims and schismatics, of traders, enslavers, and farmers, renegades and rule-makers: the firstborn of her family's new generation. The moment of birth, of nativity, is, by the very word, the root of nation.

Later, after the blood and sweat was wiped away, the newborn's father opened the family Bible and again dipped quill in ink and wrote in his fading Dutch beneath the record of his marriage: *"In hett Jaar 1756 February dou 20e to ziven in dou middagh is Geboren ons Eersten Kind un Dochter genaimt Engeltje."* In this year 1756, on the 20th day of February, at seven in the afternoon, is Born our First Child a Daughter named Engeltje.

Two days later, baby Engeltje's name was written again, this time in the book of christenings in the Dutch Reformed Church. It was a book full of other Engeltjes—a trail of names that stretched from Albany back to Holland, to a woman who had set her orphaned nephew upon the path that led to the founding of that Dutch settlement at the northernmost edge of New Netherland. In the wintry light filtering through glass stained with the emblems of those first families to colonize, the infant was sponsored by a great-grandmother and a grandfather. They were the mother and husband of Catharina's mother, Engeltje, whose bones lay nearby in the church vault.

Thus, too young to see beyond the face of the person who held her, barely more than a beating heart and drying white skin, the infant was woven into the human web of conquest, dynasty, and global power.

By the time spring came, as the tulips bloomed and infant Engeltje learned to coo and smile, the Great Powers were changing alliances like dancers in a quadrille. But each time one sovereign bowed to another sovereign, they offended their previous partners. In North America, tribal nations and confederations joined the dance or were dragged into it. Only the Netherlands managed to remain mostly neutral in what would become a great global war for empire. All that year, back-woods skirmishes between New France and the British colonies of New York, Pennsylvania, and Virginia over territory and the control of key waterways "set the world on fire."

CHAPTER 2

A Colonial Girl

About the time Engeltje cut her first teeth, the Seven Years' War officially reached Albany in the figure of British General John Campbell, 4th Earl of Loudoun, who commanded the townspeople to quarter British soldiers and officers in private homes, dismissing objections to this infringement of citizens' rights as "the Quibbles of the Provincials."

In six years of trying, the French never did gain control of the Mohawk or the Noort Rivier, nor did they hold Lake Champlain. But as the war wound down in North America, Albany found itself conquered all the same. By billeting an Englishman or a Scot (or two) to each of the town's second-best beds, the British army had infiltrated New Netherlander homes where culture was tended as carefully as embers from yesterday's fire. Where English had previously been a public language, used primarily in business and trade, now women and servants also had learned to speak it. The Noort Rivier became the North River, or, to emphasize an English claim to the province, "Hudson's River." By the time Engeltje could speak clearly, her first language was becoming obsolete, everywhere but in church.

In the tentative new peace, Engeltje's parents began to build their own house, a structure that would be both a home of their own and a physical manifestation of their place in the world. Catharina and Philip Schuyler were still in their twenties. They were active and ambitious people, and they embraced the changes in their town as positive—or at least inevitable. And they were eager to safeguard their interests. There was the sense that the British had felt justified quartering soldiers in Albany homes because, being so conspicuously Dutch, the townspeople weren't seen as true British citizens, but foreigners, and not entitled to their full constitutional rights. For provincials who had fought alongside the British in the war, this othering was disheartening. For landholders, it held a deeper threat: If the British could commandeer a bed, they could as easily commandeer private property.

Engeltje's family opted for assimilation. Relinquishing the old Dutch house on Jonckerstraet was part of this process. Philip Schuyler's brothers had already moved on—one went to a family farm on the river flats north of the town, and the other sailed to England to begin a military career in the British Army. Even his widowed sister, Geertruy Schuyler Schuyler, was moving on: She married a medic from her brother's regiment (this time, a man with a different last name from her own).

Soon the Schuylers would have a ballroom-saloon for dancing and a library full of books. Far from smelling of apples and an oil pot, the new house would not have a single cooking hearth. Not even in the cellar. No pickling steam would warp the fine wallpaper. No frying river fish or rendering tallow would "perfume" the drapery or upholstery. In this new house, Engeltje would not grow up to be a colonial Dutch matron, as her mother had been molded. Her life would take another, unfamiliar shape.

In the spring of 1761, when Engeltje was five and construction on the new house was just beginning, her father doled out farewell kisses, boarded a sloop, and sailed down the North River, bound for England. Ostensibly, Captain Schuyler was going to present accounts to the War Department, on behalf of the quartermaster, his friend and superior officer, Colonel John Bradstreet. But the trip would also be an education for the provincial militia officer: an opportunity to see England with his own eyes. He would be gone two years.

When her husband sailed from Albany, Catharina Schuyler was the mother of three daughters—Engeltje, five; Elizabeth, three; and Margarita, two—and she was pregnant. Running the household without her husband present was not new. Throughout the war, he had been gone for months at a time, but a transatlantic voyage was an especially acute risk—even the domine who had baptized Engeltje had since been lost at sea. Compounding the danger were the French privateers that would continue cruising the Atlantic in search of British ships to seize while they could still do so legally. Half a year or more might pass before Catharina learned whether her husband reached England.

In his absence, she oversaw the construction of their future home. Planks and beams felled and milled upriver were floated to Albany and dragged to the house site by oxen and hammered into place by the British soldiers Colonel Bradstreet had provided as laborers. Nearby, kilns baked blocks of clay from the Rutten Kill ravine into bricks. As the structure took form, master craftsmen were summoned from as far away as Boston: carpenters to turn the balustrades, masons to lay the stonework, and glaziers to build and hang the many-quarreled windows.

For Catharina, this structure was more than a place to live. For five years, she had lived in her mother-in-law Cornelia Schuyler's old Dutch house, duty bound as half guest, half servant. Soon she would be mistress of her own house—a house paid for by her marriage settlement, that portion of an inheritance that was paid to women at the beginning of their married life when they needed it most to set up the household in which to raise their children. Her mother-in-law would still reside with her, but it might well be on different terms, as if, with this new house, her apprenticeship was ending, and she would begin her career in earnest.

The Schuylers' new house was called "The Pastures," because it was built south of Albany, on a hillside that Catharina's ancestor had designated to be the tiny settlement's communal pastures. Now that settlement was a full-fledged town. The land was so populated that the people who sold or leased land to farmers, who owned the sawmills that supplied the building material, and who owned the ships that exported the wheat and beaver pelts and returned with cargoes of merchandise could now undertake construction of a great house. A great house, as The Pastures assuredly would become, was not destined to be just a family home. The Schuylers' house would serve as a place of industry, of business, and of hospitality—hosting dinners and serving as an inn for visitors to Albany. The amount of labor needed for operating a household was well beyond the scope of one individual. Merely tending so many fireplaces required a person dedicated to that task. The role of a housewife was thus very like that of a ship's captain, and her crew was her household staff. Some had come to their work voluntarily—hired or indentured. Others were born to their menial post—the enslaved inheriting drudgery as they inherited bondage. Catharina had grown up in houses dependent upon the enslaved people, who carried in water and wood and carried out nightsoil, who churned butter and tended the sponge for the daily bread and boiled the linens and trimmed the candlewicks. From girlhood, she had learned how to master and manage servants as she had learned to master and manage the horses she rode.

Catharina's new house would be as different in the architecture of its labor as it was different in appearance from old Dutch houses in which she had grown up. Whereas the old manor houses were built around great kitchen hearths and incorporated storerooms and granaries with living spaces, Catharina's new house was divided into a formal front house designed for genteel English-style living (itself defined by being separate from manual labor) and a one-story back appendage to which operations were relegated: a stage where elegant living was carried on and a backstage where the work was done out of sight. The kitchen, the nursery, and the business office—these would be the domain of a staff—maids and nurses and agents—separated from the home and subordinate to the family. If the front house would be for literature and music, the back of the house would be for production (the gardens, hives, coops, and hutches), for industry (soapmaking, candlemaking, cider pressing, brewing, pickling, and shoemaking), and for waste (the household dump, the manure heap, the privy). As for the front house, there would be a parlor for sipping tea and playing music, a study with a library, a dining room for giving dinners, large bedrooms in which to offer hospitality to esteemed visitors, and, on the eastern wall of the second-floor saloon, a triptych of crown glass from which the Schuyler family could look down upon the broad silver river hammocked between windmill-dotted hills as if upon their personal dominion— green in summer, burnished gold in fall, shades of gray all winter long.

All this labor had yet even to begin when Catharina's pregnancy concluded sooner than expected. At the end of July, she delivered not one baby, but twins. The boy—Engeltje's first brother—was stillborn. The girl was baptized Cornelia, after Engeltje's grandmother, and survived only seven months. Then, seven months after Cornelia died, Engeltje's grandmother followed her namesake to the grave.

In the autumn of 1762, Engeltje's father sailed home from England laden with gifts like a seafaring Sinterklaas. Philip Schuyler's first view of home from the sloop's deck was of his family's grand new house. In his travels abroad, he had seen houses vastly larger than the one that now perched upon the hillside, but this house was his own. The pleasure of his homecoming, however, was dampened by the news of the death of his mother and the two children he had never seen. Also changed by his eighteen-month absence was his wife. If in England he had entertained any fantasies of Catharina Schuyler becoming as refined as English ladies, his error was now apparent. After burying two children and the closest person she'd had to a mother since the death of her own, the frank-faced girl Philip had married that September in the early days of the war was seasoning into a New Netherlander matriarch, stalwart, independent, and wholly capable.

Fortunately, there were gifts to distract the Schuylers from feeling their losses. Philip Schuyler dazzled his daughters with gadgets—a Gregorian reflecting telescope and a magic lantern for projecting images, and a stylish new chaise for traveling. In their new house, Engeltje and her sisters might sip their syllabubs from dainty glassware especially made for that curdled treat, and when Captain and Mrs. Schuyler gave a dinner, or the little girls hosted their friends and cousins for a birth-day *fête*, their guests would spear their sturgeon steaks and bear-meat pies with silver forks.

If status could be achieved with pretty things, the Schuylers had raised theirs, at least by Albany standards, but the markers of gentility were not all available for sale in a London shop. The nobility inherited their titles and entitlements, but the gentry who came between the barons and baronesses and the laboring peasantry had to perform their class to claim it. Refinement was trained into young ladies and young gen-tlemen from their first words and steps. How a person walked, danced, spoke, held a teacup—it all mattered. Thus, the Schuylers decided to send their two eldest daughters, Engeltje and Elizabeth (called Betsy by her family), to boarding school several days' sail downriver in New York. A hearthside education in stitchery and Bible reading and a few extended stays in relatives' homes to improve their manners—all refined by a stay with their famously erudite Aunt Margarita Schuyler—might have been seen by most as sufficient for an Albany girl's education. But as members of their town's elites, Philip and Catharina Schuyler understood that the British looked down on "provincials," particularly those whose accents emphasized their non-Englishness. Philip Schuy-ler may have felt this even more acutely in England, where social rank determined one's rights, one's literal entitlements. For the sake of their rights, the Schuylers wanted their daughters to be fully fluent in the markers of class.

The sisters left for school in August 1764, when Engeltje was eight and Betsy was six. Catharina Schuyler accompanied them, along with her two younger children, little Margarita and the new baby John Brad-street, and at least one maid to help her keep track of them all in the bustling town at the tip of Manhattan Island. With almost twenty thou-sand inhabitants, New York was several times larger than Albany and many magnitudes more eclectic for being a seaport rather than a river town. The school for young ladies was run by Ann Roger—"Madame Rugee" to her pupils—in a commodious house on French-Church

Street, just beyond Wall Street. But before the sisters began boarding, they would have a holiday with their city cousins.

Amid this bustle lived the Livingston cousins that Catharina had likely lived with periodically as a child. (Sending children into other homes was common, especially if they'd lost their mothers, as Catharina had.) Brother and sister Robert (called Robert J.) and Janet Livingston had married sister and brother Susannah and William Smith, respectively, and they all lived in New York and agreed to look after the girls while they were in school. The Schuylers stayed with the Smiths and their children on Broadway—Bess Smith was right between Engeltje and Betsy in age. But the mood of that family reunion ended abruptly when the maid brought their baby brother John Bradstreet home from a walk and their mother discovered he was feverish. When the baby began vomiting blood, William Smith wrote an express letter to their father, but well before that letter reached Albany, the baby was dead.

Having lost a baby, a mother might tend to cling to her living children, but Catharina Schuyler did no such thing. The education of her daughters was an imperative for the family, perhaps even more so now that the Schuylers once again had no living son. Days after the sisters absorbed the news of their brother's death, their mother delivered them to Madame Rugee's school and sailed home to Albany with Margarita.

Catharina's decision to leave her daughters in school proved wise. Engeltje and Betsy thrived. "The young ladies are in perfect health," Robert J. Livingston reported to Albany of their progress a few months later. "[They] improve in their education in a manner almost beyond belief and are grown to such a degree of stature that all the tacks Mama put in their frocks or gowns have been let out some time ago."

The girls spent that school year in New York. Then news arrived that Parliament had passed a new Stamp Act. By the summer of 1765, the public was starting to grasp the magnitude of this latest tax scheme. The Schuylers must have guessed what was coming, because by the time mobs began burning effigies and raiding the homes of British officials, throwing furniture and sleighs onto the pyre built on New

York's Bowling Green, Engeltje and Betsy were home in Albany, where the local school seemed "more to keep us quiet than for any other purpose," in the girls' opinion. But even keeping the children home in Albany, the Schuylers could not shelter their daughters from the rising upheaval.

CHAPTER 3

The Spirit of Riots

1766

I n January 1766, a mob arrived at the Schuylers' new house outside Albany, dragging with them a stolen pleasure sleigh. If Engeltje peered out a window at these "ruffians," she would have recognized many of them. Most of Albany's chapter of the Sons of Liberty were Dutchmen who attended her copper-roofed Dutch church. Several were firemen, charged with Albany's very fine, much discussed, and greatly admired new fire engine. A few were her relatives.

Engeltje knew why the mob had come: Taxes, tyranny, and stamps were all anyone talked about that winter. The Sons of Liberty argued that requiring stamps on all printed paper products used in the colonies, from playing cards to ships' papers, so undermined the colonists' rights as British citizens that it "threaten[ed] Slavery." If taxes were an abstract concept for a child, slavery was not. To Engeltje, enslavement was entirely, even literally, familiar. There was even a ceremony performed between children in households like hers. Like a miniature wedding, the ceremony paired a master child with an enslaved child. Instead of a ring to signify their bond (or bondage), a pair of shoes was given to the child now charged to walk through life as the shadow of the other. But as much as Engeltje may have felt she loved the enslaved members of her family, she did not want to *be* one any more than she would choose to be her horse, however petted or favored.

When the mob arrived at Engeltje's house, her father—who was not a pledged member of Albany's Sons of Liberty—was not home. Nor was his friend the postmaster, whom the mob was seeking, and who had likely just left with Philip Schuyler to go up the hill to Fort Frederick, where the rioters the postmaster called "Sons of Tyranny & Ignorance" could not commit the same violence to his person that they had just done to his house and furniture. The rioters were pursuing the postmaster to force him to swear an oath that he would never serve as stampmaster. But the postmaster knew that if he took such an oath, regardless of what he thought about stamps, it would cost him the very good job he already had. This conundrum had become common. Every ship that sailed with stamped clearing papers risked vandalism to its cargo or injury to its crew. Every ship that sailed with unstamped papers risked capture by a man-of-war of the British Navy, then seizure and forfeiture.

Instead of Philip Schuyler, the mob was met by the British officer who sometimes still quartered with the Schuylers. Colonel John Bradstreet put his head out a window and addressed the rowdy crowd. "Upon my honor," he shouted out at them, "I value liberty as much as any one of you." But, he assured them, the postmaster had come and gone. The protesters weighed Colonel Bradstreet's honor against their inclination to commit mischief. They may have wavered—tempted to punish Philip Schuyler for his conservatism and his enviable English-style house. Instead, they helped themselves to the Schuylers' firewood and hay so they could set the pleasure sleigh on fire, then they dragged the flaming conveyance away to seek the postmaster elsewhere.

All that winter of 1766, protests flared throughout the British colonies. Some were violent, others were subtle. Cargoes of stamps were incinerated. Citizens dressed in mourning. While Sons of Liberty plotted their resistance late into the night in their taverns and coffeehouses, Daughters of Liberty met at dawn for marathon spinning bees, furiously twining flax for homespun cloth to replace taxable British imports. In Albany, the fire department stayed busy. There were fires to set, fires to extinguish.

In February, Engeltje crossed Benjamin Franklin's demarcation line for childhood survival and turned ten years old. Typically, Albany children of her class celebrated birthdays by dismissing their parents and hosting a company of dressed-up friends to dine. These little ladies and little gentlemen would sip cocoa and feast on sweetmeats, cracked hickory nuts, and pastries—cookies, crullers and *olie-koecken*—and lord over their enslaved waiters. By the end of the party, even the best-behaved children would have reached the outer limits of their civility, and the parents would return to set the world right again.

Then spring came in the usual way. First the ice moaned and cracked. Then the floods came. Then, from the opposite direction, came the dark clouds of passenger pigeons. As soon as every Albany household was tired of pigeon pie, the sturgeon spawned, and the fishermen went out in boats with lanterns to stalk the armor-backed behemoths.

In late April, while the Sons of Liberty were still rioting, a new group of rebels marched on New York. This group also called themselves Sons of Liberty, but the land-owning Sons of Liberty who opposed stamps and imported tea dubbed them "Levellers," after English Levellers-of-old who had chopped down the enclosure hedges landowners used to fence what had once been communal pastures. For landowners, the post-war era had been a boom time. But high land prices had exacerbated a deepening recession and tenant farmers were in distress. When tenants could not pay their rent, they could be evicted, and given the high demand for new leases, evicting a tenant allowed landlords to secure higher rents.

The crisis was rooted in the early formation of the colony, first by the Dutch patroons, Engeltje's ancestors, wealthy families that were granted large tracts of land on the condition that they would develop and administer the settlements there. When the British took over the colony, they continued the system, rewarding loyal servants of the Crown with vast manorial land grants. Typically, tenants leased farms for three lifetimes and paid rent with a share of the produce. If the leaseholder sold the lease, a quarter of that sale was paid to the landowner, so keeping the land was more lucrative for landowners than selling it.

Philip Schuyler considered himself a mere "middling" landowner. But several of the Schuylers' relatives, including Catharina Schuyler's father, Johannes van Rensselaer, owned hundreds of thousands of acres. Engeltje's grandmother Cornelia Schuyler had been born a Van Cortlandt, whose ancestors had been granted a land tract ten miles by twenty by William III, the Dutch king of England. Her other grandmother, Engeltje van Rensselaer, had been born a Livingston, whose two-branched Scottish-Dutch family had likewise amassed enormous tracts of land on both banks of the North River. By March, evictions for nonpayment on Cortlandt Manor had led to protests, which in turn led to pitchfork waving at Livingston Manor. Winter held on. Snow kept falling. The landlords armed themselves. The tenants did the same.

Azaleas blossomed. Then came the week of Pinkster, the holiday when Albany reveled in its annual play at inverting power. Engeltje and the rest of Albany's children, regardless of class, faith, ancestry, or skin color, skipped around maypoles and cheered bareback riders and watched the jubilee's appointed king, an old enslaved Black man in a velvet coat, parade to the rhythm of eelpot drums. But as the festival ended, rebellion erupted along the navigable length of the North River. It wasn't the enslaved who rose up, as critics of the festival always feared, but the tenant-farmer Sons of Liberty. Jails were broken open. The farmers threatened to level the great houses. In her great house, Engeltje watched her father prepare to leave for New York to petition the colonial government for aid to quell the violence.

To Philip Schuyler's surprise, he found New York in a state of rum-soused jubilation. News of the Stamp Act's repeal had landed ahead of the frigate that carried it, shouted from the ship's deck to the city docks and heralded through town. That night, bonfires lit the streets, illuminations glittered on shattered glass, and pistol and musket fire pierced the din. Only after Philip recovered from the twenty-eight toasts he'd drunk with his Sons of Liberty friends did he meet with General Thomas Gage.

Commander of the British forces in North America, General Gage was a veteran of some of the bloodiest battles of the previous war in the colonies, including the disastrous frontal attack by the British on Fort Ticonderoga, overlooking Lake Champlain between Albany and Montreal. Now he reported to England that he had been warned by "the better sort of people" that "The Spirit of Riot is contagious, it spread lately into the Country," and "if the provinces were left much longer in the situation they are now in, the Inhabitants would rise and attack each other."

Reluctantly, General Gage sent a regiment upriver to restore order.

When Engeltje's grandfather (and godfather) Johannes van Rensselaer learned that British soldiers had come to protect the property owners, he saw an opportunity and seized it. He sent his sons, the Albany sheriff, and a posse of armed men to deliver eviction notices to farmers on the easternmost border of his Claverack Manor. These farmers were not protesting rents—they paid no rent at all. These settlers had cleverly exploited the old dispute over provincial boundaries, gambling that the Province of Massachusetts Bay would back them against the claims of a Dutch Yorker.

Johannes van Rensselaer was not *the* Patroon of Rensselaerswijck. That quaint hereditary title belonged to a cousin. He had, however, inherited two large portions of the original mini-colony that the Dutch had granted to their ancestor. From this expanse of land—roughly three hundred thousand acres—came the family's wealth and status. The work of administering and improving the estate, as in the English manorial system, was the family business.

Years before the anti-rent riots, when the Massachusetts settlers began farming on Claverack land and claimed they owned it outright, Johannes van Rensselaer had made his case in court and appealed to the king, but it was a slow process. Claverack Manor, across the North River from Albany, stretched from the river to the border with Massachusetts Bay. The Van Rensselaer charter—granted in 1629, the same year as that of the Massachusetts Bay Colony and formally recognized by the king of England when New Netherland became New York—was the legal basis for the border between the two colonies. Thus, the problem was not a tenant problem, but rather a territorial dispute between two colonies that were, effectively, two separate countries. As paperwork crisscrossed the Atlantic, the settlers simply dug in—clearing land and building farms—plausibly confident that the king would one day favor the land's bona fide tillers, and—as New Englanders saw things—true Englishmen.

As anticipated, these settlers stood their ground when the sheriff's posse arrived with eviction orders. The skirmish was brief, but there were casualties on both sides. Engeltje's Uncle Hendrick was shot in the arm and her Uncle Robert's horse was shot out from under him. As soon as he could procure a new horse, Robert van Rensselaer rode with the Albany sheriff to report the event to General Gage and the royal governor of New York.

General Gage immediately dispatched a regiment with orders to give the landowners "all the aid in your Power." By summer's end, some sixty anti-rent rioters were in jail, and their leaders had been convicted of high treason by a jury of landowners, sentenced to hanging, disemboweling, and beheading.

Days after the "Leveller" trial ended, in a September heatwave reminiscent of Jamaica, the new Royal Governor of New York, Sir Henry Moore, and his colleague, the new Deputy Governor of Quebec, Guy Carleton, ascended the North River, "to endeavour more effectually by his Presence, to appeale sume Tumults in the Upper-Counties, as to take a View of the Country, at this pleasant Time of the Year." To signal the friendly intentions of this expedition more clearly, Governor Moore was accompanied by his wife, Lady Catherine Moore, and their daughter, Susanna.

As the governor's entourage ascended the river in two sloops, and the temperature climbed to a seething one hundred degrees, The Pastures became a tempest of preparations—boiling bedding, restuffing mattresses, perhaps vinegar-washing the saloon window quarrels so neither soot nor dust would dim the prized view through English glass of the winding river and the rolling land beyond, to the purple Taconic range, into whose woods anti-rent insurgents still vanished whenever General Gage's soldiers came near.

If getting the house clean and comfortable for guests was important, food was even more critical. Perhaps a steer had been slaughtered, on the popular assumption that an Englishman, even one from Jamaica, must have his beefsteak. Or perhaps the Schuylers would hazard the novelty of a local dish. If a sturgeon could be caught so late in the season, they might serve "Albany beef" steaks roasted, in old Dutch elegance, with cloves piercing the meat, then stewed in wine with cinnamon and nutmeg. Or North River oysters stewed in butter and mace. Or eels split and stuffed with sorrel, chervil, and rice, then tied and boiled until they floated, and served buttered and topped with an egg. Visitors from afar were always impressed by roast bear.

To the relief of all, the households' efforts were well received. Far from harboring any anti-Dutch sentiments, the jovial, jowly governor known familiarly as "Sir Harry," now in his fifties, had been a student at the Universiteit Leiden and he spoke Dutch. Lady Catherine, like Catharina Schuyler, valued fresh outdoor air and vigorous exercise—in Jamaica, a mountain was named Catherine's Peak after Lady Catherine became the first white woman to climb it. Like the Schuylers, the Moores enjoyed music, good company, and conversation (preferably without too much animosity), and they too sought to cultivate friendships that would help keep peace in the colony.

Governor Moore had been tapped to lead the fractious colony of New York for one credential above all others: He had already led one colony in rebellion. In 1760, while he was acting governor of Jamaica, a Black freedom fighter called Tacky had led a coordinated rebellion against the British. Colonial forces met this uprising with brutality, driving rebels off a cliff and displaying Tacky's severed head on a spike. For his part, Henry Moore was made a baronet and promoted to lead New York, but it was becoming clear that the lessons Sir Harry had taken from Tacky's War were not those his superiors supposed.

Instead, when he found New York in the throes of the Stamp Act upheaval, Governor Moore had joined in the fashion of wearing home-spun coats. He claimed this sartorial choice was intended to celebrate the local artistry, but the gesture also bought him time to negotiate. When a "mob" of Sons of Liberty had challenged the British officers and soldiers who had cut down the pine post they had dubbed the Tree of Liberty—calling them rascals to their faces before escalating to throwing bricks—Governor Moore never interfered. After the "Levellers'" trial, he had ordered a stay of execution for the anti-rent leader whose wife had ridden through the night in a borrowed dress to appeal to the governor for mercy. And, after the Moores' arrival in Albany, Lady Catherine Moore personally paid the fines of all prisoners in the Albany jail who were held for under £30 and sent them home to their families; for those who remained, she arranged daily provisions. Clearly the Moores had no stomach for hanging, castrating, or beheading tenant farmers. But charity was all the rebels would get for their efforts: The anti-rent movement was dead, for now.

The Moores remained with the Schuylers for a full month, first in Albany and then at the farm in Saratoga that had become the Schuylers' principal interest. Here, Philip showed off his mills and his crops and then led the governors and surveyors north to set the border. Once the men were gone, the ladies abandoned city dress for simple linen negligees and high caps and formal dinners for casual picnics on the river that at Saratoga was more like a good-size creek.

Lady Catherine Moore, formerly Catherine Maria Long of Longville, Jamaica, and Catharina Schuyler, formerly Catharina van Rensselaer, descendant of the Patroons of Rensselaerswijck, were both colonists raised on the edges of empire. Both had experienced war, and both had buried children. Both were leaders—living as examples, always on public display. Both were accustomed to status—to its privileges and responsibilities—and to the effort that came with maintaining that status. Perhaps Lady Catherine Moore and Catharina Schuyler discussed these commonalities and their corresponding challenges. Perhaps they did not need to do so. What two mothers sharing a household over several weeks could not help but discuss were their children.

Lady Moore's adolescent daughter Susanna was a very beautiful girl with "apparently no dislike to be seen," which was worrisome for her mother mainly because the Governor's Mansion was located inside a military fort where Susanna could enjoy being looked at by entire regiments. Catharina Schuyler's three living daughters, Engeltje, Elizabeth, and Margarita, had not yet crossed into puberty, but at ten, just-nine, and almost-eight, their rivalries were incessant. As for their sons, where Catharina's daughters were healthy and vigorous, her third son to be named John Bradstreet was the first to reach his first birthday. Lady Catherine also had a son Engeltje's age who loved poetry. But as the English believed boys, like horses, ought to be separated from their mothers early, lest they turn soft or sour, her boy John Henry had been sent over to England to attend Eton College, and it would be years before she could hope to see him again. At some point in their conversations, as they rambled with the children through the rugged landscape that grew more dramatic as autumn advanced, Lady Catherine decided to invite Engeltje Schuyler to live with them in the Governor's Mansion in New York for the winter.

This idea was at once entirely practical and politically significant. Mother to mother, it was a simple fix: Removing Engeltje from her siblings would reduce the squabbling, and providing a little sister for Susanna would bring her more of the attention she craved and help her to stay a little girl just a little longer. But both women were adept at tending the web of connection of friendships, alliances, and bloodlines. When New York saw Catharina's daughter, they would know what good, close friends the Moores had in Albany. As for the Schuylers, Engeltje, residing with the Moores, would represent her family, Albany, and even Dutch New York, like a little ambassador in the royal governor's court. She would be olive branch and wampum belt. And perhaps her tiny presence, and what it symbolized, could in some small way help keep peace along the North River.

Now, just as they had prepared to receive the Moores, the members of The Pastures household scrambled to prepare Engeltje to leave with them. Her trunk was packed with her whitest linens, prettiest ribbons, and, for the coming winter, stockings, quilted petticoats, perhaps a fur-lined cape. Meanwhile, the little girl was crammed with the typical admonishments given to children who will be out in public: She must behave herself, obey her hosts, use her best manners, wash her face, and keep tidy. And since Engeltje was a New Netherlander child entering an English household—even if Sir Harry did speak Dutch—she must speak English, even for her name.

When she boarded the royal governor's sloop for New York, she became Angelica.

CHAPTER 4

The Bewilderment of Liberty:
Or, a Political Education

Descending the North River, the sloop that carried Angelica glided between banks brilliant with autumn color, dotted with windmills, and patchworked with her family history. She knew each Dutch estate they passed. They were familiar by both reputation and by relation—the map of the river valley read like her family tree: Claverack Manor, Livingston Manor, Clermont Manor, and, as the river widened into the Tappan Zee, Cortlandt Manor, and onward.

Perhaps Angelica was terrified at the change to come, or perhaps the breeze of the vessel's momentum, which pulled at her skirts, roused the little girl's spirit and sense of independence. She was only half grown, and she would miss her home and her family—this time and every time she sailed away. But where the Dutch word *gezelligheid* might capture the pleasures of the home and family scene she was leaving behind, another, *uitwaaien*, named that pleasure of heading into the wind. But the river carried her along regardless.

At two o'clock on an October Saturday, to a serenade of church bells and a salute from the battery guns, Governor Moore's barge docked at New York, and Angelica—her English name already shortened by the Moores to "Anna"—entered the star-shaped fort guarding the river's mouth, the island of Manhattan, and the Governor's Mansion, which stood within the ramparts.

Thus far, Governor Moore had had no need of such protection, but the province of New York was spoiling for a fight. The governor's job as chief representative of the British Empire, of King George III himself, was to maintain control, to avert or suppress unrest, and to govern. The more rigorous Royalists in New York, those in the military especially, already found Sir Harry convivial to a fault. Meanwhile, Angelica had watched Henry Moore playing his violin and striving to placate all sides, breaking bread and telling funny stories to form friendships and alliances, parenting other family's children—all to keep the fragile peace for as long as possible. His technique may have been failing, but Angelica Schuyler absorbed the lesson well. As a girl, she would never have the option of wielding a sword. Even grasping a pen would require some audacity. A dinner table, she was learning, was as much a chess board as any battlefield. One could cut meat either place, but it was reason, not cannons, that distinguished humans from beasts.

"They pleased everyone in the circle around them," one girl of Angelica's circle would remember of the Moores' soft-power civility: "Before the tempest broke loose all its fury, it was like oil poured on agitated waters, which produces a temporary calm immediately round the ship."

Governor Moore would not live to see that tempest. But Miss Schuyler was sailing straight for the coming fury.

Angelica's winter in New York political society was the first of many. After her visit, Governor Moore appointed her father to the commission to determine the official boundary between New York and Massachusetts, and then he encouraged Philip Schuyler to run for New York's General Assembly. When he was elected to represent Albany, the family entered "the storms of public life" in New York's provincial politics. Politically, Philip Schuyler aligned with the colony's "Country" faction, who were landowners, Presbyterians, members of the Dutch Reformed Church, and held popular or whiggish views. Opposite this faction were the "City" politicians, who tended to be merchants and traders, Anglicans, and closely affiliated with the royal administration.

Had Angelica been a boy, as the precocious firstborn of a rising family, she would assuredly have spent those winters draped in the crow-black robes of the scholars at New York's King's College, squinting at Greek texts in the candlelight, learning classical rhetoric, and honing oratory skills. As a girl, however, Angelica would not receive her lessons in military affairs, governance, and statecraft from the formal study of Thucydides or Herodotus. Instead, she would learn from actual generals and governors as their careers rose and fell, and, more relevant for her future use, from the female partners whose best work was invisible. The Schuylers' dinner guests regularly included government officials, lawyers, members of the colonial government, even visiting dignitaries—a traveling European naturalist, perhaps, or a Cherokee diplomat. Some guests might have assumed that a pretty girl at these dinner tables was there for decorative purposes—an especially amusing bouquet of flowers—but Angelica spent all of those years listening.

It was a heady time and debate was growing heated, even within families. Notions of empire and enlightenment were intersecting like two turbulent rivers converging: power, domination, and absolute authority flowing up against ideas of the individual, liberty, and "natural" rights. The nations of Europe were now colonial hubs that processed raw materials from their colonial "out factories" into the wealth that built still more ships with which to conquer still more "virgin" territory. While kingdoms fought for the control of continents—swallowing up North America, South America, Africa, and South Asia—families did the same on a smaller scale. "Men of Property . . . must have it in their Power to purchase large Tracts, if they chuse this Method to lay a foundation to raise their Families," argued William Tryon, who came to govern New York in the years after Sir Harry died of dysentery and its treatment. "It [is] good Policy rather to encourage than to check such a Spirit. The subordination which arises from a distinction in Rank and Fortune, I have found from experience, to be friendly to Gov't. and to be conducive to Strengthening the Hands of the Crown, and perhaps it will prove the only Counterpoize against a Republican & levelling Spirit which the popular Constitutions of some Colonies, and the Tempers of their Inhabitants . . . so naturally excite." Meanwhile, as the military and the mercantile branches of European nations spread out across the globe in search of timber, pelts, sugar, and even human chattel, the philosophical and the theological branches sought to make sense of this work, to see its greater purpose. All met with monsters, contradictions, and moral quandaries.

The greatest of these quandaries was human oppression. Angelica's friends and family were vehement in their ideas about their colony's rights in relation to Britain, but they were less articulate in their position on liberty for those people who were born unfree or were pressed into involuntary servitude. Serfdom and slavery posed an intellectual conundrum to Enlightenment thinkers generally—how could one speak of liberty without speaking also of slavery?—but most could no more fathom their world without slaves than they could imagine giving up their horses and pulling their wagons themselves. Slavery in New York was ubiquitous: Shopkeepers, sailors, craftsmen, and widows from the highest to the lowest reaches of society were among the colony's enslavers.

Seasonal laborers were more economical than field-hand chattel slavery for northern New York's agriculture—and Philip Schuyler likely filled the barracks on his Saratoga farm with summer hires seeking the seed money with which to one day lease a farm, and he employed specialized teams to mow hay or turn the ground. Wheat, the region's primary cash crop, was farmed by tenants, who paid the Schuylers a portion of their yield, and artisans were hired to spin flax and weave it into linen. But for the labor that required practice and technical know-how—driving the horses, cooking and preserving food, operating the flax- and sawmills, dairying, and tending delicate herring nets—the Schuylers depended upon at least two families of enslaved workers. Like other enslavers, the Schuylers built the institution into the physical structures of their homes. Some great New York houses known for liberal politics had "slave pens," which were basement cells with iron-barred windows, in which to isolate unruly servants.

The same men who espoused liberty, equality, and rights expected their family—a term understood to include their wives, their servants, and their children—to submit to their absolute authority. Would-be husbands might like a spirited, high-strung wife, as they liked a horse with those same qualities, for the challenge and the thrill, but they did intend to curb that spirit to their will. What autonomy wives and daughters attained often came at the cost of others' freedom, as if there were only so much liberty to go around, or as if liberty, like daylight, depended upon its opposite to exist. For white girls and women, who understood they owed what liberty they had (the luxury of time for daily reading, for instance) to the servants who relieved them of the uncompensated drudgery that otherwise would fall to them, thinking beyond enslavement was not just conceptually difficult, it was personally threatening. Here again, Governor Tryon's logic about "The subordination which arises from a distinction in Rank and Fortune" being good for government applied: Wives and daughters who submitted to husbands and fathers in turn lorded over the enslaved.

In Jean-Jacques Rousseau's treatise *Emile, or On Education,* which came out in English translation one year before Angelica was first sent away to New York for school, the social theorist had advised: "Ye mothers that have judgement, follow my advice; do not, in defiance of nature, bring up your daughters to be gentlemen, give them the education of ladies, and assure yourselves, it will be much better for them and for us." But what *was* an education of ladies? For Rousseau, the answer lay in the purpose of that education, and the object of educating girls was to groom them to serve boys and men as mothers and partners. If this was too subtle, that great man of the Enlightenment spelled out the risks: "A witty woman," he warned, "is a scourge to her husband, to her children, to her friends, her servants, and to all the world. Elated by the sublimity of her genius, she scorns to stoop to the duties of a woman."

The duties of a woman, according to Rousseau, were to please and to serve men, which could take its form of genius. In the years Angelica spent coming of age in Royal New York's political circles, she watched many prominent women perform the balancing act of thinking and speaking while performing their roles as women. The first of these had been Lady Catherine Moore, who sought to influence public opinion through her own actions (as when she paid the prison fines in Albany), but after Sir Harry's death, the British officer with whom Susanna had eloped divorced her, and New York society froze out mother and daughter. Then came Her Excellency Margaret Tryon, who insisted upon being addressed by the same honorific as her husband, Governor Tryon. The Tryons had not been in New York long before they were dining with Schuylers "in a family way." After that, the Tryons and their daughter made a summer visit upriver, staying with the Schuylers as the Moores had done before them, giving Angelica ample opportunities to study Margaret Tryon. The daughter of a former governor of Bombay, the governor's wife was an accomplished musician who scorned chitchat at her tables and preferred to discuss military strategy. New York's glamorous Janet Livingston, who was twelve years older than her cousin Angelica and the elder sister of the rising young lawyer, Robert R. Livingston, admired Margaret Tryon's "masculine mind" and the book she had written about military fortifications—a manuscript ironically lost to a fire within the fortifications of Fort George. Like Margaret Tryon, Janet Livingston was proud and direct: "I don't like stupid people," she would say, refusing to veil her opinions or her intelligence, and secure in her high status. Margaret Tryon wasn't stupid, but she did hold views about royal governance that revolved around awe and might that jarred colonists' sensibilities. Like everyone else in New York, Angelica could see that the Tryons—separately and jointly—were proving a blunt tool for delicate work.

Of all the prominent women in New York in the 1770s—the wives of the highest-ranking men in the British colony of New York—the most useful model for Angelica was Margaret Kemble Gage. But the American wife of the commander in chief of British forces in North America set the bar for emulation very high. Lady Gage was at once exotic (her father had been born in Turkey to a Greek mother) and deeply local (her mother's family were old New Netherlanders; her mother was Philip Schuyler's first cousin). She was so refined in her manners and habits that Janet Livingston called the New Jersey-born lady the "Duchess of Brunswick." Thomas Gage had been serving in North America for as long as Angelica had been alive. Now that he was commander of British forces, charged with keeping order in thirteen increasingly fractious colonies, he was often tasked with enacting policies many colonists found objectionable (quartering British troops remained a sore point). But his striking wife, with her high social competence and her deep roots in the most prominent New York families, helped keep his professional duties from alienating him from the people he policed and protected. Yet as tensions between the colonies and Britain continued to rise, Thomas Gage was a man widely considered sociable, peaceable, and well liked. But history—at least according to the Enlightenment philosophe Baron Montesquieu—was not made by individuals.

If a teenager might study models of female power for her own purposes, to map her individual path in life, there was another reason to understand how a body submissive to a higher authority might retain her dignity and demand just treatment. The relationship of the American colonies to Britain was similar: The colonies were dependent upon Britain for protection and prohibited from trading elsewhere yet had no vote in Parliament. Most Americans accepted that they were subjects of the Crown, many professed love and loyalty to the king, but they did regard the relationship of monarch and subject as reciprocal.

One Philadelphia newspaper ran a "Letter to the Ladies" that likened this reciprocity to that of an ideal marriage, using a dialogue between a husband and a wife. It begins with the husband informing his wife that he is short of funds and has decided he shall now keep thirty percent of her "pin money."

"You cannot be in earnest," his wife protests. "You know that every farthing of it is laid out for our mutual advantage." Not only did she use that money to pay for household expenses, the lady pointed out, but she purchased everything from their tenants, "who are thereby enabled to pay their rents and employ other tenants, who, again, are enabled to pay theirs, so that your estate is improved by the whole amount."

"You question my authority, Madam?" the husband asks, insisting upon his right to rule, as England has done with America.

In turn, the wife invokes her rights. "It is my duty to run all fortunes with you, in sickness and in health. No extremity shall make me desert you. Only, do not . . . render yourself unworthy of obedience in the very act by which you demand it. I can be obedient but not base. A wife but not a slave."

"This is the language of rebellion, Madam," the husband accuses.

"This is the tone of tyranny, Sir," rebuts the wife.

Part 2

WAR FOR INDEPENDENCE

CHAPTER 5

The General's Daughter

1775

Angelica was newly nineteen, teetering between childhood dependency and adult independence in 1775, when the New York Provincial Assembly drafted a petition to King George III declaring that they and the other colonies were no longer "in a State of Infancy" and subject to "the Authority of the Parent State," but "have now reached the Period of Maturity, and think themselves intitled to their Birthright, an equal participation of Freedom with their Fellow Subjects in Britain." After finalizing this and other business of the legislative session, Philip Schuyler and the other members of the assembly dispersed. Weeks would pass before the king received this petition for more liberty, but only days passed before the colonists received their answer.

The Schuylers were at their farm in Saratoga when the news from Lexington and Concord reached them by express. "On Tuesday night the 18th instant, as secretly as possible," relayed one letter from Boston that was published that week in the New York *Journal*, "General Gage draughted out about 1000 or 1200 of his best troops which he embarked on a transport, and landed that night at Cambridge—Wednesday morning by day break they marched up to Lexington, where before breakfast as usual, about 30 of the inhabitants were practicing the manual exercise—upon these, without the least provocation, they fired about 15 minutes killed six men, and wounded several,

without a single shot from our men, who retreated as fast as possible.—
Hence they proceeded to Concord. . . . " As the story came into clearer
focus, there was no doubt that the imperial crisis had become an open
civil war.

The Schuylers considered this change in their situation. Then, surrounded by his family, his wife of twenty years, his three teenage daughters, his three young sons, and his various household servants, Philip
Schuyler penned a letter announcing their collective position: "Much
as I love peace—much as I love my domestic happiness and repose, and
desire to see my countrymen enjoying the blessings flowing from undis-
turbed industry," he proclaimed, "I would rather see all these scattered
to the winds for a time, and the sword of desolation go over the land,
than to recede one line from the just and righteous position we have
taken as freeborn subjects of Great Britain."

Angelica and her sisters were no more likely to keep their opinions to
themselves than their mother. But the family stood as one, and Philip
Schuyler announced its allegiance for the "Patriots" against those
friends and relatives who would side with the "Loyalists." "It is now
actually begun," he wrote to England. "And in the spirit of Joshua I say,
I care not what others may do, as for me and my house, we will serve
our country."

After the letter was done, Angelica watched her father ride away
for Philadelphia to take his seat in the Continental Congress. When
she saw him next, he was wearing the epaulets of a major general and
being escorted to dinner at Albany's King's Arms Tavern by a Troop of
the Horse.

In the summer of 1775, both Schuyler homes—The Pastures in Albany
and their Saratoga farmhouse—became military headquarters for
the Northern Department of the Continental Army, which was commanded by Major General Philip Schuyler. In both places, and farther
north at Fort Ticonderoga (recently seized from the British), an expedition to Canada was preparing to launch. Through both houses came
a flood of congressional delegates, tribal representatives, messengers,

and ever so many aspiring battlefield heroes—all elbowing one another for position and rank, and railing about glory.

"Let me ask you Sir, when is the Time for brave Men to exert themselves in the Cause of Liberty and their Country, if this is not?" General George Washington wrote to Angelica's father that year. For a woman, brave or otherwise, the exertion expected was hospitality—nursing, housing, and feeding.

Moving between the two households, the women and the enslaved staff of the Schuyler family went to work. Each visitor needed to be met and managed according to complex social protocols. Supplies and meals and household labor had to be performed, or at least managed, with military precision. The Schuylers and their staff were experienced hosts. "It would be seven years before I could be as intimate with half the World," one young congressional commissioner remarked of his visit at The Pastures. "There is so much frankness & freeness in this Family that a man must be dead to every feeling of Familiarity who is not familiarized the first hour of his being among them. Nature has given them at Albany what the Tour of Europe could not." His emphasis on "family"—used three times in a single sentence—was not insignificant. If the king was father of his people, then a general was father of his army. A house in order reflected on a general's abilities.

General Schuyler had many abilities—he had spent the prior war working in logistics—but he had almost no experience leading an army in battle. For this reason, the Continental Congress had appointed Richard Montgomery, a former British army officer and a kinsman by marriage, as his brigadier general. When General Montgomery arrived in Albany that summer, be brought his new wife, Angelica's forthright cousin Janet. If Angelica had been dazzled by her father's new military role, Janet was downright furious about her husband going to war. When her Richard had first presented her with a black ribbon to sew into a cockade for his hat—to signal his new rank—Janet had flatly refused to do so. But Richard Montgomery had more formal military training than most men in the United Colonies, and the Continental Army needed him. In the end, Richard left the decision to Janet, but not before he fired the shot he knew would find its mark in a Livingston's clannish pride of place: If great families like the Livingstons sat out the war safe in their congressional seats, voting "aye" or "nay" on words that would cost the blood of others, then the cause was already lost. Smarting, Janet picked up the black ribbon and stitched the rosette for her husband's hat, reluctantly joining the wives and mothers throughout the colonies upon whose support the success of the war would depend. Then she helped their enslaved manservant Dick pack the general's trunk for war—silver forks, buckles, three pairs of white breeches, Holland waistcoats, silk stockings, seven ruffled shirts, and a dictionary.

Although General Schuyler's orders from General Washington were to prepare to undertake the expedition to Canada, he felt he had to attend to more pressing business. The Six Nations of the Iroquois, as the early French explorers had dubbed the tribes of that large, powerful confederacy, or the Haudenosaunee, as those tribes called themselves, had been formal allies of the British since the war against the French. Now, however, as the Continental Army prepared to fight the British, that alliance posed an enormous risk, so the Continental Congress had sent a team of commissioners, several of them Southerners, with experience negotiating with the Cherokee, to keep the peace between the colonies and the Haudenosaunee. Philip Schuyler had been tasked with other duties, but he was not inclined to leave such delicate diplomacy to outsiders who did not have his personal history with the tribal delegates and sachems whose ancestors had known his ancestors.

General Schuyler dispatched General Richard Montgomery to Fort Ticonderoga, to survey the soldiers and supplies there, and he tasked his two elder daughters with amusing one young conference delegate who seemed especially green. (Betsy took the young gentleman hiking, Angelica may have sent him off to a Netherlander funeral.) Still, the negotiations went slowly. The Haudenosaunee were protective of their alliance with Britain. One senior clan leader and cultural interlocutor was particularly vehement. For fifteen years, Molly Brant had been the life partner of the recently deceased superintendent of Indian affairs, Sir William Johnson, with whom she had had eight children, but she arrived at the Albany conference dressed not as the widow of a British baronet but as a Mohawk stateswoman. Like her brother, Joseph Brant, she opposed any alliance with the rebels. The colonists, she understood, wanted land, but the king of England had promised the Confederacy that Britain would not permit settlement west of the Appalachians.

Philip Schuyler knew Molly and Joseph Brant, and he had often worked with Sir William Johnson. He knew the Haudenosaunee would not join the rebellion; he just wanted the powerful confederacy to remain neutral. He and the commissioners argued that this was not a war between enemies, but rather a family quarrel. Finally, they agreed upon a covenant of neutrality, and General Schuyler rushed off to invade Canada.

It was September by the time the Continental Army finally set off for Quebec from Fort Ticonderoga. Officially, it was an invasion, but it was also an invitation to the colonists of that British province to join the other thirteen in rebellion. Philip Schuyler half expected the Canadian colonists to join them willingly. Indeed, Montreal fell quickly, but General Schuyler would not see this happen. Before the Northern Department of the Continental Army had reached the northern mouth of Lake Champlain, its commander was too ill to walk. When Catharina Schuyler heard that her husband had been rowed back to Fort Ticonderoga in a precarious state of health, she packed supplies, doled out orders to her daughters and her staff, and left with her driver, Lewis. The first day's journey north and across the Mohawk River by ferry was familiar and easy, and she and Lewis likely made it in the relative comfort of a chaise. But after Saratoga, there were "corduroy roads" made of logs laid one against the other, so the chaise was left behind and she made the next bone-rattling leg of her trip by wagon, despite the risk such jolting was believed to pose to a woman in her eighth month of pregnancy.

Philip Schuyler recovered quickly in his wife's care, but he did not follow his army northward. General Montgomery had captured Montreal, but the expedition wasn't unfolding as the two generals had envisioned. The Canadians had not rallied to their cause. Nor were the Continental soldiers much of an army—at least not in comparison to the army model General Montgomery knew: "There is such an equality among them, that the officers have no authority," he complained about his American troops to his brother-in-law, the Continental congressman Robert R. Livingston. "The privates are all generals but not soldiers." Further complicating the situation, winter was coming and smallpox was spreading.

General Schuyler had written that he hoped to rejoin the army, but by the time the prisoners of war from Montreal began arriving, he had contracted "a violent Flux," so he traveled instead to Albany. Now The Pastures became a hospital as well as a military command post, giving new meaning to Philip Schuyler's pledge at the war's onset: "As for me and my house, we will serve our country."

The course of human events flowed on. Catharina Schuyler's baby was born. General Schuyler marched three thousand soldiers up the Mohawk River to parley with representatives of the Mohawk—one of the Six Nations—about a Loyalist agitator under that tribe's protection. He had returned to Albany by the morning of January 7, in time for his new daughter's baptism.

The baby was named Cornelia, after Philip Schuyler's mother and the baby who had died while her father was in England. In honor of her name, the young lady who carried the baby to church was Angelica's cousin Cornelia, her Aunt Geertruy's daughter, who had lived with her long ago in their grandmother's house on Jonckerstraet. The name Cornelia was important for yet another reason. In Roman history, Cornelia was a widow who turned down a king's proposal of marriage so that she could educate her sons and tend to their careers as political reformists. This was seen as model womanhood, and Philip Schuyler's own widowed mother had lived by it.

Immediately after church services and the baby's baptism, Albany turned its attention to the train of sledges slung with cannons attempting to cross the river. Suspense was high; warm weather had weakened the ice and the oxen, and the cannons were extremely heavy. These were the cannons captured with Fort Ticonderoga, and they were bound for Boston, which General Washington's Main Army was holding under siege. As soon as the first cannons successfully reached the opposite shore, General Schuyler wrote happily to General Washington that, "this Morning I had the satisfaction to see the first Division of Sleds with Cannon cross the River, should there be Snow all the Way to Cambridge, they will probably arrive there about this Day Week." Later that day, one cannon did break through the ice, but the townspeople, experienced with fishing things out of the river, joined in the effort of raising it again. The effort would pay off, but it was the last good news of the winter.

Less than a week later, General Schuyler's next letter to his commander left Albany by urgent express: "I wish I had no Occasion to send My Dear General this Melancholly Account," he wrote to General Washington. "My Amiable Friend the Gallant Montgomery is no more . . . & we have met with a severe Check, in an unsuccessful Attempt on Quebec." On New Year's Eve, General Richard Montgomery, while leading a last-ditch effort to take the town of Quebec, had been shot in the head and had died in the snow where he fell.

The invasion of Quebec Province began with a few thousand Continental soldiers, the officers' servants (many of them enslaved) and the camp staff (some of them women) whose half rations were now reduced by necessity. These soldiers and their retinue starved, froze, and fought both the British and smallpox. But in the synecdoche of the military— the head standing in for the whole—it was General Montgomery's death that was significant. It was so significant, in fact, that it was evolving into myth. At his funeral, Richard Montgomery was eulogized as "an American Cincinnatus," after the Roman model of civic virtue who had left his plow to lead an army.

CHAPTER 6

Loyalties and Petty Treasons

The week Angelica turned twenty, the *Connecticut Courant* committed its entire front page to reprinting *Common Sense,* the slim manifesto that was just then spreading through the United Colonies like a fever in an army camp. The anonymous author rallied American patriots to go beyond fighting for rights and representation and move to make a full separation of the colonies from Britain: "Britain is the parent country, say some. Then the more shame upon her conduct. Even brutes do not devour their young."

Common Sense promised that "the birthday of a new world is at hand." As Angelica faced becoming twenty, she likely craved a little independence herself. When she was a little girl, her celebrations had been comedic inversions—children playing at adults, hosting their friends at table, gorging on chocolate and *olie-koecken*—a festival of fools, a saturnalia. When the world was right side up, she was just a child. She had no rights, only privileges granted by her parents or extended to her through them. It was a child's duty to submit to a parent, but it was also a wife's duty to submit to a husband, as it was a subject's duty to submit to a monarch. The hierarchy—king to noble, noble to peasant, father to wife, wife to child—was a rigid structure, power and dependency girded with love, as delicate and strong as a whalebone birdcage.

During that first winter of the war, everyone in the United Colonies was anxious for news. Buried amid the usual advertisements offering snuff, lace, and whale oil, or wanting wet nurses or the return of run-away indentured or enslaved servants, came bureaucratic announcements that Congress had formed a committee to superintend the treasury, for instance, which was welcome news to those in Albany who supplied and transported the army and hoped to settle their accounts. Or, as if printed specifically for her eyes, there was the news that Congress had appointed Benjamin Franklin to lead a diplomatic delegation to Canada. For Angelica, this meant one thing: The Pastures would soon have more houseguests.

In March, reports came from Massachusetts that the cannons from Fort Ticonderoga that Albany townspeople had hauled over the weak river ice were now arrayed on Boston's Dorchester Heights, compelling the British under General Gage's replacement, General William Howe, to evacuate the town. But now came the question of where the British Army would turn next: North to reinforce Quebec? South to attack New York? The Americans still held Montreal and had Quebec under siege, and regiments from Boston began marching to join them even before the last of the British transports embarked, but the invasion of Canada was foundering.

Seventy-year-old Benjamin Franklin arrived in Albany in April 1776 "disguised in furs" and already so fatigued by the journey that he felt he should write farewell letters to his friends. For a week, he remained in the care of the Schuyler household, waiting out a spring snow while General Schuyler went ahead to assess the state of the ice on the lakes. The small party of diplomats now sought to accomplish what the invasion had not: to bring Britain's fourteenth North American colony into the rebellion. But the weather was severe and the Canadians chillier still, and when Dr. Franklin passed through Albany again on his return from Canada in May, all he had to show for his journey was a fine marten-fur cap.

In addition to her usual duties, Angelica made herself useful by sifting through the news—from newspapers and by word of mouth. She dispatched summaries to her father as he rode that spring between the northern forts. They were clever, formal letters—the sort that would be passed around and read by other people. She spoke of political and military affairs and did not mention that Betsy had the mumps or speak of herself. Instead, the young lady reported on the infighting over who should captain the newly built ships coming off the stocks along the North River, the most experienced sea captains or the men of highest rank: "We hear no news from the Army at l'île aux Noix [Quebec] and the idea of a Ministerial Fleet is Lost in our disgust of American Perfidy."

There was a growing rift between so-called Patriots and Loyalists, and those who tried not to take sides—such as the Schuylers' relative William Smith—were finding themselves in a dangerous no-man's-land. Meanwhile, even within the rebellion, rivalries and personal ambitions impeded military strategy, and conspiracies threatened to unravel what was left. Angelica was fluent in these factions: "Mr. Mathews is Condemned," she quipped to her father about the mayor of New York who was arrested for conspiring to assassinate General Washington and spike New York's cannons, should General Howe attack New York. No one was above suspicion, and New York was full of Loyalists who might sabotage the war from within. "The fleet were to have attacked the city on the day on which the conspirators were to have assassinated our Worthy Generals," Angelica reported of the alleged plot.

Angelica also kept an eye on a distant cousin, Lady Mary Johnson, the twenty-five-year-old wife of a powerful Loyalist New York landowner whom her father was keeping under house arrest in Albany. Like her cousin Janet Montgomery, now an icon draped in black mourning clothes, Lady Mary had become a figurehead of the war—although she stood for the other side.

When they were girls, Lady Johnson, then called Polly Watts, had come to Albany with Governor Moore's entourage. Since then, Angelica had known her in political circles in New York, where the Watts family lived at 3 Broadway, and Polly's father sat on the governor's council. In July 1773, the New York *Gazette* announcement of Miss Watts's June wedding had described the bride as "a young lady highly distinguished for the advantages of person, as well as mental accomplishments." Sir

John Johnson was far from being known for "mental accomplishments" (his academic career at Benjamin Franklin's school in Philadelphia had been brief and unimpressive), and although he was an heir to a fortune, that fortune was in wilderness acreage and human chattel. But Sir John had knelt before King George III, and his loyalty was unflagging. Likewise, Polly Watts was so firmly a Loyalist that she had been a member of a delegation that had traveled up the North River to rally influential families, including the Livingstons, to the side of the king. Now Sir John and Lady Mary Johnson were joined in cause and matrimony, and they were causing General Schuyler a great deal of trouble.

When the war began, and General Schuyler had been conferring with the Haudenosaunee and assembling an army to call on Canada, Sir John Johnson had done likewise, but for the British. So General Schuyler had led a militia force up the frozen Mohawk River to put a stop to Sir John's efforts. But, given Sir John's kinship ties to the Mohawk, and the value General Schuyler placed on the agreed covenant of neutrality, he had granted Sir John parole, on his word as a gentleman. This compromise had not worked out. The public accused General Schuyler of sharing Sir John's loyalties, and Sir John remained a threat. When General Schuyler sent a regiment to take Sir John into custody, Lady Johnson received them at Johnson Hall with the news that Sir John had "resolved to retire into the woods." Opting not to pursue a man known for his abilities as a wilderness warrior, the officers instead arrested his pregnant wife and two toddlers and took them to Albany. General Schuyler put the family under house arrest as insurance against what he called "the effects of her husband's virulence." Holding a woman hostage, especially a woman of Lady Johnson's status, proved challenging. She trafficked in information and undermined General Schuyler in angry letters. She wrote to General Washington, complaining that she had been subject to "threats from General Schuyler too indelicate & cruel." Soon, even the enemy were referring to Lady Johnson: "Arbitrary imprisonment, confiscation of property, persecution and torture . . . are among the palpable enormities that verify the affirmative," wrote one British officer to justify harsh measures against the rebels.

Angelica handled her furious cousin gently. "There has been a report in town that Sir John Johnson was dead, some person had told Lady Johnson and made her very unhappy," she wrote to her father. "I desired a Lady to tell her that he was not Dead, but not to mention my name as I should not wish her to imagine herself under an obligation to me for what was only an act of humanity; if you approve of this I shall applaud myself for it; if not my future conduct must be Improved by your example." Then she concluded her letter with a verbal curtsy, "I am with affection your dutiful child Ange: Schuyler."

The chivalric code that all her male friends invoked when they spoke of valor and honor insisted that one care for those weaker than oneself. But it was not clear which of the two young ladies had more power. Angelica Schuyler was not under house arrest as Lady Johnson was. She could still saddle her horse Fly and go off for a gallop, if she chose. But she was still a child. And she would be for as long as she owed her duty to her parents.

On July 4, 1776, Angelica Schuyler wrote to her father that she hoped the future would bring "news favourable to our Cause." That same night, printers in Philadelphia pressed the first two hundred copies of the newly ratified Declaration of Independence. When this broadside reached The Pastures, Angelica's father was away at a conference with the Six Nations, enabling her to read it first, before forwarding the shocking document up the Mohawk River.

"We hold these truths to be self-evident, that all men are created equal, that they are endowed by their Creator with certain unalienable Rights, that among these are Life, Liberty and the pursuit of Happiness," the document began. Then it charged the king with a catalogue of "abuses and usurpations" committed against the colonies and concluded that the United Colonies "ought to be Free and Independent States; that they are Absolved from all Allegiance to the British Crown, and that all political connection between them and the State of Great Britain, is and ought to be totally dissolved; and that as Free and Independent States, they have full Power to levy War, conclude Peace, contract Alliances, establish Commerce, and to do all other Acts and Things which Independent States may of right do."

Even if she agreed with every word in the Declaration, which her own cousin Robert R. Livingston had helped to write, Angelica understood the terrifying significance.

Common Sense had compared the war to a separation: "It matters very little now, what the king of England either says or does; he hath wickedly broken through every moral and human obligation, trampled nature and conscience beneath his feet," the pamphlet had argued. "It is *now* the interest of America to provide for herself. She hath already a large and young family, who it is more her duty to take care of, than to be granting away her property, to support a power who is becoming a reproach to the names of men and Christians." By this metaphor, the Declaration of Independence was a motion for divorce, something that then was only legal in Connecticut.

Continental Army officers were ordered to read the document to the soldiers. Each word was treason. There would be no turning back now.

Treason, under English law, was the betrayal of a state authority to whom one owed allegiance, and it was a popular word in 1776. Petit or petty treason was the betrayal by a servant, wife, or child of their master, husband, or parent. If a subject killed a sovereign, the crime was worse than ordinary murder because the crime was not against only one person, but rather against the order of things: A woman convicted of any form of treason was to be burned at the stake.

The War of Independence was very much against the order of things. "We hold these truths to be self-evident, that all men are created equal," Angelica read along with every literate American alive. But what of women? What would their independence look like? A woman was required by law to be the dependent of a father, a husband, even a younger brother—or, absent these, a ward of the state. Like a child, she required a guardian. Even a widow, a "relic," was seen as bound to a man and beholden to his interests, albeit a man not even physically present. And yet, if these were truly new times, if an individual had natural rights that came from somewhere other than an anointed king, the structure of marriage and family would necessarily become different.

Such logic likely seemed at once as ludicrous and thrilling as the Pinkster festival or her childhood birthday parties when inversions of power played out only to revel in their absurdity, like the interludes of chaos in a Shakespeare comedy, when a Bottom is on top. Everyone understood that the world would be righted by the play's end. But the revolution taking place around Angelica was not a game or a play. When the chaos ended, what shape would the country take?

Angelica could not wait to know the future if she wanted to play a part in making it. She was a foot soldier in her current position, and for all the public mourning for General Montgomery, no one had reported the names of foot soldiers who had died with him in Quebec.

Angelica—properly *Miss* Schuyler, the honorific due the eldest unwed daughter—adored her father, who indulged her in return. With no male sibling old enough to supersede her, she reigned over her five siblings: her two closest sisters, Betsy and Margarita (who was called Peggy), and their three younger brothers, John Bradstreet (Johnny), Philip (Phil), and, toddling after them, little Rensselaer. With her white skin, she outranked the enslaved Black members of the household, but some of them had raised her and held standing that would have prevented her from pressing the point. Rank and authority did not always correlate, a point a pretty girl could not help making now and then to the aides-de-camp and junior officers who flocked to The Pastures when the war began, jockeying for rank.

She was twenty now, still a minor but not a child. As for her rank, there was only one way for Angelica to change her station, and that was to marry. Marriage was a gamble. Nearly every novel warned young women of rakes and charlatans. And the examples around her—widowed Janet Montgomery, imprisoned Lady Mary Johnson, her own overworked mother—were hardly storybook romances. Still, if Angelica wanted a greater say than she had as a general's daughter, in a country where "the privates are all generals," she would have to find the right man.

From books and by example, Angelica had been instructed in an art of matchmaking that verged on blood sport. An ambitious young lady seeking a husband ought to calculate a prospect's pedigree, training, conformation, temperament, and observable health, possibly even his teeth, just as one would judge a horse or hound. Or, like her father assessing soldiers' merits, she might weigh a man's intelligence, honor, and "activity." Or, like her mother, she might measure a man by the acres he owned on the North River and his pew in the Dutch Reformed Church.

At least in 1776, the country's most promising young officers flowed through The Pastures. Angelica's father's military family—as he called them—consisted of young gentlemen chosen for their promise and their family backgrounds. There was her father's aide-de-camp, Brockholst Livingston, the son of the governor of New Jersey, whose sister Sarah had been married for two years to the rising New York lawyer John Jay, but Brockholst was only nineteen, a year younger than Angelica. There was Nicholas van Rensselaer, a young gentleman farmer from just across the river, with all the attributes her own father had claimed when he had wed Angelica's mother. And Philip van Cortlandt, who'd come to The Pastures from Fort Ticonderoga the previous autumn to convalesce from a fever and recovered so fully that the next time he visited the Schuylers, he departed on ice skates and dined the second night with the Livingstons in Rhinebeck, sixty miles downriver.

Men with skills the army needed—like Philip van Cortlandt, who might have served as the engineer General Schuyler sought—would settle for no role save one of action. And they certainly weren't settling down. To them, the battlefield was all that mattered. Even those men who valued pure erudition—the would-be poets and philosophers—had abandoned Latin and Greek for blood and glory.

If fighting men were not disposed to thoughts of marriage, Angelica would have to look elsewhere, perhaps to men whose contributions to the war came by way of a pen, rather than a musket. In this category were her father's two military secretaries, John Lansing and Richard Varick, both newly minted lawyers. John Lansing, who had been raised and educated in Albany, often traveled with the general. Richard Varick more often remained at The Pastures, where he opened the mail and did odd jobs like hiring wagoners or finding nails for the shipwrights madly building boats on Lake Champlain. When the general was away, he remained at The Pastures to meet official callers, copy the mail, and carry out commissions for Catharina Schuyler, whose household needs—such as pickling supplies—were in no way separate from military needs. If Richard Varick was not sufficiently established to undertake a marriage, he was evidently besotted with the Schuyler girls: "Your amiable lady daughters also claim no small share of my love and sincere respect for their goodness and attention," Richard Varick wrote to their father. "I wish ever to cleave a line of conduct which may merit their as well as your approbation." It seemed most likely sweet, steady Betsy to whom he would cleave, given any opportunity. John Lansing kept his thoughts to himself.

Before she had become a widow, Janet Montgomery had bemoaned in verse the sudden death of romance: "Marriages now are so much out of fashion/That even Love is Esteemed an unworthy Passion." But time for making light had passed, Janet's own husband was dead, and it's entirely possible that Angelica Schuyler had seen a draft of her future plans succumb to the snow in Canada, where so many young Americans had died.

All around Angelica, even in her own home, were her male friends, those ambitious aides-de-camp—young, bright, active men, all with family connections like her own—who salivated for both cause and personal advancement. These young men spoke incessantly of glory, honor, and rank. As for Angelica—*Miss* Schuyler—only one change in rank was available.

Marriage was described to young white women like Angelica as "the haven of matrimony." When she arrived at that "haven," a wife ceased to be a person and became, in legal terms, an extension of her husband: a *feme covert*, a "covered woman." She could not sue or be sued. She could not make a contract. She could not serve as a witness, even in trials concerning crimes committed against her person. Her marriage vow was her own prerogative: "I do" was her sole vote. With it, she consented to be bound, for life, to the government of a husband. She became a subject in political body, a *polis* of one—that is, unless one counted the servants, the enslaved, and any preexisting or eventual minor children, who also lacked individual rights. But of course, these states were not equivalent: An enslaved woman was not legally entitled to marry at all.

As for keeping the rank of daughter? Unlike a widow, who could stand proxy for her dead spouse, or a bachelor who might live freely, in the world Angelica inhabited, a spinster was forever a dependent, vestigial, legally a perpetual child. Marriage might go badly, but for women like Angelica, spinsterhood could only offer a stunted life. A marriage might be just a change of masters, but at least a change of master could be a choice, an act of agency.

That is, if she got to choose. Jean-Jacques Rousseau had reasoned that, as love—or "mutual inclination"—was the first duty of a married pair, and love was not within anyone's control, thus love ought to be felt before a couple were united. But for parents, leaving so enormous a choice to a child, even an intelligent adult child, was difficult.

That summer, a man did come to The Pastures seeking to supplant General Schuyler, although not in his daughter's heart. A bespectacled major general in his fifties, Horatio Gates wasn't interested in Angelica. He wanted General Schuyler's command of the Northern Army.

Courtesy required that supper come before business, and the family made room for the new arrivals at the dinner table, where they had just sat down to eat. By this time, members of the Schuyler family were

practiced at hosting and had a protocol for dealing with political adversaries. So too was the liveried servant Prince, who laid plates and silver
and poured Madeira. While the men bided their time, the young ladies
chatted and laughed, effervescent in the candlelight, their conversation
playfully witty and pitched to ease and charm. The Schuyler women
understood that when a man's blood was up, it was their duty to sit on
his pistol case—metaphorically or otherwise.

One young officer who had accompanied General Gates to Albany
was struck by the elegant style of everything he saw: the beautiful
house, the lively black-eyed young ladies, the panorama of the river up
which he'd just spent seven days sailing. Then again, Colonel Trumbull's eye for beauty was exceptional. Plus, he missed his own sister,
who had suffered a breakdown after witnessing the aftermath of the
1775 Battle of Bunker Hill and had hanged herself. Angelica already
knew the governor of Connecticut's older sons—one was in Albany as
paymaster, the other was commissary general. Colonel Trumbull was
the youngest, just her age. He had attended Harvard, learned French
on the side, and was expected to study the law next, but even though
he had been blinded in one eye by a childhood fall down a flight of
stairs, he wanted to be an artist. He was called Jack by family and
friends to avoid confusion with his elder brother Jonathon, but this
was no night for first names and familiarity. All were given their rank,
from General to Miss. Neither Miss Schuyler nor Colonel Trumbull
expressed any romantic interest in one another, but perhaps at that
first fraught dinner each recognized in the other the makings of a
good friend.

After civilities had been performed, the two generals went into General Schuyler's study to sort out the confusion. Each officer produced
his commission. Reading General Gates's orders, General Schuyler concluded that they very clearly placed him in command of the army in
Canada, whereas his own orders very clearly placed him in command
of the army in New York. The only hitch was that there was no army in
Canada. General Schuyler pointed out that General Benedict Arnold,
who had assumed command of the Northern Army after General

Montgomery's death, despite being wounded himself, had just obtained permission to retreat beyond Île aux Noix, reentering New York.

A few days later, Generals Schuyler and Gates and their retinues rode off for Lake Champlain to see "the wretched remnant of the army"— half of them sick, all of them suffering—and to discuss how to secure the lake, now that the British were preparing their counterinvasion.

CHAPTER 7

The Breach of the Fortress of Ticonderoga

1777

In September 1776, the Continental Army abandoned Manhattan to the British. Nine days later, the town of New York burned. Meanwhile, three hundred miles of river and lakes to the north, General Benedict Arnold was leading a flotilla of galleys and "gundolas" to meet the new British fleet on Lake Champlain.

That same month, a team of auditors arrived from the Continental Congress tasked with reviewing and settling the accounts of the Northern Army. Promptly on arrival, Commissioners James Milligan, John Carter, and John Welles opened an office in Albany, hung out a sign, printed broadsides, and sent announcements to the nearest newspapers, bidding all persons, civil or military, employed in the service of the United States, to produce their accounts for settlement.

General Schuyler welcomed the audit. Over the course of that summer—especially in places where old stereotypes of Dutch greed blended with rivalries and cultural differences between Yankees and Yorkers—rumors had promulgated that the Dutch Yorker leading the Northern Army was embezzling funds. Now, New England regiments were refusing to serve under him. Even Congress had questions.

Compared to would-be heroes who traipsed through The Pastures that autumn, the treasury commissioners with their ledgers and quills were bureaucrats, but each had proven his loyalty to the rebellion. One was an Englishman—John Carter, Esquire—who had emigrated to the colonies before the war. In the first weeks of the war, he had been a passenger on a merchant ship bound for Portugal that was captured at sea by the British Navy and taken into Boston. When he secured his release—paroled on his honor as a gentleman, as was customary—he had supplied the Continental Congress with intelligence gleaned during his visit with the British. To further prove his bona fides, Mr. Carter carried a letter to General Schuyler from one New York delegate vouchsafing that he was not a "tory" who supported royal authority, but rather, "though young in years, an Old fashioned English Whig."

General Schuyler was too busy to pay much attention. He opened his house to the auditors, introduced them to John Lansing and Richard Varick, and showed them his books. Then he left Albany, accompanying Mrs. Schuyler and the younger children to their house at Saratoga, then traveling on to the several northern forts under his command to assess their readiness to receive the counterinvasion from Canada.

John Carter may not have been chasing military promotion and battlefield laurels, but he was as ambitious and as vehement in his opinions regarding the American cause as the rest of the young gentlemen in General Schuyler's orbit. If the Schuylers had perceived the extent of his ambition, perhaps they would not have thought it wise to leave their pretty firstborn in charge of the house in Albany while the rest of the family was away.

If her parents underestimated John Carter, Angelica did not. She soon deduced that he was more than a tabulator of accounts. He spoke French. He didn't just read poetry; back in England, he'd known poets, even female poets. He was in his early thirties, a slight man, and beautiful, with languid blue eyes and passionate political opinions. And he was very good at cards.

Angelica loved to play cards. Perhaps it was the even footing with the young men who sat down to play with her. Perhaps it was the flex of the intellect, the thrill of the win, the rush of a risky wager, the silent communication with a whist partner. For John Carter, however, the best part of the game was the gamble and he loved a big, all-in play. In Albany, as he sat at the table, contemplating his thirteen cards and the remarkable brunette across from him, he saw that the odds were long, but might not be impossible.

While John Carter considered his strategy in Albany, General Horatio Gates, who now commanded Fort Ticonderoga, wanted urgently to see the commissioners. Even as the fort braced for attack, he summoned them. When the auditors failed to arrive, he wrote more forcefully, insisting that, "If that request is not complied with, I shall be under the necessity of acquainting Congress that their order is wanting to bring you here."

With equal arrogance, John Carter replied that he and his colleagues "were not under the direction of any officer in the army." Besides, he continued, "There are accounts here of much greater consequence, which will render it impossible to leave this place."

John Carter had chosen his side in this war-within-a-war.

Next, John Carter wrote to General Schuyler: "I am sorry to tell you, that Miss Anna had yesterday a very serious attack from a fever." He was already using Angelica's first name to her father.

Philip Schuyler was unimpressed by John Carter. The young Englishman courting his daughter had no family connections, no estate or hope of one, and no fortune save what coin he carried on his person.

John Carter's only credentials for his current posting was that he had provided useful intelligence to Congress in the first weeks of the war, having witnessed what he suspected was a Loyalist plot to supply the British. The capture of the *Charming Sally*, five hundred miles into a voyage to Portugal, had felt almost prearranged. The ship's captain had made no attempt to escape the *Glasgow*, or to resist seizure. Then, when the ship was brought into Boston, the British commander, General Thomas Gage, flouted naval wartime custom—in which a condemned ship and its cargo was a prize—by initially offering to purchase the *Charming Sally*'s cargo of wheat flour at a fair market rate and let the captain and the ship go free.

None of this was good news, but it had been useful to Congress and

General Washington, then besieging Boston from Charlestown. The information was less useful to the Schuylers: Whether John Carter was a spy for the Americans or for the British, he was still a spy. According to the rules of war, a captured spy did not merit an honorable death, but rather a hanging.

The Schuylers rejected John Carter's suit for Angelica. "The match was exceedingly disagreeable to me," wrote her father.

But John Carter didn't go away.

When March 1777 bowed its way out of Albany with a three-day sleeting blizzard, Angelica's condition was as foul as the weather. She ached. She had another fever. The whites of her eyes and her winter-pale complexion had turned a sickly yellow hue. When Richard Varick wrote to her father, who was en route to Philadelphia to defend his record before the Continental Congress, the secretary relayed that all was well, "Except Miss Schuyler, whose malady, tho not mortal, keeps her exceedingly weak and is probably of a nature different from common disorders."

Indeed, Angelica suffered for reasons beyond the jaundice she'd likely contracted while helping her mother treat the sick officers who were carried into Albany. John Carter, who also had business with Congress, had accompanied her father on the dangerous, two-hundred-mile journey. Spring travel was treacherous in any year. Rivers ran high. Roads turned to sucking mud. But the war made the risks much worse. Bands of deserters prowled the no-man's-land between the rival armies. The enemy's depredations had been explicitly covered in the newspapers:

> From Fishkill: "As usual, these Heroes of Britain, have burnt some houses, plundered the inhabitants of what they could conveniently take away with them, frightened the women and children."

> From Brunswick: "Scarce a day passed without an attempt to forage and plunder, but the Vigilance and bravery of our troops obliges the enemy to return commonly without plunder and often with a very great loss of their men and Baggage."

From Newark: "Great have been the ravages committed by the British troops in this part of the country. . . . Their footsteps with us are marked with desolation and ruin of every kind. I, with many others, fled from the town, and those that tarried behind suffered almost every manner of evil. The murder, robbery, ravishments, and insults, they were guilty of are dreadful."

Angelica's mother's anxiety for her husband's safety was high, but Angelica had an added fear. Her beau hoped to convince her father to let him marry her, but her father probably hoped just as much that he could convince John Carter to fold his hand and go away. Even if the general hadn't needed convincing, Catharina Schuyler—with her Van Rensselaer and Livingston roots—would never bend. Family, bloodlines, and property were her core priorities, and John Carter possessed none of them. No wheedling or whining or even straight-up begging would sway Angelica's mother.

Meanwhile, observing her daughter's state, Catharina summoned the doctor to bleed her. Conveniently, bloodletting was a common treatment for both heartache as well as jaundice, but rarely a cure.

Spring came gradually, and as the ice broke open, the Northern Department began to prepare for the inevitable counterinvasion from Quebec. General Horatio Gates returned to Albany to take command in General Schuyler's absence, and the young gentlemen of his military family made themselves at home at The Pastures. The distraction of their presence may have been balm for Angelica's nerves, but they agitated her mother.

In his unanswered letters to General Schuyler, Richard Varick had complained that these gentlemen who passed the time of day at The Pastures "keep the ladies in alarm" with their talk of imminent invasion. One aide-de-camp, Robert Troup, announced that a fleet of frigates and transports was already sailing up the North River. Another, James Wilkinson, an impulsive twenty-year-old from Maryland whom Mrs. Schuyler had nursed through a dangerous bout of typhus that past winter, erroneously informed her that her husband was now serving as

General Washington's second-in-command on the Delaware River. At this revelation, Catharina Schuyler, having made up her mind to visit headquarters herself, had to be dissuaded.

"These unguarded expressions would alarm even men," Richard Varick conceded. The fear that General William Howe's forces at New York would attack in concert with an invasion from Canada was not far-fetched, making Albany the likely bull's eye of the British Army's summer strategy.

What no one expected was the speed with which the summer campaign began. The townspeople of Albany were just seeding their garden plots along the North River when an express rider crossed the brownstone bridge at a brisk clip to deliver the news that British ships—two schooners, six gondolas, and forty bâteaux—had been spotted through the fog off Split Rock on Lake Champlain.

Horatio Gates, who had yet to brave the muddy spring roads to visit Fort Ticonderoga, was as shocked as anyone: "I never thought it was possible, for the Main Force of the Enemy to come so early up the Lake," General Gates marveled. It was only the second of June.

The weeks that followed were frenzied. On the fourth of June, General Schuyler arrived home. Now that he was back, and—to General Gates's irritation—back in command, he made up for lost time. A Seneca chief and his delegation had been waiting at The Pastures. The covenant was fraying—the Mohawk were petitioning for permission to buy necessary goods from the British at Fort Niagara. General Schuyler scribbled off letters to Congress, pleading again for the goods necessary to maintain the covenant and deter the Haudenosaunee from turning to trade with the British for necessities. Philip Schuyler had hoped that General Gates would remain in command at Fort Ticonderoga, but he refused and left town to contest directly to Congress his removal from command. In his place, Philip Schuyler appointed another general—Arthur St. Clair—to command Fort Ticonderoga.

After ten days of meetings and letters, General Schuyler traveled north with his wife and daughter Betsy, leaving them at Saratoga and traveling onward to inspect the North River forts, Edward and Ann, before going off to Lake Champlain to see what defenses were in place. When he reached Fort Ticonderoga, he found it woefully ill-prepared for the coming invasion. The army had been busy building redoubts and running a boom chain across the river to impede ships from reaching the fort. But there were not enough soldiers to defend the position fully. The salted meat had turned rancid and the flour had not arrived. General Schuyler wrote to the Massachusetts governor the first day he was there: "Every moment's delay is attended with Danger and may prove fatal to us."

With all attention directed northward, Angelica reunited with John Carter. The ten weeks he'd traveled with her father had changed nothing. The couple were as determined to wed as her parents were opposed. Angelica had spent the previous weeks in the company of General Gates's officers, one of whom may have influenced her thinking: Colonel Tadeusz Kosciuszko was a young Polish nobleman who'd been caught attempting to elope with a young lady. He'd been beaten and banished for love.

Angelica saw that she had two choices: She could submit to parental authority or she could rebel, separate, and declare her independence. On the morning of June 21, Angelica had made her choice. She and John crossed the river by ferry, as if visiting her grandfather; instead, they crossed the border into Massachusetts, where they received a marriage license.

On that same day, a vanguard of canoes glided across the 45th parallel, into Lake Champlain. Following these guides were two armed schooners and a vivid column of bâteaux loaded with rank-and-file soldiers. The red coats of British Army regulars contrasted with the uniforms of mercenaries hired from German principalities as reinforcements: Hessian *Jaegers* in green, Brunswickers in blue. Each rank and station was indicated by headwear: beaver-felt tricorns, feathers and cockades, mitre caps, great grenadiers' bearskins, and turkey feathers, angled just so. In all, the invading army was three times the size of the sick, shabby Continental Army now preparing to defend Fort Ticonderoga.

Angelica and John's Monday wedding was succinct and to the point. Neither the bride nor the groom expected more. Protestant weddings, in any event, were deliberately minimal affairs: All that was required was a simple expression of voluntary consent before witnesses and a clerk. Informing the Schuyler family would be another matter. For this, the couple sought help from Angelica's grandfather and godfather Johannes van Rensselaer, who likely made matters even worse.

The couple stayed at Crailo, the Van Rensselaers' manor house directly across the river from Albany, and one of Angelica's uncles was dispatched to Saratoga carrying letters to her parents announcing the news. A few days later, Angelica's parents returned to Albany, but they did not cross the river to see the newlyweds or invite the couple to call on them. Angelica and John each wrote a letter but received no answer. Annoyed, Johannes van Rensselaer finally summoned his forty-year-old daughter and the major general for a dressing-down.

"The General scarcely spoke a dozen Words all the Time, and Mrs. S. was in a most violent Passion and said all that Rage and Resentment could inspire," John Carter reported to the Livingstons. "He told her that he did not know who she took after he was sure not after her Father and Mother." But after Catharina Schuyler's temper had burned down, the Schuylers sent a chilly note inviting the Carters to "come in Person and make their Peace." When John and Angelica crossed the river, they were met at the ferry landing by a chariot sent to carry them to The Pastures, as if they were formal guests, or even strangers.

Twice humiliated—first by her daughter, then by her father—Catharina Schuyler did not yield beyond performing cold civility, but Philip Schuyler threw up his hands. He wrote to the gentleman who had first recommended John Carter to him as "an Old fashioned English Whig": "Carter and my eldest daughter ran off and married, but as there is no undoing this gordian knot, I took what I hope you will think the prudent part: I frowned, I made them humble themselves, forgave, and called them home."

By July third, Philip Schuyler was already using Angelica's marriage as a smoke screen. Twelve wagons of stores and goods were removed that day from the Schuylers' Saratoga farm. To prevent people from thinking he lacked courage or confidence in his army at Fort Ticonderoga and was moving his possessions out of the path of the invasion it was his job to prevent, he explained that these items were for his newly married daughter, as she set up her own household. No one was fooled.

"General Schuyler hourly expects a reinforcement from Peeks Kill with which he intends to march himself," John Carter wrote to one of his fellow commissioners in Philadelphia. "I think the Enemy will get a Drubbing." Philip Schuyler's old friend William Smith, living under house arrest at Livingston Manor, was more savvy: "With 3 or 4000 Men at Ticonderoga he has not Alternative but a Captivity, Death, or a Conduct which will be called Cowardice or Desertion."

Indeed, on July 4, 1777, the first anniversary of the ratification of the Declaration of Independence, the soldiers at Fort Ticonderoga noticed the glimmer of campfires atop a nearby hill. It was nothing to celebrate. One year earlier, Angelica's friend Jack Trumbull had anticipated this scenario when he sketched the terrain surrounding Fort Ticonderoga. The other officers had insisted the hill was too far to pose any risk, but this was easy to test. Unfortunately for them all, Jack was right: A cannon fired from the fort did hit the hillside. They all knew that if the British could hoist their artillery up that steep hill, Fort Ticonderoga would be as indefensible as Boston had been when Fort Ticonderoga's guns were arrayed upon Dorchester Heights. Seeing the lights of fires on the hilltop was warning enough. Rather than risk being forced to surrender, the Continental Army evacuated Fort Ticonderoga in the predawn hours and fled.

Without specifying whether he meant the retreat from Ticonderoga or Angelica's elopement, Richard Varick wrote to Philip Schuyler: "I was sorry and much disappointed to receive the confirmation of so igno-minious a flight."

CHAPTER 8

Join or Die

Even in a crisis, life goes on. Even in the heat of war, people and animals must be fed. Gardens must be tended. Children must be bathed and put to bed. The day after Fort Ticonderoga fell to the British, the manager of the Schuylers' Saratoga farm wrote to report that "Several of our negroes are Sick & has been this three weeks past & not yete able fore Service." The grass had not been mowed. The ploughing had only just been finished. And the garden was overrun with weeds. Angelica's mother set off for Saratoga with her baby, Cornelia, and her maid, Jenny, likely relieved to have an excuse to leave Albany, even though "a band of miscreants" had recently attempted to set fire to her Saratoga house.

The British Army was at least thirty miles away and moving slowly. As they advanced, the Continental Army retreated. Too outnumbered to risk engagement, General Schuyler had assigned the engineer Colonel Kosciuszko the task of devising ways to slow the enemy's advance. Trees were cut across creeks so nothing could be floated. Bridges were demolished so no cannon could be hauled across without rebuilding. Meanwhile, farmers were urged to burn any provisions they could not harvest yet or could not carry away. People said Catharina Schuyler herself put the torch to the Schuylers' wheatfields in Saratoga. As the British chopped their way steadily southward, repairing bridges and clearing blocked roads so wagons and cannons could pass, nimbler foraging parties ranged widely, pilfering chickens and vandalizing as they went. Some took scalps, for which General John Burgoyne, the commander of the invasion, had offered hard coin. Then a letter appeared in newspapers in Boston and New York that further inflamed public imagination. It claimed that a band of men, allied with the British, "took a young woman, Janey McRea by name, out of a house at Fort Edward, carried her about half a mile into the bushes, and there killed and scalped her in cold blood." With each retelling, the young woman of this fresh captivity narrative grew more lovely, virtuous, and virginal. As to whether Miss McRea's first name was Jane, or Janet, or Jenny, whether she possessed golden locks or red or black hair, Angelica likely knew precisely: They were Saratoga neighbors. The detail that Janey McRea was captured while traveling to Fort Ticonderoga to meet her Loyalist fiancé was particularly raw. Not even a month had passed since Angelica's own brash elopement.

Neither Janey McRea's death nor General Burgoyne's army reaching the North River, ten miles upstream, could compel Catharina Schuyler to abandon her farm. Even when Philip insisted she return to Albany, she refused. Evidently, she was still too furious to face Angelica.

Meanwhile, in Albany, Angelica tried to be a wife and did not excel. "She is a young housekeeper and wants to gain experience," her husband wrote to a friend in Philadelphia, with a request that he send the best cookbook he could find to help her improve.

Angelica was probably realizing that she had a lot to learn if she aspired to be anything like her mother. And learning to cook was the least of it.

By August of 1777, everything was unraveling. Sir John Johnson's King's Rangers and a Mohawk force ambushed a militia of Continentals and Oneida allies marching to Fort Schuyler. The Battle of Oriskany was not just a bloodbath, it severed the covenant of neutrality and it ruptured the Haudenosaunee Confederacy itself. Angelica reported the news to Livingston Manor, where her kinsman William

Smith recorded in his diary of the war: "Mrs. Carter says the Sennecas have sent a bloody Hatchet to the Oneidas who are to meet her Father Genl. Schuyler this week at Albany to join the Congress & implore Assistance." Meanwhile, General Burgoyne's army could no longer be checked without a direct confrontation, and, without reinforcements, the Continentals were too outnumbered to withstand battle with a professional army, even if that army was looking a little worse for wear. As these two storms loomed, Philip Schuyler received the news from his replacement, Horatio Gates, that he had been formally relieved of his command for the loss of Fort Ticonderoga.

The first week of September, Angelica, with her new husband, her sister Betsy, and their servants, ferried across the North River and rode east across Claverack Manor, land their family had occupied, for better or worse, for a century and a half. When the evacuees crossed the now-settled border into Massachusetts, they must have looked back. If General Burgoyne captured Albany, they might lose it all. Some were calling 1777, with its numeral 7s like a line of gallows, "the year of the hangman."

Indeed, the noose seemed to be tightening. The British held Newport and Montreal. General Howe's division of the British Army was marching on Philadelphia, General Henry Clinton's division was firmly entrenched at New York and Long Island and would likely attack up the North River, General Burgoyne's force was now advancing down the North River, and yet another prong was descending the Mohawk River to converge at Albany.

Two hundred miles lay between Albany and Boston. If Angelica and Betsy traveled by chaise or wagon, they might have managed thirty miles a day, and if they each rode, and didn't wait for their luggage, they might make fifty. But covering the expanse of cultural difference between their home state and this "country" of Massachusetts—making friends with Bostonians—surely would take more than days or weeks.

Like siblings, the thirteen British colonies in North America shared the same parentage, yet they had little else in common. Like siblings, time and reason for their coming to be and their distinct physical traits, ideological pursuits, and individual interests had formed and informed each one differently. Pennsylvania and Virginia had discrete political structures and economic systems. The character of the Royal Province of New York—polyglot, pluralist, and just a little piratical—had developed under conditions wholly unlike those that had engendered the puritanical theocracy of the early Massachusetts Bay Colony. Rivalries inflamed these differences. In the eyes of Massachusetts, New York had been built by beaver-hatted burghers who were loose in their morals and over-fond of lucre. In the eyes of New Yorkers, Massachusetts was a realm of witch-burning, Indian-warring religious extremists. One visitor wrote of Massachusetts that year, "Puritanism and a spirit of persecution are not yet totally extinguished."

Living in Boston would not be easy. Angelica's Dutch roots made her not just a stranger in Boston (Old Boston's label for all but the purest of Puritans), but a foreigner. Worse still, Massachusetts didn't just loathe her father as a Dutchman or a Yorker. Before the war began, Philip Schuyler had represented New York on the commission that fixed the contentious boundary dividing New York and Massachusetts. The residual animosity over that affair now made Bostonians willing to believe the outlandish rumor that General Schuyler had forfeited Fort Ticonderoga after General Burgoyne fired silver cannonballs over the rampart walls to buy his surrender.

But something unexpected was happening now. As Angelica, Betsy, and John traveled eastward through New England, away from the war, they found they were moving against the flow of traffic. For Yankees who had objected to serving under the Yorker General Schuyler, perhaps it was the change of leadership that made them willing to enlist. For those New Englanders raised on the terror stories of their ancestors' own Indian wars, perhaps the news of the murder of Janey McRea had kindled their fire to fight. Some may have been roused by General Benedict Arnold's success turning the British back on the Mohawk River, or by news of the militia victory against a British foraging party at Bennington. But the most probable reason was visible to the travelers in each fresh haystack and shock of drying wheat they passed:

New Englanders had put up their harvest, their families had provisions for the winter, and now the farmers marched to defend those harvests against invasion. Individual interests had aligned, and at last, reinforcements were flowing toward Albany.

In 1754, two years before Angelica's birth, Benjamin Franklin had traveled to Albany to propose that the colonies join in a "league of friendship." The Philadelphia printer had promoted this idea in advance with a woodcut of a snake chopped into eight pieces, each labeled with the name of a colony, above the caption "Join, or Die." The Albany Plan— loosely modeled after the Confederacy of the Six Nations—failed to pass. But that autumn of 1777, as Angelica and Betsy and their attendants left the country of their past, Congress finally was drafting, and redrafting, the Articles of Confederation, a document that would join the thirteen very different colonies into a more unified nation that just might win the war.

It was counterintuitive—that the states would have to bind themselves together to become "free"—but even the tract *Common Sense*, in making the case for independence, had argued that "the continental belt is too loosely buckled." The success of this long-shot war depended upon friendship between the so-called united states, those in Congress agreed, but law cannot force friendship any more than Johannes van Rensselaer was able to force a reconciliation between Catharina Schuyler and her rebel daughter.

The Articles of Confederation would need not only to be ratified, but also to be enacted—not just as law, but as practice. As General Schuyler's daughters, Angelica and Betsy could not expect a warm reception in New England, but with some grace, crossing the contentious border into the country of Massachusetts could position them to serve a purpose greater than their individual safety. Certainly, for kin, cause, and country, as well as for their own happiness and success, the sisters had to try.

CHAPTER 9

The Maiden Voyage
of the *Angelica*

In Boston, the Carters leased a stately house on Frog Lane, which stretched from the stump of the felled Liberty Tree, past the burying ground at the foot of the Common, to the tidal salt marsh of sedge grass and darting curlews of the bay. Once situated, Angelica Carter and Betsy Schuyler set out to learn the lay of the land and assess their position.

Since the British evacuation of Boston the previous spring, the Common's full quota of seventy cows had returned to graze, so, once again, the sisters lived beside a public pasture. For air and exercise, they could promenade along the mall that divided the Common from town, or, to satisfy Betsy's taste for a vigorous hike, they could climb the hill to Boston's tar-bucket beacon. The British soldiers had felled every tree worth the effort during the siege (the Liberty Tree alone was said to have yielded fourteen cords of firewood), so the view was expansive. Angelica would be particularly interested in the Dorchester Heights, the hills across the bay where the cannons the Albany townspeople had helped to cross the ice had ultimately been arrayed (their number supplemented by a few "Quakers," as they called the painted logs they had positioned to look like cannons). As had happened since then to the Americans at Fort Ticonderoga, the British had realized their disadvantage and evacuated without a fight. Turning clockwise from Dorchester, beyond her own house, she could see the Neck, the strip of land that connected Boston to the mainland. Turning to face due north, she could see the mouth of the Charles River, up which lay the village of Cambridge, once the summer retreat of Boston's better-off, and once again the scholars' haunt: Now that General Washington's Main Army no longer used Harvard's halls as hospitals and barracks, young gentlemen had resumed studying there. Another turn revealed the ruins of Charlestown, and the Mystic River. Out of sight was the famous blood-fed slope upon which the Battle of Bunker Hill had been fought.

From this vantage point, Angelica could also survey Boston's social terrain. Nearest the beacon on the crest stood the Hancocks' mansion—a stone house very like those in which she'd grown up, but badly damaged by the British and empty now, save for the servants. John Hancock was serving his final weeks as the president of the Continental Congress. Dorothy Quincy Hancock was with her family, grieving the death of her daughter. Until the Hancocks returned to town, Angelica would aim her sights lower down the hill, perhaps with neighbors on Frog Lane. These included Mrs. Loring, who was running the family's bakery business while her husband was away fighting in the war, and the Snider family, who, before the war, had lost their eleven-year-old son Christopher when he was shot in the chest by a Loyalist shopkeeper during the riots of 1770. Neither of these households was as welcoming as that of Hannah Breck, who well understood being displaced by the war: During the siege, an artillery shell had exploded in her garden, shattering windows and mirrors. After that, Hannah Breck had left with her two small children to live in Philadelphia, while her husband remained in Boston to safeguard their home and import business. When the city returned to what passed as "normal," they had returned.

As his wife explored the social strata, John Carter trawled Boston for business opportunities, and he found plenty. If Angelica was a stranger, Boston was almost familiar to John. The smells of turpentine, fish, and tidewaters must have reminded him of his childhood home on England's North Sea coast. Angelica's people were land people: They made their fortune in acreage, rents, and timber. But John's people harvested the sea. His forebears had made and lost fortunes fishing for herring and cod and engaging in the Muscovy and Levantine trades, stocking their merchant houses with goods from the Russian and Ottoman Empires. In poor fishing seasons, herring luggers might double as smugglers, making night runs across the sea to trade illegally with the Dutch. This personal history, though he kept his story close, primed John to join in Boston's zeal for privateering.

Shortly after John Carter had first come into Boston in 1775, as a prisoner off the captured *Charming Sally*, Massachusetts had drafted "An Act for Encouraging the Fixing out of Armed Vessels," which permitted civilians to "equip any vessel to sail on the seas, attack, take and bring into any port in this colony all vessels offending or employed by the enemy." By the autumn of 1777, Boston had become—as one privateer termed it—"privateering mad." Stories spread of sailors coming into staggering wealth. As his share of a prize, one fourteen-year-old sailor received one ton of sugar, forty gallons of rum, twenty pounds of ginger, and $100 in gold. Of course, it was risky. In sea battles, wooden and canvas vessels loaded with gunpowder exchanged broadsides until one lowered the flag and accepted capture or exploded. Even those privateer backers who remained safe on shore risked financial cataclysm.

For those who questioned the morality of legal piracy, their scruples were counteracted by the staggering wartime prices. Butter, candles, and common butcher meat were expensive, but flour could not be had for any price. As the prices inflated, paper currency depreciated. At the beginning of that year, $1.25 Continental Currency could purchase one Spanish dollar in specie (milled gold or silver coins), but, due in part to British counterfeits that had diluted that year's printing, it would soon take twice as much paper money to purchase the same in coin.

Want of money was not the sole motivation spurring the Americans' desire to chase down British ships and seize them as prizes. In England, where the prices of imported goods were soaring, the newspapers blamed American "pyrates." Observing this irritation from the relative proximity of France, the diplomat Benjamin Franklin encouraged American privateers: "We expect to make their merchants sick of a contest in which so much is risked and nothing gained."

General Washington was more conflicted. True, privateers were forcing the British to divert resources to defend trade, but they also siphoned off the supply of able-bodied young men the army badly needed. On the other hand, the Continental "Navy," such as it was, proved no match for the formidable British. In the first sea battle of the war, the *Glasgow*—the same twenty-gun ship that had taken the *Charming Sally*—had independently fended off a squadron of five Continental ships. Strengthening Continental sea power, when the army was so undersupplied, would be slow and politically tedious. If merchants and whalers would refit their vessels with funds from private investors, that would increase American naval power without further exacerbating the Continental Army's financial straits.

For John Carter, privateering held another perk. In times of war, a captured gentleman might be set free by an enemy simply by pledging, upon his honor, not to take up arms in the present conflict. Certainly, Commander Thomas Gage would have extracted this pledge from John Carter when he was brought into Boston by the *Glasgow*. Such a pledge would explain why John did not seek a commission in the Continental Army, as most ambitious men of his age and political persuasion were eager to do. But investing in privateer outfits offered a convenient loophole to a pledge not to take up arms. If his ships were successful, he would not only get rich—he would also have the pleasure of "returning the compliment" paid to him personally by the *Glasgow*.

Many Boston women had even greater cause to seek revenge than John Carter. Some had lost sons or husbands on Bunker Hill. Some had had their homes burned or bombarded, or they had faced other forms of violence from an occupying army in a time when the rape of a woman was perceived as an act of a man or men inflicting pain, insult, and property damage upon another man or men. And all were living under the strain of wartime economics—shortages, inflation, and currency depreciation.

One Boston lady who invested in privateer ventures was Lucy Knox, wife of Brigadier General Henry Knox, who had come to Albany the previous winter to transport the cannons from Fort Ticonderoga to Dorchester Heights. Lucy was twenty-one, like Angelica, and had been raised in a comparably elite family in Boston, although hers had evacuated with the British. She was well read, finely educated, and even had fine handwriting, which was unusual for a woman, even one of her social status. If anything delayed the two women from becoming friends, it was that Lucy Knox was one of those Bostonians convinced that "Master Schuyler"—as she called the general, denying him his rank—"cannot be guiltless."

With her family having fled to England, and her husband at the front, Lucy Knox was struggling to live within her means. "When the price of every thing is so exorbitant indeed it is difficult to get the necessarys of life here, at any price," wrote Lucy to her husband that year. "For butter we give two shillings a pound—eggs go for two pence a piece . . . as for flour it is not to be had at any price, nor cyder." And another time: "I am ashamed to tell you what I have spent."

Backing privateers offered a chance for making up the difference, and her husband supported the idea. "I can see no reason why [individuals] may not make war as ever on his own account as to assist it on account of the public," the general reasoned. First, Lucy Knox backed the privateer *Yankee Hero*, on credit, but it was captured. When she could not pay the £100 the *Hero*'s owners demanded, she went in double-or-nothing on the *American Tartar*. When the *Tartar* was run down in a squall by a sixty-four-gun warship, she tried to stay philosophical about the losses when she wrote her husband that "fortune my friend seems against us."

Lucy Knox's losses were not unique, however much they mortified her, but the risks did not deter John and Angelica from trying their own luck. That fall, the Carters backed the ship *Portsmouth*, on a voyage to Bordeaux, France, ostensibly to buy wine but in fact carrying twenty-two guns and a letter of marque—a license to privateer—from the state of Massachusetts.

At the end of September 1777, while Boston was gazing out to sea, chilling news arrived by land. It was not from New York, but from Pennsylvania: Despite the Continental Army's efforts to check their advance at Brandywine Creek, the British Army, led by General William Howe, had seized the city of Philadelphia. This was a surprise. Most had expected General Howe to move in concert with General John

Burgoyne and invade up the North River. Still, the fall of Philadelphia, seat of the Continental Congress, was a significant blow to morale.

The following week, a second express rider reached Boston. From their house on Frog Lane, Angelica and Betsy may have heard the hoofbeats, at three in the morning, as the courier clattered into Boston. This time, the news was better: A "smart action" had taken place upon the rolling hills on the west bank of the North River.

Still more news eclipsed the rest: On the seventeenth of October, just half a mile downstream from the charred remains of the Schuylers' family farm in Saratoga, General Burgoyne had ceremoniously handed his sword to General Horatio Gates.

In November, it was General Burgoyne himself who arrived in Boston, followed by his entire army. To save these prisoners of war from ignominy, after they had surrendered honorably and pledged not to take up arms again in the current war, the Americans dubbed them the Convention Army, after the Convention of Saratoga. The soldiers would be billeted under guard near Cambridge until the British could certify the surrender and arrange for transports to carry them home. The officers, meanwhile, moved into houses vacated by Loyalists, which were far more comfortable. They were free to come and go, within a ten-mile circle, on their word of honor as gentlemen.

Locals who observed this arrival were surprised to see that the Convention Army was no longer the fearsome invasion of fresh reinforcements it had been when it embarked upon Lake Champlain, but rather a motley throng of "poor, dirty, emaciated men." More shocking still was the condition of the women of that army. Over the course of the year's expedition, approximately two thousand women had been attached to the invading army. Three hundred of them were officially listed on the rosters, for cooking and laundering. Others were officers' or soldiers' wives or servants. As with the soldiers, these women had set out from Canada at first thaw, traveling over rough terrain in wagons and over water in bâteaux when available, walking when they were not, from Quebec to Ticonderoga to Saratoga—about two hundred miles. From Saratoga to Cambridge was that distance again, but at least there were roads for walking. The women of Boston and Cambridge had seen their share of war as well, but it was startling to see what one woman described as "great numbers of women, who seemd to be the beasts of burthen . . . [Some] having a bushel basket on their back, by which they were bent double, the contents seemd to be Pots and Kettles, various sorts of Furniture, children peeping thro gridirons and other utensils, some very young Infants who were born on the road, the women bare feet, cloathd in dirty raggs, such effluvia filld the air while they were passing, had they not been smoaking all the time, I should have been apprehensive of being contaminated by them."

These women were so ragged by the time they reached Boston that the local selectmen urged that "these wenches not show themselves outside of camp for fear the pregnant women in Boston should be marked."

The revelry celebrating the American victory at Saratoga was only just subsiding when an invitation arrived at the Carters' house on Frog Lane asking the couple to a ball being given by General Burgoyne and the other Convention Army officers. There were many reasons Angelica might not attend a social event given by the British. For one, Boston's selectmen had forbidden townspeople from associating with the Convention Army. For another, although General Burgoyne would not celebrate the coming Christmas at The Pastures, as he had predicted, he had issued the orders that the Schuylers' farmhouse, outbuildings, and mills at Saratoga be burned.

Angelica's sense of etiquette was informed by a code rooted in old chivalry, however, so honor, valor, and mercy were as integral to her as they were to those gentlemen who stared down the mouths of cannons or dueling pistols. Her father had excused General Burgoyne's actions regarding his Saratoga home as "the fate of war." Her mother and Peggy and the servants at The Pastures had hosted the officers of that army in a style befitting their rank for nine long days, even though the necessity of guarding the potato field from half-starved prisoners of war left the household shorthanded. Now it fell to Angelica and Betsy to recognize and enact the hard-won peace at Saratoga by performing the requisite courtesy of friendship. To this end, the sisters dressed, curled and pouffed their hair, and, flouting Boston's selectmen, crossed the Charles River to dance with their recent enemies. They were the only American ladies who deigned—or dared—to do so.

In associating with the Convention Army, Angelica met the Prussian-born Baroness Friederike Riedesel. Called "Mrs. General," even by her husband, she was an impressive woman by any measure. Since leaving her husband's sovereign principality in the Rhine River Valley to join him at war, the thirty-year-old noblewoman had sailed to England, where she met the German-speaking Queen Charlotte and gave birth to a third daughter. Then she crossed to Quebec, where her husband and General Burgoyne were preparing to invade New York. With her children, a cook, and a maid, the baroness followed the invasion—from Montreal, to Fort Ticonderoga, to Fort Edward, and on to Saratoga, where she and her children had sheltered through the final battle in a cellar, listening to cannonballs rolling across the floor above their heads.

The baroness impressed Angelica, and vice versa. Friederike Riedesel had been raised in the court of one of Europe's "enlightened absolutists": Prussia's Frederick the Great envisioned a government where intellectual illumination merged with political pragmatism. Furthermore, the baroness presented a model of modern womanhood that was both heroic and novel. Prominent American women were being cast as heroines of the war. Angelica's own mother was among them, for burning her own wheat. Margaret Livingston, the widowed mother of Janet Montgomery and Robert Livingston, was another. When the British attacked up the North River, Margaret Livingston had refused special treatment, though it was offered to her because she had recently nursed back to health a British officer (who was in fact her kinsman). Instead, she had buried her silver, hauled out the best of her furniture, and now Clermont Manor and Robert Livingston's Belvidere were nothing but char and rubble. Also like Angelica's mother, who propelled her husband forward through his maladies and piques, even if it meant arduous travel and danger to her person, Friederike Riedesel elevated the spirits of her sometimes depressive husband and assisted him with the work of caring for and leading his soldiers. And yet, Mrs. General was also different. The womanhood manifested by the baroness was not independent, but it did present a model of equality and of individual rights for women, albeit separate from those of men. She was not an appendage of her husband, and she was not a brigadier to his general. Rather—in the dualism that was becoming increasingly popular as the pendulum of intellectual discourse swung from pure reason toward the romantic—if he was the head of their conjoined being, she was the heart.

Mrs. General admired Angelica in return: She called her "gentle and good, like her parents." And the two women, each needing friends, began to visit one another regularly, despite the admonishments of Boston's selectmen and the tendency of Boston women to spit on the baroness.

In January 1778, despite rumors of its capture, the privateer *Portsmouth* returned from her nine-week cruise, having done "considerable mischief." Among her prizes were the brig *Emperor of Germany*, laden with beef and butter; the brig *George*, with dry fish; the eight-gun brig *Swan*, with beef, butter, and fish; and the ship *Duckenfield*, a three-decker mounting twenty carriage guns and richly supplied with dry goods and wine. If John Carter had been bluffing when he dared Angelica to disobey her parents, risk her inheritance, and marry him, if in fact he had been, as some suspected, an all-out charlatan conning his way up the colonial hierarchy, it was all moot now: As a part-owner of the *Portsmouth*, John Carter was now publicly and verifiably a rich man. That is, he *was* a rich man until the night of January 15, when the Carters' fortunes veered again.

The fire started in one of the chambers of the house on Frog Lane and spread with incredible speed. Housefires were such common calamities that Boston had outlawed thatched roofs and wooden chimneys for more than a century, but candles still tipped onto carpets, embers leapt from hearths, and chimney soot combusted. Rooftop balconies and buckets were of some use, but the Carters' fire bloomed so quickly that there wasn't even time to save the furniture. Angelica, now clearly pregnant, must have clutched Betsy as they listened to the bells of Boston's #9 fire engine coming nearer and watched the fire lick the night sky, then leap from the house to the barn. Only the deep snow on house roofs prevented the Carters' fire from incinerating the city.

At some point, someone—probably Angelica's sympathetic neighbor, Hannah Breck—ushered Angelica and her sister into her home for the night.

In the weeks following the housefire, while the Carters were reassembling the life they had only just begun to make for themselves in Boston, General Henry Knox made a visit home from Valley Forge. Lucy Knox's husband was a large, likeable man—his comrades in arms compared him to an ox—and he had been a trusted member of General Washington's inner circle since the first days of the war, when he and Lucy had slipped out of occupied Boston with his sword stitched into her cloak. For Lucy, who had not seen her "Harry" for a year, his visit was a relief. Like many women, she had borne the strain of the war the best she could, enduring solitary parenthood, smallpox inoculations for herself and her daughter, financial anxiety, and the loneliness of being separated from both her Loyalist family and her rebel spouse. For Angelica, who had likely met the general when he had been in Albany to usher the Fort Ticonderoga cannons across feeble river ice, Henry Knox was both good company and a reliable firsthand source of news from General Washington's camp as well as the Continental Congress now displaced from Philadelphia.

Much of what Henry Knox had to report was dismal. That winter had been severe, and the undersupplied Continental Army had been racked by dysentery and typhoid. If the abject suffering of the soldiers made individual suffering of food shortages and high prices and an accidental housefire seem small, they did not deter the Continentals from infighting and partisanship any more than they deterred Bostonians from complaining about butter. One happy effect of factional wrangling, at least in the eyes of Angelica and Betsy, was that Philip Schuyler's reputation was now on the mend.

General Knox, like others close to General Washington, had tended to sympathize with General Schuyler. After the loss of Fort Ticonderoga, he had written to Lucy: "As we have not heard Genl St. Clairs account of the matter we suspend our Judgement with respect to the propriety of the evacuation tho we Dread the Consequences." But there was no stopping that myth of the silver cannonballs. Now, however, the pendulum of scandal had reversed course, and General Horatio Gates, "the hero of Saratoga," was on the receiving end of public scorn.

The so-called "Conway Affair" began with a leaked letter to General Gates that criticized General Washington as "a weak general [with] bad Councilors." From this whiff of treason against General Washington unspooled what appeared to many to be a covert plot to unseat the commander of the Continental Army and replace him with General Gates. Then, though it reflected badly on a senior officer to do so, Horatio Gates had fought a pistol duel with his twenty-year-old protégé James Wilkinson, the man who had boasted of the letter to other officers without realizing what it insinuated.

For supporters of General Schuyler, the Conway Affair was a vindication: The idea that Horatio Gates had the audacity to connive to unseat General Washington shone stark new light upon his earlier efforts to besmirch and supplant General Schuyler. John Carter was delighted by this change in the political tides. He had felt that his own honor was impinged upon when General Gates resumed command of the Northern Division and he had felt it necessary to resign. "How strange is it that Congress cannot or will not open their Eyes to the Blunders and Inconsistencies of that man," John crowed in a letter to Albany. "His infamous attempts against Genl. Washington have ruined his Character with the People here who begin to hold him in Detestation, and to see that our success to the Northward are owing to Arnold and not to this Blusteur."

The final weeks of Angelica's pregnancy were lonely ones. Lucy and Betsy had both left Boston. Lucy, eager to emulate Mrs. General, had persuaded her husband to take her and their daughter to live at headquarters—all Angelica had left of her friends now were the furniture and mirrors they lent to her when they left town. Betsy had been recalled to Albany by her father, and although John was "exceedingly concerned at the Consequence of their Separation," he would not go against the wishes of the general, so Angelica, though distressed, was forcibly parted from her sister. Even John was often away in New Hampshire, where the ship *Portsmouth* was refitting for another cruise and a new venture was in the works, which John described as "a large Privateer that none of their Merchantmen can oppose."

Meanwhile, Boston ran low on food. As the poor turned to eating quahogs dug from frigid beaches at low tide, the selectmen decreed that "the more opulent Inhabitants of the Town . . . will on no occasion whatever have more than two dishes of meat on the same day on their table, and . . . that the inhabitants agree universally to make two dinners per week on fish, if to be had."

At last, in April, the waiting ended. First the newspapers announced a new opportunity: "To all Gentlemen Volunteers, who are desirous of serving their Country, and making their Fortunes," aboard the new privateer *Angelica*, a brigantine "built on purpose to chastise British insolence." Fresh off her stocks, the nimble *Angelica* carried sixteen six-pound guns, and carved on her stern was a rattlesnake, its body whole, joined, and united.

That same week, with no grandmothers, no sisters, no tipsy Dutch matrons to support her spirit and ply her with caudle wine, and no newspaper announcements, Angelica gave birth to a son they named Philip. If anyone attended Angelica's labor and spoke to her in the old hearthstone language, it might have been an enslaved maid—perhaps a woman with whom she'd been joined since childhood, perhaps a woman who had raised her—but, either way, she was a person whose presence was as ordinary and beneath Angelica's notice as her own shadow, and no mention of this person was ever made.

Only after Philip was born did Angelica's younger sister Peggy arrive from Albany to replace Betsy and stand as godmother at the baptism, along with a cousin, John Livingston, and, representing his father's side of the family, John's privateering partner Adam Babcock. As a gift, and with John Carter's agreement, Adam Babcock had procured his new godson a "Negro Boy."

The Carters' enslaved boy was called Ben, and he may have been part of a privateer prize (the *New Duckinfield*, named for a Jamaican sugar plantation, may have been a slaver). Objections to slavery were strident, but in 1778, slavery was as legal in Boston as it was in Albany and everywhere else in the freedom-fighting United States.

On the third of June, Angelica reemerged from lying-in to attend the baroness's spectacular birthday party for General Riedesel. The baroness had illuminations in her garden and, despite the selectmen's rules about limiting meat, eighty different dishes were served at dinner. At midnight, the party broke into spontaneous song to commemorate King George III's birthday on the fourth of June.

Only John Carter was not especially amused. While they all played at peace in Mrs. General's illuminated gardens, the British were still very much a threat, and he felt it particularly strongly that week because the newspapers had just reported that the privateer *Portsmouth* had been seized by the fifty-gun HMS *Experiment*. Angelica's politesse never seemed to crack, but John could not always keep his temper, and the loss of his privateer was a severe blow. Once, when the British had been on another burning spree, John had horrified the baroness by suggesting that Americans ought to send a general's pickled head in a barrel to England for each fire General Howe had set. The baroness had never liked John, who gambled regularly with some of the Convention Army officers. She called him "wicked and treacherous" and only tolerated him because she loved Angelica. Tonight, however, he kept himself under control and the baroness noticed. "Even the Carters had not the heart to hold themselves aloof," she recalled with delight after her successful party.

Had John known that night what General Howe had just done to his *Angelica*, his beautiful brigantine with the rattlesnake carved on her stern, the evening might have gone quite differently.

Two weeks out at sea, the *Angelica* had seen a lone vessel and mistook it for a Jamaican merchant ship. By the time the brigantine's green crew realized their error, the frigate *Andromeda*, one of the British Navy's fastest vessels, had come about to face them.

The *Andromeda* was not cruising. She was traveling fast and light, and her primary cargo was none other than General William Howe himself, who had been recalled to England to explain the surrender at Saratoga to King George and Parliament. General Howe's decision to capture the city that was the seat of the rebellion, instead of collaborating with General Burgoyne, now looked like vanity. Already his successor was preparing to abandon Philadelphia and return to New York. To cheer up this honored guest, the crew of the *Andromeda* made sport of the American privateer. When they caught her, the *Angelica* lowered her pine-tree flag, but the *Andromeda* wasn't done yet. First, they transferred the crew of the *Angelica* aboard the *Andromeda*, told them to strip to their skivvies, and then locked them up in the frigate's hold. Next, they waited there, in the open Atlantic, for sunset—precursor to the real entertainment. Once it was dark, General Howe and the *Andromeda* crew gathered on the deck to watch the American brigantine *Angelica* blow up.

CHAPTER 10

Independency and Happiness

1778–1779

When Peggy's visit to Boston ended, Angelica decided to leave with her sister, three-month-old Philip, and likely Ben. Their escort, John Lansing, estimated the trip home to Albany would take ten days. This didn't bother Angelica. Newly a mother, she was eager to see her own mother, all the more so because forty-four-year-old Catharina Schuyler had just delivered another baby boy and was suffering from "a most violent pain & swelling in her leg." "Curdling of the blood," or clotting, was not uncommon after childbirth, but the condition was excruciating and could be fatal. When they arrived, the sisters found their mother and new baby brother both very much alive. If there was bad blood left, it was between Mrs. Schuyler and her firstborn daughter. Not even being presented with her first grandbaby seemed to move Mrs. Schuyler to treat her daughter with anything more than cold politeness.

Maybe she was old-fashioned, but clearly Mrs. Schuyler's ideas about marriage were strong and intransigent, and so were her ideas about duty. Given her own life's work, it was likely she had expected Angelica to further the family and country—meaning New York—and to tend their deep Dutch roots in North River soil. As for Angelica, she was smart enough to see how her elopement made her look like a spoiled child, running off in the middle of a public emergency to satisfy her own heart's desire. But from her vantage point—as a member of a generation that came of age amid constant talk of liberty, individual rights, and even free will—the situation looked different.

If her choice mirrored the ideals of the War of Independence, so did the criticism of her choice. Powerful British politicians were calling the Americans' Declaration of Independence "false and frivolous." They said the American people had been duped by bad actors who set about "alienating the affections of the Colonies from the Kingdom." They were appalled at the colonies' ingratitude.

But perspectives change with time and circumstance: Angelica was now a mother, and, as any new parent, she was forced to reevaluate her own history from this altered state. As old-fashioned or provincial her mother might have seemed to her, Angelica could not fail to comprehend to what extent Catharina Schuyler had secured for her every advantage it was in her power to give. Likewise, her pride and love for her son Phil would be fierce and blind.

Angelica wanted to find a way back to her mother, but she failed to find it that summer. A scant month later, Catharina Schuyler loaded her youngest children in a wagon and set off for her rebuilt farmhouse at Saratoga; Angelica packed up her own children, baby Phil, and her enslaved boy Ben, and set off in the opposite direction.

The Livingston enclave had always welcomed Angelica as one of their own. After all, she was the namesake of Engeltje Livingston. Janet Montgomery, her brother Robert, the Continental Congressman, and, closer to her own age, their younger sister Kitty, of Clermont Manor, were as near to her as siblings. Since Angelica's Jonckerstraet nursery-mate Cornelia Schuyler had married Walter Livingston, of Livingston Manor, she too was a regular presence, as was her mother Geertruy Cochran and her doctor husband, John Cochran. Angelica was eager to show off her son to them all, but likely more pressing was her desire to see William and Janet Smith, second parents to her since her days at Madame Rugee's boarding school, who were now slated for exile. William Smith had declined to take any loyalty oaths to the revolution, especially once independence was part of the equation. The Livingstons—his wife's family—had sheltered him, letting him live at the manor under house arrest. But the political rift had become too wide. "The common Felicity is our Aim," William Smith had written to Angelica's father, once his closest friend and ally in provincial politics. "We differ in Judgmt. respecting the Means. Some think Independency and Happiness synonymous Terms. My Opinion always was, *Le Jeu ne vaut pas la Chandelle*"— The game is not worth the candle—"I don't esteem it equal to the Value of one Man's Blood." But many more men's blood than that had been lost, and when Angelica's cousin Bess Smith had died two years earlier, her parents attributed her death to stress related to the revolution. There was no room now for nuance; that summer, the New York Legislature had served William Smith with an Act of Banishment. As for Janet Smith's opinion, she had simply asked for permission to visit her family's graves before she left the country of her ancestors. Angelica arrived in Rhinebeck just in time to say good-bye. Then she stayed on among the Livingstons while her father and General Arthur St. Clair stood trial at White Plains, a day's ride downriver, for dereliction of duty in the loss of Fort Ticonderoga.

That year, the revolution had seemed to lose its way. Its heroes were tarnished, its purpose was muddled, its resources were exhausted. Angelica's own family had ruptured, their farm had been destroyed, her father was on trial. Loyalty oaths lacked the power of conviction; individual glory trumped cause.

Was William Smith right? Was the game not worth the candle?

From the court-martial at White Plains came news not of honor restored but of affairs of honor: General Gates and General Wilkinson, both summoned to testify, had dueled yet again. This time, as Angelica likely read in the Fishkill newspaper, her husband was involved.

John Carter had come from Boston to support his father-in-law, but he had agreed to serve as James Wilkinson's second; their acquaintance Tadeusz Kosciuszko, the engineer, had done the same for Horatio Gates. Once again, however, no blood was spilled. Unsatisfied, James Wilkinson demanded a statement attesting to his honor as a gentleman. John

Carter wrote it up, and Colonel Kosciuszko signed it. And then things devolved further.

"As Col. Kosciuszko has threatened to take liberties with my Character," John Carter wrote to the newspaper, "I think it necessary to publish the following facts." The evening after the duel, he related, Colonel Kosciuszko had called at General Schuyler's lodgings asking to see the statement. The document, he had realized, attested only to General Wilkinson's honor and made no mention of General Gates's. When John said he could not change the statement without consent from General Wilkinson, Colonel Kosciuszko pocketed the paper. John called him a thief. In return, the colonel told him to meet him at the smith's shop with his second and his arms.

John met the challenge not with sword or pistols but with his pen: "A midnight robber, who steals a purse, or an assassin, who attempts a gentleman's life might with equal propriety offer to make amends with his sword," he reasoned to any and all who read the newspaper. "But every man of common sense would look, upon the person who met him on such terms, as a madman."

Tadeusz Kosciuszko retaliated—also in print—by accusing John Carter of cowardice and questioning his loyalty: "Whether the wretch be a mercenary calumniator, in the pay . . . of our enemies, for injuring our cause, by abusing our Generals, I shall not determine," the colonel insinuated. "But I firmly believe, with many others, that, should he return to Boston, and visit the Convention troops, they THEMSELVES would tar and feather him for having presumed to mention so irreverently the character of Gen. Gates."

Killing a man in a duel was as illegal as shooting him in any other fashion. A spontaneous crime of passion might be ruled manslaughter. But the spat between John Carter and Tadeusz Kosciuszko had unfolded publicly, over weeks, and in print. If they dueled and one of them died, the other might be hanged for murder.

Some people speculated that the reason John Carter kept his past a secret was because he had killed a man in a duel. Others had heard that he'd faked his own death, leaving a sword and a coat in a field. Rumors aside, if John dueled in this place with Tadeusz Kosciuszko, there would be no hiding from the consequences. There were thirteen thousand Continental soldiers encamped nearby. George Washington was there. Also there was his father-in-law—the very man he had likely sought to impress by setting himself opposite to General Gates. On the other hand, declining to duel would prove he was a man without honor. John's choice would define him indefinitely.

Rather than risk charges of either manslaughter or cowardice, John stormed into the courtroom where the inquest was underway, brandished his pistols, and shouted for the "rascal" Colonel Kosciuszko to show himself. But the colonel was not there. The guards moved in, but John eluded them, ran outside to his waiting horse, and galloped out of camp.

This outburst averted the duel and, surprisingly, even more. After it was over, Angelica's uncle, Dr. John Cochran, visited the Carters and reported back to the Schuylers that John Carter's conflict with General Gates had "done him much Honor & gained him universal esteem. It has most effectually broke the neck of all that infamous Cabal who wanted to destroy him. His whole conduct in this affair was uniform, spirited & genteel, which I am sure will give you & all his friends much pleasure."

"Anny was happy to see me & they both treated me with the utmost hospitality," the doctor assured her father. "[They are] in good health and spirits, blessed with the finest boy in the world."

Dr. Cochran, who was married to Philip Schuyler's older sister Geertruy, was himself a father and grandfather to other boys, so his diagnosis of the baby's fineness rang of propaganda or, rather, avuncular kindness—he seemed to want to suture the family back together. Young and spirited, Angelica and John had careened into their conjoined life like a rudderless ship, leaving wreckage in their wake. But no blood had been spilled and the doctor had seen worse.

The problem, of course, was not really one of individuals or individual families. The entire young, spirited not-quite-a-country seemed almost as rudderless. What had happened to "Join, or Die," to *Common Sense*? What had happened to the Declaration's "We the People of the United States"? How would this splintered, erratic army of touchy individuals ever win a war? And if they miraculously did, how would their independency ever arrive at happiness?

The conflict had begun with a clear cause—the colonies objecting to a subordinate status within the empire—which one was for or against. Then the war for greater rights and representation had transitioned into a war for independence, and again, people were for or against. As the struggle dragged on, however, factionalism, regionalism, individual ambitions, and contrasting objectives shattered the delicate unity of shared purpose. Sometimes it seemed as if every chess piece were playing for itself.

Whereas 1778 had begun with the scandal of the Conway Affair, and the year's most significant battles against the British (at Monmouth, New Jersey, and Newport, Rhode Island) had both ended in defeat and accusations of dishonor, 1779 promised early to be the grimmest year of the war. After the court-martial cleared General Schuyler of dereliction of duty in the loss of Fort Ticonderoga, he formally resigned from the Continental Army. He promised George Washington that he would render the cause any service, but only as a private man.

Unfortunately, his offer would prove too little too late. Throughout the autumn, while Philip Schuyler was tied up in the business of the court-martial, the Mohawk and Seneca—two tribes of the fractured Haudenosaunee Confederacy—had joined British rangers in raids on New York border settlements, starting in Cobleskill, only forty miles from Albany. Other tribes—the Oneida and the Tuscarora— now fought with the Americans when they retaliated: They lived close to settler communities and for generations had been linked to towns such as Albany by trade and defense—which they now needed themselves, against the powerful Seneca. Philip Schuyler, whose ancestor had escorted a delegation of sachems to meet Queen Anne half a century earlier, did what he could to deserve these neighbors' trust, but he had lost much of his former influence. This was only partly due to his role as a general: Back when New York was its own country, when the Schuylers and the Moores or the Tryons dined informally as one family, he had been a large man in a small country. Now New York was uniting with Massachusetts, Pennsylvania, and Virginia, and he was one man in a crowd. His pleas to Congress to temper the retaliations to prevent an escalation of the border fighting met with as little success as his earlier pleas for the goods necessary to preserve the covenant of neutrality.

Now that the court-martial was completed, the Continental Army was planning a second invasion of Canada. General Washington sent Philip Schuyler a long list of questions related to the means and merit of the proposed campaign. Philip Schuyler answered in careful detail: "The Enemy Are In possession of Niagera, the Senecas, Cayugas, part of the Onondagos, and the Delawars and Mingos nearest to the former are all in their Interest," he warned. Still, he saw the advantages of wresting Fort Niagara from the British. Foremost, he thought possession of that fort would mean a return to peaceful relations with the Six Nations. "The Advantages of Maintaining Niagera would be; that the Senecas Cayaugas and such other of the Six nations and their dependants who are now so hostile would never venture to Molest our frontiers and their trade would benefit the States," he replied to General Washington, in particular emphasizing "The Valuable furr trade of the upper lakes."

"I cannot foresee any disadvantages," Philip Schuyler concluded, revealing a profound lack of imagination. When the army's plans shifted focus from targeting the British fort to targeting the tribes who had allied with the British, the extent of his error became clear. Now his counsel took on a desperate tone: To "supercede the Necessity of an Expedition," he recommended kidnapping women and children to force a negotiation. Too weak in his position and conviction, he was unable to stand wholly in the way of what was coming.

The "extirpation" Molly and Joseph Brant had warned of began in the early spring of 1779. The Continental Army marched up along the Susquehanna River after the spring floods, crossing into Haudenosaunee territory south of the Finger Lakes. From June to October, following explicit orders from General Washington to "lay waste all the settlements around . . . that the country may not be merely overrun but

destroyed," the Continental Army's scorched-earth campaign razed villages, girdled orchards, burned food stores, and slew livestock, driving
families from their longhouses and forcing an exodus from the Susquehanna, along Cayuga and Seneca Lakes, sweeping westward all the way
to the Genesee River.

CHAPTER 11

A Change of Situation

1780–1781

I n the first true days of spring, 1780, the frigate *L'Hermione* sailed into Boston Harbor and was met with fierce celebration. She carried gold—600,000 *livres* worth—to help fund the war and the much-needed news that France would soon deploy an expeditionary force to come support the Americans' fight for independence. To Angelica's delight, *L'Hermione* also carried Gilbert du Motier, the twenty-two-year-old Marquis de Lafayette.

Even from a distance, the tall, broad-shouldered, hazel-eyed Frenchman looked far better than when she'd seen him last, in January 1779, when her uncle Dr. John Cochran escorted his patient to Boston to meet his ship bound for France. Then, the marquis was just recovering his natural ebullience after a dangerous brush with a hemorrhagic fever. To regain his strength, Dr. Cochran had encouraged him to drink Madeira, and the Carters, who had returned to Boston after the fiasco at White Plains, had plenty of that. Plus, the hospitable couple spoke French. "Whenever I meet with Crowing, howlowing, and drinking," the marquis wrote to his doctor once he was aboard the French frigate *Alliance*, "I call again to my mind the happy days you have past in Boston."

Like Angelica, Gilbert du Motier had annoyed the people who mattered to him—in his case, his pregnant wife and his king—by running off at nineteen to join the American war. He had fought and even been injured in the Battle of Brandywine Creek, but as he matured, he had come to realize that his noble blood could be put to better use than personal glory. Now he had decided to return to France to reconcile with Their Majesties, King Louis XVI and Queen Marie-Antoinette, and with Adrienne de Lafayette. Then he planned to use his influence as a high-ranking nobleman to urge France to commit more fully to the American cause.

Now that the marquis had returned, his mission successful, more "howlowing" ensued, but a Franco-American alliance, if easy to announce, would be difficult to realize. In 1778, the American diplomatic team in France, led by Benjamin Franklin, had forged a Treaty of Amity with France, but, by that summer's end, the Battle of Newport, in Rhode Island, had proved how two armies, speaking different languages, answering to different leaders, might fail to achieve anything like "amity."

As for Boston, where a young woman from New York could feel like a foreigner, welcoming the French who'd come to aid the war caused some dissonance. During the previous war, the colonies had been awash with anti-French propaganda, and just one year earlier, Boston's anti-Catholics had burned effigies of the pope and the devil in observance of Guy Fawkes Day. The same day in September 1778 when John Carter had brandished his pistol in the courtroom, threatening to shoot a "rascal," a Boston mob had beaten a French officer to death outside a bakery set up to supply the squadron's rations. (Whether this eruption of violence was caused by culture clash or by the smell of baking bread wafting through a town long starved for flour was ambiguous—either way, blame was carefully pinned upon the British deserters from the crew of the privateer *Marlborough*.)

But even good intentions could miss the mark: When Samuel and Hannah Breck, the Carters' Frog Lane neighbors, attended a dinner given to welcome the allies to Boston, one French officer fished an object from his soup and exclaimed, *"Mon Dieu! Un grenouille!"* His bowl contained a full-grown frog, "just as green and perfect as if he had hopped from the pond into the tureen." The guests' amusement embarrassed

their host, who had caused every swamp in town to be searched so he
might make his guests feel welcome.

A long, disappointing year of war had dragged past since those initial culture clashes between Americans and the first French squadron
that had come to assist in fighting the British. Now, expectations and
assumptions on both sides had been tempered by reality. Language bar-
riers, religious differences, and even ancient prejudices now seemed less
critical than winning the war.

Also aboard *L'Hermione* was a mild-mannered bureaucrat in his fifties, whom France had likely sent as ballast to the full-sails zeal of
the young marquis. Commissaire Louis-Dominique Éthis had only
recently appended "de Corny" to his old if modest bourgeois family
name. He had not come for glory, but rather to establish a hospital
and prepare for the arrival of the coming army, General Rochambeau's
Expédition Particulière.

The only problem was, the commissaire did not speak English. Nor
did Samuel Breck, the merchant who had previously managed most of
the French trade in Boston, speak French. But the Carters did. Bostonians were so indignant when Monsieur de Corny tapped a "stranger"
to supply the coming army that objections made it all the way to General Washington's desk. But John Carter didn't just know French, he
knew the intricacies of purchasing, storing, transporting, and distrib-
uting wholesale foodstuffs.

Since his return to Boston, while Angelica had a second baby, John
had turned from investing in privateer ships to supplying them. His
store on Long Wharf even sold cannons from the Salisbury, Connecticut, forge. For John, this was not new work, but a return to what he
knew. In his past, before he left London, John had served an apprenticeship to London's top wholesale grocer, Davison Newman & Co., Ltd.,
a firm best known in Boston for the sixteen chests of its fine tea that
had been pitched into the harbor in 1774 during one of that town's "tea
parties." Then he had been a partner in his own firm. But England was

not America. And he was not the man he had been. Even if Monsieur de Corny liked him, John would have to prove himself capable of so massive an undertaking as supplying an army.

John's first major gaffe occurred on the eleventh of July, when the lifting fog unveiled the flotilla of French ships on Narragansett Bay, off Newport, Rhode Island. There was a convoy of eight double-decker ships-of-the-line, plus two fighting frigates, and several transport luggers, but not a single state or military dignitary was present to greet General Jean-Baptiste Donatien de Vimeur, comte de Rochambeau, commander of the *Expédition Particulière*, when he disembarked at Newport and wandered the town in his full French military regalia, looking for a cup of tea.

"The fields became major deserts and those whom curiosity led to visit Newport could scarcely perceive a human form in the street," one Frenchman observed.

When the French fleet was spotted in Narragansett Bay, the traumatized people of Newport—Loyalists, Patriots, and antiwar Quakers alike—panicked. The British Army had occupied Newport for three years, commandeering the town's new library for an officers' lounge, quartering troops in Trinity Church, and compelling the citizens to supply the occupiers with bread, meat, and beer. The 1778 Battle of Newport had ravaged the town further. The British had only left Newport, of their own accord, a few months prior to the arrival of the French. So, at the sight of warships, the townspeople had hidden their children, barricaded their homes, or left town entirely.

Hearing what had happened, patriot dignitaries rushed to Newport to assure the French allies that they were in fact welcome. General William Heath came on behalf of the American army. Governor William Greene appeared on behalf of the state. And John and Angelica Carter came to see what they could do to help. Finding that a great deal of help was needed, the couple found lodging in Newport and stayed.

Newporters and the newly arrived French gaped at one another in those first weeks. Where the Continentals had little in the way of uniforms, the French officers dressed in brilliant white coats with tails and colored facing signifying their corps, wore high boots or knee-high spatterdashes, carried ornate sidearms, and topped their uniformly queued hair with plumed hats embellished with brightly colored pompoms. And where the Continentals marched to fife and drum, the French paraded to the music of a full military band. But the awe ran in both directions. The French officers—men qualified by social rank attached to property and title—marveled at Rhode Island farmers who both owned *and* worked their land, and they were struck dumb whenever Americans would ask a nobleman what trade he practiced back home. And the Abbé Robin, a priest who traveled with the army, was stunned one summer evening when he rode through "a meadow covered by sparks of fire."

Sometimes, little cultural clashes led to laughter. Americans, one Frenchman noted, "do not waste kisses on men. They shake-hands which means gripping hand for a more or less long time, often very strongly." Other differences were mere annoyances. Americans drank their coffee too weak and their tea too strong. Worst of all was what passed for bread in New England. But the situation remained delicate. Any little friction could easily spark the tinderbox of difference and the end of the alliance.

General Rochambeau, a thoughtful, "abstemious" man experienced in foreign warfare, understood that polite relations between the American hosts and his uninvited army and navy were essential to a successful military mission. He insisted that officers and soldiers remain on their best behavior: Nothing was to be taken—not a fruit from a tree, not a stick of firewood—that was not freely offered and fairly paid for. Drunkenness was *verboten*.

But the general needed American counterparts who also understood, and who could assist with the delicate work of translation—not merely of language, but also of all the other ways different peoples can misunderstand one another. He needed people who knew how and when to sit on pistol cases.

Angelica Carter was one of the women who filled this role. Adding to the French she had begun to learn at Madame Rugee's boarding school were her friendships with aristocrats—from Sir Harry to Mrs. General—and her experience as a "stranger" in Boston. So, while her husband grappled with procuring food and fodder for twelve thousand French officers, soldiers, sailors, servants, and dependents, as well as their horses, in a time of low supply and high prices, Angelica made friends.

Soon the social scene in Newport became a stream of dinners, dances, and picnics. One commissary officer described a party of gentlemen and ladies gathered to feast upon a four-hundred-pound turtle: The turtle he found unpalatable, but the American ladies were very handsome, even if they danced with their arms extended in a style not to his taste.

There were also formal events. A delegation of Catholic Oneida—one of the Haudenosaunee tribes that had allied with the Americans—came from New York to Newport to pay respects to the French. Orations and gifts were exchanged. Then the French soldiers paraded their maneuvers and urged the delegates—many of them elders—to dance for them in return. "Their singing is monotonous, they interrupt it with sharp and disagreeable cries. In singing they beat time with two little bits of wood," Commissaire Blanchard remarked of the experience that was at once otherworldly and familiar. "In dancing . . . they remind me of those peasants in my province when they tread the grapes in the winepress."

When the French sought explanations for words or manners they did not understand, Angelica translated and explained. Often, as with all travelers who find gender norms to be the most startling of cultural differences, it was American women the French sought to understand.

American women, one Frenchman observed, "are of a large size, well proportioned, their features generally regular, and their complexion fair, without ruddiness. They have less cheerfulness and ease of behaviour, than the ladies of France, but more of greatness and dignity." Then again, he lamented, American women had terrible teeth: "[T]he women, who are commonly very handsome, are often, at eighteen or twenty years of age, entirely deprived of this most precious ornament."

As to sexual mores, the French were amazed to see young, unmarried women galloping their horses and traveling alone, even late in the evening, while grown married women mostly stayed in their homes. Angelica tried to explain this to the Marquis de Chastellux, a high-ranking French general in his mid-forties who regularly sought out her insights for a book he planned to write. "It is not a crime for an unmarried girl to kiss a young man, but it would be a crime for a married woman, who had just intended to please," the marquis recorded, knowing his French readers would find this shocking. In France, the exact opposite was true: Virgins were kept under close watch or behind closed doors (some young girls were sent to convents for their educations), while married women were free to go where they liked.

If the French were more shocked by the freedom of unmarried women, Angelica's unmarried sister Peggy provided an example. When the Carters departed for Newport, they deputized Peggy as acting mistress of their household in Boston. "During my stay in Boston, I dined at the house of a young American lady," Angelica's friend Commissaire Claude Blanchard recorded in his diary. "It is a great contrast to our manners to see a young lady (she was twenty, at the most) lodging and entertaining a young man."

Rules for women's clothing were as confounding to the French. The Marquis de Chastellux illustrated his bafflement with an anecdote about Angelica, whom he described as "a young and pretty woman, whose husband is interested in the supplies of the army, and now lives in Newport. . . . One morning, when she entered her husband's office, without being dressed, but in a rather elegant French *déshabillé*, a Farmer from the State of Massachusetts, who was there on business, demanded to know who the young lady was."

"Undress" was a category of lighter, more practical dresses without rigid hoops, boned or metal stomachers, or doorway-catching hip paniers that permitted a woman greater freedom of motion. From riding habits to housedresses, "undress" was clothing made of softer, more relaxed fabrics, such as cotton or diaphanous silk, instead of heavy, stiff brocade. In France, these more "natural" styles were coming into vogue partly due to that country's fascination with American simplicity. But gowns made for movement revealed more of the female form than the "upholstery" women typically donned for public wear, and not all freedom-fighting Americans approved.

The Massachusetts farmer was one who did not. According to the marquis, when the farmer was told that the lady was Madame Carter, he was appalled. "'Well!' he said loudly enough for her to hear. 'A wife and a mother, truly, has no business to be so well dressed.'"

As the French learned about America from Angelica, she learned from them about France. François-Jean de Beauvoir, Marquis de Chastellux, was a scholar and a philosophe. Even Louis-Dominique Éthis de Corny boasted Enlightenment credentials: He was the author of two books—the most recent a treatise on the dangers of frivolous talents—and he had once exchanged letters with Voltaire. Certainly, being in the presence of European intellectuals was thrilling to a twenty-four-year-old lady from Albany, but she was probably surprised that they—accustomed to women versed in philosophy and literature who orchestrated intellectual events in their living rooms—wanted to know what she thought.

Many people felt that an overly intelligent woman was an aberration, a grotesque, a "hen who crows," and Angelica knew that revealing her intellect in some situations could be as offensive as baring her kneecap for all to see. But whereas in Albany she was one of a scant few girls who'd done more than stitch her alphabet on a sampler and learn to tabulate shillings and pence, French courtiers like the titled officers among whom she now lived were not so easily shocked. Rather, her new French friends were beginning to draw Angelica further out into the intellectual open.

John Carter was also flourishing because of the French. Serving these allies who might save the foundering war was challenging work; the

French were demanding clients. If American soldiers were accustomed to being underfed, underclothed, and unpaid, the French soldiers were not. "A European army would not put up for a month with the frightful misery the American one has been plunged in for more than a year," one officer remarked. But when the job was well done, John Carter's new employers showed their appreciation in hard coin—a small percentage of each and every purchase made to feed an army.

Such a lucrative post incited jealousies, but John fortified his position by partnering with a man who possessed a superabundance of the attributes he himself lacked: land, capital, and friends. Jeremiah Wadsworth was a wealthy, well-known, well-liked sea captain-turned-farmer who had done some commissary work for the Continental Army earlier in the war. He spoke no French, but he came from Connecticut, which, unlike its neighbors, had not yet suffered a British occupation and thus was able to serve as the war's breadbasket. Soon, the Carters' toddler, Phil, called him "Papa Wadsworth," and the supply firm Wadsworth & Carter was counting hard currency by the cask.

The French Army was eager for action, but it was not until late September of 1780 that General Rochambeau and his naval commander, Admiral Charles de Ternay, left Newport to meet in person with General Washington at the Wadsworths' house in Hartford.

General Washington also wanted to attack the British at New York, and he worried that waiting was becoming as dangerous as fighting. General Rochambeau and Admiral Ternay were just as determined to delay. The British were well fortified in New York, and the French preferred to await their promised reinforcements before engaging an entrenched enemy that outmatched them in troops and cannons.

Before the Americans could press their case, the Hartford Conference was interrupted by reports that the British were on the move. These reports proved imprecise—only a single British sloop, the *Vulture*, had come up the North River. But when the dust settled, the Americans discovered that the British had indeed struck a profound blow. A spy, John André, had been captured with Tadeusz Kosciuszko's architectural plan of West Point hidden in his boot, and General Benedict Arnold, famous for having assumed command of the siege of Quebec after the death of General Montgomery and for leading an unauthorized attack in the Battle of Saratoga, had turned his coat and joined the British.

Angelica knew both Benedict Arnold and John André. The former had defended her father; the latter had been a gentleman-prisoner in Albany after he was captured by General Montgomery's army at Montreal. After the spy had been hanged, there wasn't much to say.

As the French and Continental armies went into their winter camps, having made no attempt to attack New York, the officers' ennui increased.

In Newport, some officers passed the time dancing in the pavilion General Rochambeau had the soldiers build behind his own quarters on New Lane—having heard from officers who had wintered previously with General Washington's army that dancing was healthy. Others, such as Angelica Carter's friend General Chastellux, left town to tour the country.

By the close of 1780, it seemed only dancers and suppliers had plenty to do. Wadsworth & Carter had just been contracted to serve as the French Army's exclusive suppliers—a great compliment to the firm, but one that would keep John Carter tied to the French Army, day in and day out, for as long as he could meet the terms of the contract, which would be no easy feat. With ice already forming on the rivers, a thousand quintals of flour that John Carter had purchased for the French Army had been confiscated for the use of the Continental Army. After this, the French soldiers' daily ration of bread had to be reduced from the standard two pounds per day. With their own militias to ration, states began blocking the sale of wheat outside their borders. "Send on immediately what [flour] is already at Hartford and the rest as fast as it arrives, the Admiral is almost distracted about it," John Carter urged Jeremiah Wadsworth. "They are only now supplied from Hand to Mouth."

When Admiral Ternay died a few weeks later—not from want of flour but from a putrid fever, or typhus—Angelica Carter joined the rest of the town at his elaborate funeral, while another much simpler ceremony took place at The Pastures in Albany. Angelica's sister Betsy had been waiting all fall for her wedding to Captain Alexander Hamilton, but General Washington hadn't been able to spare his French-speaking secretary until a few weeks before Christmas. Unlike her older sister, Betsy had obtained her parents' permission before marrying, but that permission came with a caveat: "You will see the Impropriety of taking the *dernier pas* where you are," General Schuyler had warned the young officer in the spring, lest he consider the more expedient route to matrimony and elope with Betsy in New Jersey rather than returning to New York to do things properly. "Mrs. Schuyler did not see her Eldest daughter married. That also gave me pain, and we wish not to Experience It a Second time." Peggy made the journey home to see her sister married and spend Christmas with her family, but Angelica sent her best wishes by way of the Marquis de Chastellux.

"I am the happiest of Women," the new bride gushed in a letter to Peggy when she arrived at her new home at military headquarters, ninety miles downriver at New Windsor. "Get married I charge you."

Peggy was nonplussed. She had admirers. One French officer, "Lewis" Fleury, had written to Alexander Hamilton that he hoped to marry Peggy. But she was in no rush to join her sisters in the state of matrimony. She had seen Angelica's marriage up close, and—between fleeing an invasion, the housefire, the dueling, and all their other struggles— their example did not inspire Peggy to follow suit. Even Betsy's new felicity had a tinny ring to it. In the same letter, the new bride remarked of social events in distant Newport: "There has been a ball given to Mr. Carter and the only one." Their older sister never ceased to absorb the greater share of attention.

In fact, the officers of the Royal Deux-Ponts Regiment had organized a ball in honor of all the ladies in Newport, not just for "the
only one." But there were precious few women available for the French
Army to celebrate. The French *Expédition Particulière* had found too
few ships to transport its army, so wives and warhorses had been left
to await the next convoy, which still had not arrived. In February,
yet another party was held, this time to celebrate the birthdays of
Angelica, now twenty-five, and the black-haired, violet-eyed Catharine Greene, twenty-six.

Caty Greene, the wife of Rhode Island's General Nathanael Greene,
had been a spirited fixture at General Washington's camps since the
war's beginning. When a bout of pneumonia had prevented her from
traveling to Morristown to join the army in winter camp in 1779,
George Washington himself had urged her to rejoin the army the following year. Rumor had it that one night, on a bet, Caty Greene and
George Washington had danced for three hours straight without sitting down. That year, General Greene had gone south to relieve General Horatio Gates of his command of the Southern Army, and he
had pleaded with his wife not to follow him. Valley Forge had been no
picnic, but the South was a horror. Caty Greene had stayed home in
Rhode Island, lonely and bored and oppressed by family cares, until
the French officers began calling to meet the wife of the famous General Greene. Now she was again the light of the army's long winter
night, this time reviving her schoolgirl French to do so and drinking
better-than-usual wine.

Lovely, lively young women, intelligent and amusing, Angelica and
Caty were both married and mothers to young children. For these traits
alone, they were valuable to the armies. They stood in for the thousands
of women whose absences were felt by the officers and soldiers at war.
They were a comfort and, to military men steeped in chivalric notions,
they embodied the cause. They were also useful. Angelica and Caty, being
attached to major generals, were sometimes better informed than any
of the French officers. Caty Greene received letters from the Southern

Front; Angelica Carter received them from the North. Between them, they knew just about every Continental officer in the war.

No ball given to any lady in Newport measured up to the *fête* the French put on to honor General George Washington when he came to town. The officers in charge of decorations went to great lengths to please. Mirrors were collected from houses all over Newport to decorate the assembly room to look at least a little like what noblemen who had danced at the Palace of Versailles felt a ballroom should be. Candles were distributed to be put in house windows so that the town would be illuminated.

When the legendary forty-nine-year-old commander of the Continental Army finally arrived, tall and broad and straight, the French outdid themselves paying him homage. When the first musical number was played—a popular air called "A Successful Campaign"—General Rochambeau and other senior officers commandeered the band's instruments and played it themselves.

Angelica Carter expressed as much reverence as anyone for George Washington, but that night her attention was focused mostly on her new brother-in-law. Betsy's new husband was very like her own husband, albeit a decade younger. Both men were compact, slender men, with fair complexions. But where John Carter's blue eyes were languid pools, Alexander Hamilton's were more intense. They were both ambitious and—Angelica learned right away—hot tempered. When he derided George Washington as "a man to whom all the world is offering incense," the sacrilege had to make her laugh. How many mirrors the French officers had carried through the streets of Newport!

Alexander Hamilton had come to Newport in a temper. He had just quit his job as General Washington's secretary, only to be chided by everyone he knew and compelled to come to this conference anyway (though he had traveled separately, on principle). As to his plans, the three-months-married twenty-five-year-old had his heart set on a battlefield command.

Philip Schuyler had responded cautiously to the news of his new son-in-law's unemployment. "Long before I had the least Intimation that you intended that connection with my family, which is so very pleasing to me, and which affords me such entire satisfaction I had studied Your Character and that of the other Gentlemen who composed the Genrals family," he had replied to Alexander's announcement. "In you only I found those qualifications so essentially necessary to the man who is to aid and council a commanding General."

Angelica and John were kind to their new brother-in-law during his visit. John paid his hairdresser bill and Angelica confided that she was pregnant. Alexander had understood that family connections were valuable. Their mutual friend, the Marquis de Fleury, had written to Alexander before his wedding: "Mrs. Carter told me you was soon to be married to her sister, Miss betsy Schuyler. I congratulate you heartyly on that conquest; for many Reasons: the first that you will get all that familly's interest, & that a man of your abilities wants a Little influence to do good to his country." But, having grown up without family support, the young man may not have grasped quite how such a family worked. He had expected his marriage to change his station, and when his position remained exactly the same, he was furious. Now, however, as Alexander indulged in self-destruction, quitting his job and breaking with George Washington, his new family spread wide its safety net to catch and protect him.

Even as Alexander was in Newport, with Angelica gently pulling the whole story out of him, his new bride, Betsy, was with Martha Washington in Albany. On the twenty-fifth anniversary of the day she delivered her first child, Catharina Schuyler had given birth to her fourteenth and final baby. The baby was named Catharina and when she was carried to the copper-roofed church to be baptized, Peggy Schuyler and Martha Washington (and George Washington, by proxy) were named the new baby's godparents. This small ceremony formalized a friendship and a long alliance between the Schuylers and the Washingtons but may also have attested to the Washingtons' parental feelings toward Alexander Hamilton. Linking their families by this baptism—as was not possible in a wedding, since Alexander was not their son—strengthened the bonds that would help Alexander rise. Perhaps Alexander would never learn to see the work of the women around him—the perpetual sewing, knitting, and spinning, so many millions of nearly invisible stitches, not just in linen and wool, but in weaving a social fabric. Whether or not Alexander recognized this, their threads were wound around him, now that he was bound to Betsy.

Angelica was performing the same kind of work in Newport, making Alexander part of the intimate family by introducing the new uncle to his toddling nephew, Phil, and dimple-chinned baby niece, who was named Catharine, but called Kitty.

Even John seemed happy to have this new connection, if only to commiserate about his father-in-law, who was then causing him some grief and threatening to challenge Jeremiah Wadsworth over some matter of honor, even as the old general urged Alexander to calm himself.

"I felicitate you on your Change as you seem'd so much to desire it," John wrote to Alexander after he left Newport. "I wish much to be inform'd, as independent of myself a certain Laidy (who has not yet made her appearance this morning) is very anxious for your Happiness and Glory."

CHAPTER 12

Home Front

After General Washington's visit to Newport, the *Expédition Particulière* lumbered into action. Now John Carter was swept up in the work of hiring oxcarts and drivers and stockpiling supplies along the route to the North River, where the French and American armies would finally converge.

John hoped that Philip Schuyler would come to Newport to help his wife travel back to Albany with the children, Phil, Ben, and Kitty (who was already one and a half), since he could not leave the French Army now.

"I have been in constant Expectation of Genl. Schuyler's arrival here to take Mrs. Carter and the little ones with him to Albany, but I hear not a Word of him," John wrote to Alexander Hamilton. "If he does not appear in ten Days, I must send Mrs. Carter as in her Situation the Journey in the middle of June will be too fatiguing."

Philip Schuyler had his own worries, however, and did not come for his pregnant daughter. He had been bled twice that month for a "quinsy," or sore throat. Besides, spies reported British and Loyalist forces were gathering at the northern end of Lake Champlain, and, rumor had it, a "skulking party" intended to capture General Schuyler for the two-hundred-guinea bounty the British offered.

Left to her own devices, Angelica likely departed from Newport with one of the first French regiments to march, so she would have company, extra hands, and protection as far as the North River. Once in New York, instead of staying to witness the two allied armies join, she turned her attention northward, tracing the river back home over terrain she knew like her own skin. While his wife traveled home, John scrambled to tie up loose ends in Newport. "This damn'd service has given me more Trouble than every Thing else belonging to the army," he wrote to Jeremiah Wadsworth on the eve of his departure. At least his exertions on behalf of the French had not gone unnoticed: Alexander reported to Albany that "the principal French officers express great satisfaction at his conduct."

When Angelica arrived home, the entire Schuyler family was together again for the first time in two years, and the house, so large when it was built, was full to bursting. When Angelica, Betsy, and Peggy were young, The Pastures had been a house of girls. Now, their brothers Johnny, Phil, and wild little Rensselaer were fifteen, twelve, and seven, respectively. (Cortlandt, whose birth had caused his mother's blood to curdle, had not survived his first year.) Then came their littlest sisters, Cornelia—her father's "dearest love"—was now four, and the new baby Catharina—called Kitty—was six months old. Now adding to their numbers came the Carter children—Philip and Kitty, and likely Ben.

In an ordinary summer, with this many children, Catharina Schuyler would have preferred to be in Saratoga, where there was more space for them to romp and less upholstery for them to damage, but there had been more warnings that the British and their Loyalist allies intended to capture Philip Schuyler. So the family remained in town, with a few guards rotating round-the-clock watches.

August came, and so did the heat. One day, Angelica walked into the entrance hall and saw that some of the guards had gone down to rest in the cool cellar and left their muskets at the ready in the hall. Thinking of the children, she put the guns in a closet. Meanwhile, someone else propped open the front and back doors to let in a cross breeze. Then, during dinner, there was a scuffle at the back gate, followed by the crack of a musket, and a maid came in to say that a Captain Meyers wished

to see General Schuyler. Captain John Walden Meyers was also Hans
Waltermyer, or, within his Palatine community, Johannes Waldenmeier. Before the war, he had been a tenant farmer on a patent downriver; now he lived in the woods, a spy for the British.

After this point in the telling, memory and myth and multiple
perspectives diverge, but the sum of the stories is this: By taking the
trouble of being formally announced, Captain "Meyers" had given
the guards in the cellar time to join the fray and the family time to put
down their silverware and bolt for the stairs. Up they went, as quickly as
two pregnant women, two grandparents, and so many children could
go. The guards held the invaders back, but, without their muskets, they
were soon overwhelmed. Meanwhile, as the Schuylers barricaded themselves in the bedroom, someone remembered that they had forgotten
six-month-old Kitty—the Washingtons' goddaughter—downstairs in
her cradle.

Peggy realized that rescuing her littlest sister fell to her. Her mother
was too recognizable. If Philip Schuyler could hold women hostage,
so might a band of Loyalists and redcoats. Her brothers (though they
would all disagree, right down to little Rensselaer) were too young.
Both of her older sisters were pregnant. Peggy went back downstairs,
reached her sister's cradle, scooped up the baby, and began her retreat
when someone finally noticed her.

"Wench!" shouted one of the invaders, assuming she was a maid.
"Where is your master?"

"Gone to alarm the town," Peggy answered.

Then, according to some embellished tellings, the ranger threw a
hatchet at Peggy, but it stuck in the banister. She ran, but the attacker
did not pursue her. Outside, there were pistol shots.

"Come on, my lads," boomed Philip Schuyler's voice. "Surround the
house, And Secure the Villains who are plundering."

But there were no "lads." People in the village had heard the shots,
but The Pastures was well outside of town. And most good soldiers,
like John Carter and Alexander Hamilton, were away, downriver with
the armies. But the ploy worked. The raiding party hadn't seen which
way Philip Schuyler had gone. They thought he was hiding, or that he'd

slipped out the open front door, or that he'd jumped out the second-story window. Those who had pursued the family upstairs heard the general shouting and ran back downstairs. Then there was the temptation of all those silver dishes.

When the chaos was over, and the attackers had fled, two of General Schuyler's men and a soup tureen had been taken away. Philip Schuyler wrote immediately to "request the Oneidas Tuscarroras, and the Cajhnwajas to turn out" and capture every suspected person. The band of attackers had expected this, and their network was in place, a chain of Loyalist households through which people and news flowed north to the British in Canada. So, even though Johannes Waldenmeier and the two British regulars were injured (at least one of them had been bayoneted in the fight to enter the house), the invaders vanished.

The supposedly covert plans for the combined French and American Armies to march to Virginia reached The Pastures a few days after the Albany house invasion. All summer, General Lafayette's regiment had played cat-and-mouse with the British army in Virginia, but if the French and American forces were brought to bear, along with reinforcements at sea, they might just achieve another victory like that at Saratoga—four long years earlier. Writing to Betsy of the scheme, Alexander Hamilton tempered his enthusiasm: "It is ten to one that our views will be disappointed by Cornwallis retiring to South Carolina by land."

By mid-September, when her labor began, Angelica's friends—those affections forged in the heat of strange, adverse circumstances—were five hundred miles south, staring down General Charles Cornwallis's encampment at the mouth of the York River. Angelica called her new baby John, but she did not have him baptized. If she had longed for the old customs when she gave birth to her first two children, her priorities had changed. Now, experienced at childbirth, she was clearly impatient to be gone. As soon as her requisite six weeks of healing passed, and her conveyance was packed, Angelica headed for Virginia with Peggy and Phil, and probably Ben, plus the baby at her breast. Only Kitty, her two-year-old toddler, was left behind in the nursery at The Pastures.

From Virginia, where the French and the Continentals were erecting new camps and digging trenches, Alexander sent congratulations on the new baby: "Tell Mrs. Carter I partake in the joy of the adventure she has made a present of to the world."

Then, on October 19, after eleven days of bombardment, General Cornwallis's army surrendered. From the Carolinas to the northern forts of New York, war-worn Continentals pummeled the sky with exuberant "feu de joy" as each received the happy news from Virginia.

If victory in childbed or battlefield in fact brought joy, neither Angelica nor Alexander chose to savor theirs for long. As she had flown from the childbed, Alexander flew from the battlefield and the negotiation of that battle's resolution. Alexander rode north to his pregnant wife in Albany as quickly as horses and weather permitted—or perhaps faster, since he wore out one set of horses midway and had to find new ones to finish the journey. Angelica and her babies, meanwhile, traveled slowly.

By mid-November, Angelica and Peggy and their retinue had completed the first leg of their cumbersome journey: down the east bank of the North River, to rest with their Livingston relatives, then onward to Continental Village, where the military assisted them in arranging for ferries over the river near West Point. Once across, they traveled wide of British-held New York, through countryside regularly visited by red-coat raiding parties. As women traveling with young children, their greatest defense and their greatest vulnerability were one and the same.

If Angelica and Peggy crossed paths with Alexander on the road, perhaps he told them of his glorious ten-minute sprint across that pitch-dark Virginia battlefield, with an unloaded musket, to overrun Redoubt Ten, at the same time their friends of the Royal Deux-Ponts regiment, whose officers had held the New Year's ball for the ladies of Newport, simultaneously stormed Redoubt Nine. But as much as Alexander liked to talk and write, he had little to say after the Battle of Yorktown. He had had his glory, but now he was running from all that preceded the white flag flapping from the parapet at Yorktown—the stench of the horse carcasses floating in the tidewaters after the British killed the herd that the siege had prevented them from feeding, the wasting roadside corpses of the enslaved people who had run toward the British promise of freedom. He was exhausted and racing toward Betsy, and his home.

As for Angelica, she was racing, as best she could, toward her army of Virginia friends who had no wives or mothers near enough to welcome them in the aftermath of battle.

A few weeks later, Alexander would write to his friend Louis-Marie de Noailles, the brother-in-law of General Lafayette and an officer of the Royal Deux-Ponts Regiment: "I chuse rather to find the cause of our victory in the superior number of good and regular troops, in the uninterrupted harmony of the two nations, and their equal desire to be celebrated in the annals of history, for an ardent love of great and heroic actions."

Heroic actions might take eleven days, like the siege of a fortified town, or ten minutes, like the storming of an enemy redout, but maintaining harmony within the alliance would take every day and minute in between. A battle had been won, but not the war. Politically and diplomatically, it would be a long winter.

CHAPTER 13

Esprit de Corps

When Angelica and Peggy reached Philadelphia, the two young women found the city on the Delaware River in a state of zealous celebration. From the windows of one house on Sixth Street shone an illuminated transparency, a back-lighted painting that depicted a rooster standing upon a lion pierced by thirteen arrows with the motto *"Gallus victor super leonem cantat,"* or "The cock sings victorious over the lion." Not to be outdone, the painter Charles Peale had decorated the upper-floor windows of his house on the corner of Third and Lombard with portraits of Generals Washington and Rochambeau ringed with stars and flowers, palms, laurels, and rays of glory, along with the motto "Shine Valiant Chiefs." The light through the lower windows revealed a painting of a ship named *Cornwallis,* which flew French colors above the British ones. Those who did not paint provided dinners and various modes of entertainment. At the house of the French ambassador, Anne-César de La Luzerne, an "oratorio" set to music was performed. At the Southwark Theatre, the comedy *Eugenie* was followed by an illumination of thirteen columns, above which Cupid supported a laurel crown over the motto "Washington, the pride of his country and the terror of Britain."

Just as pleasant as Philadelphia's self-professed "panegyrics" was the presence in that town of so many of the sisters' friends. The charismatic brothers-in-law, the Marquis de Lafayette and the Vicomte de

Noailles, were in Philadelphia preparing to sail to France to deliver to their king the capitulation certificates from the recent Battle of York-town. Caty Greene was there, preparing to join her husband in South Carolina—where the British still held Charlestown and the fighting was still desperate. Their uncle Dr. John Cochran was also in town, in his new post as director of military hospitals for the Continental Army, as was their cousin, Congressman Robert R. Livingston, who had recently been appointed superintendent of foreign affairs.

The warm light of good society and so many friends gathered in one place may have drawn the sisters into Philadelphia, but the parties were not what delayed Angelica and Peggy. It was Martha Washington's exam-ple that likely compelled them to stay. This was a precarious moment—and so critical that Martha Washington had come from attending the fresh grave of her last living child, her son with her late first husband: Just shy of twenty-seven, Jack Custis had died, with hundreds of others, of the typhus outbreak after the Battle of Yorktown.

Yorktown had put the British king in check. But if the states now recalled their regiments or failed to pay their requested share of war expenses—or if French military and financial support for the war flagged—Britain would simply regroup and reinforce and return the following year, and the year after that, and the recent victory would end up meaning very little to the overall war. "Our Success in Virginia, hap-pily effected with little Loss of Time & Blood, cannot fail, if properly pursued," General Washington wrote to Angelica's father from Phila-delphia. "All my Powers will be exerted this Winter . . . to stimulate the States to vigorous Preparations for another Campaign."

Like General Burgoyne's surrender at Saratoga, the surrender of General Cornwallis was worthy of celebration, but the war was by no means over. Capitulation certificates did not constitute a treaty any more than General Cornwallis's army of eight thousand soldiers—now interred in prisoner-of-war camps—stood for the entire British force in North America, an estimated forty thousand in 1781.

General Washington held that war was made on a battlefield with can-nons and bayonets, not peace. Peace was made at a table with a pen. And until pen was put to paper, it was imperative to continue the war. George and Martha Washington had come to Philadelphia to rally Congress to see the matter through. "It is an old and true Maxim," General Washington insisted, "that to make a good peace, you ought to be well prepared to carry on the War." And General Schuyler's daughters and General Greene's wife and all the friends they could muster in Philadelphia's vivid demonstration of unity and support—all this applied pressure on Congress.

The financier Robert Morris, the new superintendent of finance, held that wars were won and lost with money. "People flatter themselves with the hope of peace," he remarked after General Cornwallis's surrender at Yorktown. "But on what is [the hope] founded? Has the enemy given the slightest evidence of a desire for it? Instead of suing for peace they talk only of war, they prepare only for war. . . . [England] enjoys full credit and therefore she *can* carry on the war, and the object of it on her part is so great that therefore she *will* carry on the war."

Where the British Army still had funds and funding, the Continental Army's finances were dire. Without a large injection of funds, the Continental Army would soon be bankrupt. London papers were already reporting that it was. If credit and capital could not be raised, and soon, the British would win the war by default.

Without credit or taxation, funding the war for another season—if there were to be another season—would take both foreign investment and creative financing. Taxes were out of the question. Even the new Articles of Confederation, which had gone into effect that year, did not authorize Congress to levy taxes. Nor could many people afford them after six years of war and the havoc of paper money: That year, Continental currency had devalued so much that a single Spanish dollar in hard coin cost $100 Continental—at which point states revoked its legal-tender status. Credit required some proof that the money could be repaid, but again, without a reliable revenue stream, Congress could make no promises.

This is where Angelica came in. She was not just a pretty woman at the parties she attended. Nor was she now just a representative or extension of Philip Schuyler. Now, Angelica was also the wife of a man of significance—and those who sought any business with him treated her accordingly. She had been married to John for four years, and they had three children, but representing him was new. Few had heard of John Carter before that year, save for his capture off the *Charming Sally*, his marriage to her, and his non-duel with Tadeusz Kosciuszko, but the firm Wadsworth & Carter had become a primary spigot through which actual hard money flowed into the country. And Robert Morris wanted to open a bank.

The proposed Bank of North America was to be a national (albeit private) bank that would sell shares for hard money, then extend credit to the Continental Army at six percent per annum. Alexander Hamilton had already shared his opinions on the matter with the Robert Morris—during the months between quitting his job with General Washington and accepting the command of an infantry regiment, he had been reading about financial systems. But ideas meant little without capital. So, before the French army had left its encampments on the North River to march to Virginia, Robert Morris had paid its suppliers a visit. When the plans were finalized, the bulk of the bank's shares were held in equal parts by three men: Robert Morris, Jeremiah Wadsworth, and John Carter. Some states had objected to the idea of a national bank, out of the usual concern that it might supersede their internal decision-making bodies, but plans were moving forward, and Robert Morris was optimistic that they would get the votes to approve the bank's charter.

On Christmas, the families of Robert Morris and George Washington sat down together for the holiday dinner, Angelica very likely among them, as a member of the Washingtons' "family." Then, on the last day of 1781, Congress granted the bank charter, and the following week, with great pomp and many of Angelica's friends in attendance, the first branch of the Bank of North America opened its doors.

As with privateers, the public had little love for bankers (or "stock-jobbers"). John Carter had now been both. Perhaps the whole tentative project was motivated entirely by the siren call of a windfall, with John as hope-struck as any dice-player, but perhaps this was his way of fighting for the cause without taking up arms. Motivations aside, Robert

Morris, Jeremiah Wadsworth, and John Carter were effectively the venture or "creative" capitalists whose risky investment might just take a good idea—an independent United States—beyond the concept phase, and make it real. More simply, as Alexander Hamilton had written that year, "Tis by introducing order into our finances—by restoring public credit—not by gaining battles, that we are finally to gain our object."

"Mrs. Carter and Miss Schuyler leave us tomorrow," George Washington wrote to inform their father on the day after the bank's ceremonial opening. Since Philip Schuyler's departure from the Continental Army, the two men had continued to write to each other at least monthly, and sometimes weekly, and their friendship had grown beyond their shared work. General Washington also gave Angelica a letter to carry to General Chastellux. Messengers rode regularly from Philadelphia to the camp at Williamsburg, Virginia, where the French expeditionary force would spend the winter, but this was not a military letter: General Washington was writing in his personal capacity, by the hand of a mutual friend, to implore the marquis to help persuade France to send more money.

With that, the sisters were finished with Philadelphia. They loaded up the children and began the second half of their journey southward.

More than two months after they had set out, the travelers reached Tidewater Virginia, and, at last, Williamsburg, where the French Army was now encamped. Half the size of Albany (when not home to an army), the former capital of the wealthiest and most populous of the thirteen former colonies was bookended at east and west by the Virginia Capitol building and the College of William and Mary, both now repurposed to serve the war. As they rode through Williamsburg, the sisters would not have thought much of the town, but instead they sought out familiar faces. Angelica had heard word-of-mouth reports—names of the living and the dead—but no news was as reliable as what she could now verify with her own eyes and ears.

Those faces were all more weathered after the long march and south-ern exposure, and many were still gaunt from surviving the typhus out-break. Now, among the survivors, there was the pleasure of reunion. In French and English, greetings and congratulations were exchanged—joy of the victory, joy of the baby. Amid all of this, Angelica's gaze met the deep blue eyes of her husband. After six months of separation, this was an emotional moment, but the timbre of those emotions was known to her alone. Had she come for family, or friendship, or country—or were all three one? Of course, she had come because she was necessary, because she was part of the movement. But what part that was lacked a name. Like the foot soldiers whose deaths in battle were numbered but not named, or the unremembered slaves who had almost assur-edly made her journey to Williamsburg possible, or, for that matter, the horses that bore her over those five hundred war-torn miles, women were essential components of the clockwork, but not its face.

Lives are the sum of actions, whatever their intent. For whatever rea-son she had come, Angelica's next action was to present her husband with his son and namesake.

CHAPTER 14

The Long Road from Yorktown

1781–1783

"We are still in this wretched little hole of Williamsburg, where we are bored to death," one of General Rochambeau's aides wrote home. Peggy agreed. "You cannot think how anxious we are to see you and Papa," she wrote to her mother. "I am quite tired of this place."

The main Continental Army had returned north, to deter the British from ranging beyond their stronghold on Manhattan. The Southern Department was doing the same in South Carolina, where the British still held Charlestown. As for the French, General Rochambeau's army remained in the middle, so no new incursion could be made upon Virginia. Everywhere, Americans hoped that the British surrender at Yorktown would bring about the end of the war, but in the spring of 1782, it was too soon to know.

Then these hopes were all but dashed when news reached them that the British had triumphed over the French Navy in a sea battle near the islands called Les Saintes. Among the ships lost was the three-decker *Ville de Paris*, the flagship of the French naval squadron that had prevented General Cornwallis's army from retreating to sea by way of the Chesapeake. Those who had hoped Yorktown would bring about peace began to think again.

John called the naval defeat at the Battle of the Saintes "a cursed blow" that would force the army to remain in Virginia all year.

Since the army would stay put a little longer, John Carter sought a new source of hay to feed the army's horses and cattle. An early summer had withered what supply wasn't already exhausted or trampled by the armies on the York Peninsula, but he heard of one plantation that had hay it was unable to cut. Westover Plantation was thirty miles up the James River, a long way to go for hay, but he had no choice. Even in hard times, Virginians famously grew one crop above all others, but neither horse nor human could eat tobacco any more than they could eat Continental currency. Mary Willing Byrd, the widowed executrix of Westover, hadn't always been a Virginia "planter." She was the daughter of a Philadelphia banker (her brother had been appointed president of the new Bank of North America), and her fields were diversified.

When John went to see Mary Byrd about hay, Angelica and Peggy went with him. Apparently, the sisters were not concerned about visiting a woman who had been charged with treason by the State of Virginia and was currently awaiting trial.

A thirty-mile carriage ride across Tidewater Virginia ought to have been a pleasant journey. And it was, at first, despite the heat. John Carter rode his black stallion, and the sisters took in the Virginia scenery. They passed through the sparse woods and orchards of the York Peninsula to reach a ferry across the broad Chickahominy River. Then the road ran parallel to the James River, alongside field after field of tobacco, not yet in pink bloom, baking in the sun.

What travelers to Virginia usually noticed most was not the crops in the field, but the field hands. Angelica and Peggy had grown up in a household wholly dependent upon enslaved "domestics," and Angelica and John had kept Ben, and possibly others. But Northerners and foreigners were invariably shocked by Virginia's stockyard system of chattel slavery. Here, enslaved laborers were penned and prodded like oxen or mules, and put to work in all weather. Neither system was moral, but there was no question that the Southern system, if more honest in its stark brutality, was startlingly inhumane.

It was the nakedness that resonated most, exposing more than skin:

"The children, boys and girls, go naked until ten or twelve years old; the others have nothing but a shirt or some miserable rags," remarked Angelica's friend the Commissaire Claude Blanchard after he visited Westover. "The inhabitants of these southern provinces do not cultivate their estates themselves, like those of the north; they have negro slaves, like our colonists in our islands, and they themselves lead an idle life, giving themselves no concerns about anything except their table." Without "our colonists in our islands," as Claude Blanchard was savvy enough to acknowledge, France would not possess the surplus wealth to fight America's war.

Stripped of niceties, this slavery was a slap in the face for many who reasoned away their complicity. If the enslaved in Albany were prettily treated, the threat of being sold to Virginia or the West Indies manifested the same threat as if the New York enslavers held the cat-o'-nine flail themselves. As well read as she was, Angelica understood she was a beneficiary of both models, but slavery seemed as intractable to those accustomed to the practice as giving up horses and carriages and pulling one's own plow. Still, Virginia was an education.

Since the beginning of the war, Angelica had traveled throughout the former colonies, regions so different from one another that it was incredible that they had joined in common cause to fight this war. She had spent time with the Marquis de Chastellux, who was trying to make sense of regional differences he encountered. With input from Angelica, he had characterized New Yorkers as concerned first for family and their domestic economy. "It is only from necessity that these families are formed into a state," the marquis judged the former Dutch colony. As for Pennsylvanians, he said they "have no characteristic assimilation, that they are intermingled and confounded, and more actuated to individual than to public liberty, more inclined to anarchy than to democracy." But Virginia received the marquis's harshest verdicts. He traced its distinct qualities to the initial transplantation, "a strain of adventurers inspirited by notions of nobility (and disdain for agriculture or commerce)—warlike and romantic." Slavery had exacerbated the princely attitudes the marquis observed.

It was necessary to understand how the different former colonies had formed, because the war would end one day. And what then? Virginia's way? Or that of Massachusetts? A confederacy of allied but distinct tribes like the Six Nations? A union of semiautonomous states joined under something like the States-General of the Dutch Republic? A constitutional monarchy like the British government they were so avidly shedding? Or would it take the strong hand of an "enlightened absolutist" like Prussia's Frederick or Russia's Catherine to lead so disparate an empire? Would the states even try to remain conjoined or go their separate, sovereign ways after the war was over?

Pride was certainly evident in the visage of Westover Plantation, despite the deprivations of the war. The Carters approached the plantation house by a lane shaded by oaks and tulip trees to arrive at the riverside mansion—three stories of red brick overlooking the slow green river.

Many of Angelica's French friends had visited Westover already. The Marquis de Chastellux had seen his first hummingbird in the gardens there, and he was just as awed by the sturgeon jumping in the evening. But Angelica must have been as intrigued by Mary Byrd as she was by the statuary and paintings by European masters. Mary Byrd was an educated elite woman like herself whose marriage to a third-generation, land-rich Virginia "planter" had taken her life on a dark road of debt so insurmountable that on New Year's Day of 1777, her husband had put a pistol to his head and fired, leaving Mary Byrd, a thirty-six-year-old mother of ten, to manage the foundering plantation on her own. Most of the slaves and the books in the library and everything else the Byrds felt they could live without had been auctioned off, but apparently they had more to lose.

When the British Army, on the way to sack Richmond, commandeered Westover as a temporary headquarters, Mary Byrd and her children retired to the upper floor and stayed out of the way as the army slaughtered and ate her dairy cattle and trampled her fields. Afterward, she wrote to the British under a flag of truce to request the return of the items the soldiers had taken with them—her boats, horses, blacksmithing tools, and human chattel. In answer, the

British sent her daughter's riding horse and some assorted goods, possibly looted from Richmond. But the shipment was intercepted, and the Continentals raided Westover themselves, seeking proof of treason.

"What am I but an American? All my friends and connexions are in America; my whole property is here—could I wish ill to everything I have an interest in?" wrote Mary Byrd to the governor of Virginia. It was an important question: As a woman, she was expected to pay taxes, but with no vote, a single woman had no representation. A "freeholder" could only be male, but "all persons" could be deemed a traitor. "I think I am called on to say something on the subject, as a duty I owe myself, the public in general, and you in particular as Supreme Magistrate of this State."

This "Supreme Magistrate," was Thomas Jefferson, a man Mary Byrd knew well enough to speak to in conciliatory terms. "I consulted my heart and my head, and acted to the best of my judgment," she said of the "hospitality" she had shown the British officers and her subsequent communication with them. "If I have acted erroneously, it was an error in judgment and not of the Heart. . . . No action of my life has been inconsistent with the character of a virtuous American."

Thomas Jefferson wrote back to explain the law to her: As she had provided "aid and comfort" to the enemy and, by soliciting and receiving goods, had engaged in commerce, both defined acts of treason.

At the time of Angelica and Peggy's visit, Mary Byrd's trial had again been postponed, though the stream of guests through Westover suggested that the court of public opinion was very much in session. The sisters were clearly not afraid that they might be labeled as Tory sympathizers; they had danced with the British and Brunswicker officers in Boston, and Angelica had remained close with their Smith relatives right up until their extradition to British New York. This case was different, however. The sisters were backing Mary Byrd and the underlying question her case posed: In this new republican government that people like Thomas Jefferson espoused, where would women like them fit? What were their rights and liberties?

The sisters' Westover sojourn proved a fiasco. The first night, another guest, a young doctor from Williamsburg, developed a fever and became delirious in the night and raved so loudly that no one slept anywhere in that large house. The Carters knew they ought to leave immediately—they were only in the way—but leaving was complicated by the heat that had already worn out the horses. In compromise, they sent their heavy coach ahead to the Chickahominy and followed it there the following day in the Byrds' carriage. They then ferried across to meet their horses, fresh for the final leg of the journey. But in such intense heat, even dividing the trip across two days was not enough. Miles from Williamsburg, the horses were spent, and a fresh team had to be sent from town to pull the coach home. By nightfall, John Carter's prized black stallion was dead.

Back in Williamsburg, the Carters learned their travails were not over: Despite the deadly heat wave, the army would march immediately. "Should we unfortunately march in this hot weather we shall lose half of our horses," John warned his partner in Connecticut. And horses would not be the only fatalities.

Before the army could move, however, it needed money. The French expected a shipment of funds to pay the soldiers and the suppliers, but the frigate hadn't yet come in. As a stopgap, the French now needed a loan from the Americans. John's concern for the horses was not so great that he would pass up a chance at a fortune.

Wadsworth & Carter had earned a percentage for each head of cattle, each wagonload of bread, and each pipe of wine the army consumed for nearly two years. The firm had made a great deal of money in the process—not paper money that promptly lost its value, but hard coin. They had made so much that they *could* supply General Rochambeau's army with enough specie to pay and feed their soldiers for a month or two. But doing so was risky. If the frigate didn't come, or French bills of exchange suddenly lost value, or the suppliers suddenly needed capital to make good on their contracted obligation, Wadsworth & Carter could be caught out over the precipice of financial ruin. So, without time to consult Jeremiah Wadsworth in Connecticut, John Carter cut a deal and reported the outcome: "I told the General . . . it was equally your Intention with mine when a military Operation was in Question to afford them all possible facility. . . . I told him very coolly that I had made a generous proposal and would admit no alterations and that he could find no man in America who would have made so liberal a one."

After agreeing to late payment on 150,000 *livres*, which they would receive whenever the French frigate came, Wadsworth & Carter now supplied an additional 400,000 *livres* to General Rochambeau's army. In return, they were given bills of exchange totaling 460,000 *livres*. The difference was easily enough money to build and outfit a fine naval frigate or purchase a country estate.

As soon as the French Army had the money, the march to New York began.

The first few days of the march to New York, the French Army traveled no more than seven or eight miles a day, most of it in the predawn dark. Even so, twenty horses had died before they reached the hamlet of New Kent, twenty-seven miles from where they'd begun. It took the army train that long just to reach the Potomac River and ferry from Virginia to Georgetown, the tobacco port on the Maryland bank. Hospitals had to be established along the route to house the soldiers who succumbed to heat, fatigue, or fever.

"The drought has been extraordinary," one officer wrote home. "All the brooks are dry and our army has the greatest difficulty in finding water." For the trip, Angelica and Peggy had made new clothes out of lightweight cotton chintz and calico, and they rode with the children and the officers while the foot soldiers walked, but still they suffered.

In Baltimore, the army had a reprieve. Through seven years of war, while other major ports had been occupied or blockaded or both by the British Navy, Baltimore's nimble merchant fleet had managed to keep most of Europe's snuffboxes and pipes supplied with tobacco. The sisters set out to enjoy themselves, and Angelica shined.

"Mrs. Carter is a fine woman," a Maryland friend wrote to Alexander Hamilton. "She charms in all companies. No one has seen her, of either sex, who has not been pleased with her, and she has pleased every one." Baltimore was less impressed by Peggy's brilliance. "Peggy, though, perhaps a finer woman, is not generally thought so. Her own sex are apprehensive that she considers them poor things." He then compared her to a character in a popular poem who is imbued by the gods' trickery with "the Seeds of Knowledge, Judgement, Wit" reserved for males, and suffers for it. As for John, the gentleman dismissed him as a "mere man of business."

There was more talk of peace, but General Washington and General Rochambeau remained skeptical.

John left before the army, riding a new horse with his four-year-old Phil up in the saddle with him. It was time for Phil to start school, and John's Philadelphia associate John Chaloner had agreed to board the child in his own family. After leaving Phil, John continued ahead to New York, to prepare a new encampment for the French army.

One by one, the French regiments began to leave Baltimore, despite the prevalence of a violent intermittent fever. The French blamed the marshy terrain, but locals associated "this plaugy fever" with the visiting army. Even General Rochambeau was having fits of fever and ague.

Angelica and Peggy, with the baby and the servants, rode in lockstep with the slow-moving army. It took five tedious days to reach the Head of Elk; two more brought them across Wilmington's Brandywine Creek (where the French officers all set off to see where the battle had been); and another day was needed to reach Chester. From there, it would be less than a day's ride to Philadelphia. But the sisters did reach town.

When fever felled Angelica, Peggy, and one-year-old Jack all at once, they could go no farther. The army continued to march, but when their friends reached Philadelphia, they informed the French minister about the waylaid ladies, and Monsieur La Luzerne sent immediate help. Among their rescuers was Marianne Craik, a doctor's wife who had been a nurse in the hospital at Williamsburg after the Battle of Yorktown. Before that, she may have known the sisters at Newport, when John was involved in setting up a hospital for the French Army. Marianne Craik recognized the severity of the situation, and she wrote immediately to John, at army headquarters on the North River, and to the girls' parents, in Albany.

The malady was more than an ague. It began with a high fever that, after the first phase, came and went in waves. Between the fevers, the young women suffered fatigue and excruciating joint pain. Angelica must have been vomiting also, because it took days before she could tolerate the tonic of cinchona bark in wine that the eminent Dr. Jones prescribed when he came to see her.

When John received letters from Marianne Craik, he sent for Jeremiah Wadsworth to come take his place with the army. Then, leaving at first light, he ferried across the North River and rode all that day and night—only stopping to change horses and order flour in Morristown at nine o'clock that evening. By the next morning, he was at Angelica's side.

He found his beautiful wife wracked by illness. "Few persons have ever been more severely handled than they have and you must not be alarmed if their recovery should be tedious," John Chaloner had warned him. "Their present reduced situation renders it impossible to be otherwise."

For "a mere man of business," John had come quickly to his family's emergency, but he didn't stay long at their bedsides. He had another crisis to deal with: There was no flour to be had for either army.

The morning he arrived, having ridden through the night, he called on the financier Robert Morris to see what could be done. John already had an inkling that something was deeply wrong. His friend Walter Livingston, who supplied the Continental Army in New York, had told him that his firm had been reimbursed for supplies so irregularly that farmers would extend them no more credit. The money to pay for food and fodder for the army came from the Continental Congress, if and when states made their nonbinding contributions. When no funds were forthcoming, Robert Morris, as superintendent of finance, filled in the gaps with money borrowed on his personal credit, promissory notes, and, as in the case with his suppliers, by spreading the debt widely. By reputation, Robert Morris was the wealthiest man in the thirteen states, but skeptics suggested he could "dazzle the public eye with the same piece of coin, multiplied by a thousand reflections."

The extent of the army's financial problem was far worse than John imagined. Robert Morris wasn't even coy about it: "Money I have none," he confessed openly. But even if he had, he now felt that paying the debts "would only increase the mischief for I see no Prospect of Payment." The states simply did not pay their quotas. He described the situation in terms of the problem he now faced supplying clothing to the army: "We have lately had an arrival here of Linnens which the Clothier says are sufficient to make thirty thousand shirts. . . . But he is already so much indebted to the poor People who have worked for him and who are starving for want of their Wages, that he can not procure Credit to get them made. . . . Thus while People who live in Ease and even in Luxury avoid under various Pretexts the Payment of taxes," Robert Morris complained, "a great Portion of the Public Expense is borne by poor Women who earn their daily Bread by their daily Labor."

If no one could lend the Continental Army money on long-term credit, the financier concluded, General Washington would have to "subsist his Troops by military Collection"—as in, seize supplies from the local citizens, an act of tyranny that contradicted the war itself.

Robert Morris's confession was not without motive. He wanted Wadsworth & Carter to supply the Continental Army as well as the French. The superintendent offered generous terms for the long credit the undertaking would require. He would argue to Congress that the difference in price would be made up by reducing competition in prices—with only one army supplier buying wheat, farmers could take it or leave it.

It wasn't the first time that Robert Morris had made this proposal, but John had refused him in the past. It was enough work to supply one army. But French Minister La Luzerne had just announced to Congress that the expeditionary force would ship out to the war's new front in the West Indies by the end of the year. This would leave the Continental Army to its own depleted resources in North America, should the British send reinforcements for the coming year's campaign.

This created two incentives for John to agree to Robert Morris's proposition: First, if the army could not be fed, the war would be over. Second, when the French Army sailed, John would be out of a job. Whether one or the other motivation factored more strongly in his calculations, perhaps even John could not say for sure. Either way, he would have to speak to his partner.

As John fretted over flour and credit, Angelica's fevers came and went in waves. The pain in her feet and ankles was so intense that she could neither stand nor walk. As for Peggy, her twenty-fourth birthday found her unable to rise from bed. Only little Jack was fever-free and recovering. John wanted them to move into town, but Angelica resisted. She knew that as soon as she was in town, despite his promises, her husband would leave.

She wasn't wrong. Angelica could barely walk when John Carter rushed back to army headquarters on the North River.

But Angelica and Peggy were not left alone in their new Philadelphia house for long. Their seventeen-year-old brother, Johnny Schuyler, was the first to arrive, bringing with him Angelica's daughter Kitty. Then came the Honorable Alexander Hamilton—after a year telling people he was rocking his son Philip's cradle, he had passed the New York bar and run against his father-in-law in the race for Albany's congressional seat and won. A few days after the congressman appeared, Philip and Catharina Schuyler arrived with their own toddler, Kitty. Angelica and Peggy's father had tried to keep the severity of their illness from their mother but failed.

"Mrs. Carter is weak, but not in any dangerous way," Philip Schuyler wrote home to Betsy Hamilton. "We have hopes that a fortnight will restore them both to so much strength as to commence the journey to Albany with your mama and me." When Angelica's recovery appeared to slow, he sent a letter under a flag of truce to the latest British commander in New York—a onetime guest of the Schuylers', Guy Carleton—requesting permission to sail through enemy-controlled waters. But it was Angelica who prevented the scheme.

John Carter was still gone at Christmas. In addition to provisioning the French transports for the voyage to the West Indies, he had convinced Jeremiah Wadsworth to go in with him on a new project. Their new privateer *Angelica* was to be a 104-foot square-sterned ship with a copper-sheathed hull and a figurehead of a woman. The war was moving out to sea—and John wanted in on it. But he was home by the New Year.

Soon after that, Betsy Hamilton and her own baby Philip joined the family. For a brief wintry moment, Angelica had near her the people she loved most. And then, like the ice on the river, they broke up and floated onward.

In March, the *Hyder Alley* sailed into Philadelphia's harbor crying the news: Britain had begun to treat for peace. When this news reached the Carters at Sunday dinner at the Morrises' house, the dinner gave way to celebration.

After that, Angelica had no peace.

First, John sold the new privateer—complete but for rigging. Instead of prowling the Caribbean, the *Angelica* would be refitted as a merchant ship and renamed *Empress of China*. Her new owners hoped she would be the first American ship to trade in China. Next, John began planning a voyage to France. "I doubt not but you are fully convinc'd how essentially necessary our voyage is when you consider our Fortunes are at stake," he wrote to Jeremiah Wadsworth. John wanted to cash in his French bills of exchange, and any additional bills he could get his hands on for less than face value. Then, the man who had supplied two armies went to work supplying his family for the Atlantic crossing.

Angelica intended to visit Albany before they sailed, to see her home and her family one last time, but Phil came down with scarlet fever and the doctors advised against so long a journey. Kitty and Jack would have to travel with Betsy, who was also leaving Philadelphia. (Alexander had lost his patience with Congress—they would go to Albany until the British left New York, then move there.) As for Ben, Angelica would not risk taking him to France. Slavery was still very much in place in the

French colonies, but the principle of "free soil" was well established in France itself. Any enslaved person who set foot in France became legally free. Angelica might have prevented Ben from leaving her—many people did that—but her friends might not forgive her for it. Instead, she transferred him temporarily to a new master, on the condition that he never be sold to anyone but herself. With so much going on, neither Angelica nor Betsy was home in June when Peggy married.

Nor was their mother present at Peggy's wedding. To avoid being thwarted or made to wait to marry her six-years-younger cousin, Stephen van Rensselaer, Peggy had followed Angelica's lead and eloped. Stephen's youth aside, the future patroon had all the qualities of an excellent match, but Catharina Schuyler was still furious with Peggy. What spared the newlyweds was that Peggy had better timing. When Mrs. Schuyler heard of the elopement, she was preparing to receive George and Martha Washington for an extended visit. On the eve of the Washingtons' arrival, rather than risk his honored friend's opinion of him, General Schuyler wrote his new teenage son-in-law a kind note.

Angelica had nothing to say about Peggy's choice or her methods. What surprised her was that, after living in Boston, Newport, Williamsburg, and Philadelphia, and among the French—her independent-minded sister had gone home and attached herself firmly to her roots.

"Must she always be within the sound of the Dutch bell?" she would marvel.

Angelica would regret not hearing Albany's Dutch bell one last time before the Carters sailed for France.

As they embarked, Angelica looked forward to seeing the French friends she'd lived with through two intense years of war, to meeting their wives and families, to seeing the places they told her about when they were homesick. And it pained her to think of leaving her siblings and friends, her parents, her small children, and all the places she would miss when she was homesick—the country of her birth, the country for which she had fought, in her own way, for eight incredible, difficult years. And between those two halves of her heart lay six weeks at sea, a thousand roiling miles—a sickening prospect even if she weren't deep in the first trimester of a fourth pregnancy. But the world had turned upside down, and she and John, together and separately, had to find where they fit in the new world order.

Part 3

AMERICAN ABROAD

What are Kings and Queens to an American
who has seen a Washington!

—*Angelica Church*

CHAPTER 15

Siècle des Lumières /
The Age of Enlightenment

1783

In the summer of 1783, as the Carters sailed to France under a sun that shone a blood-tinged hue, the sky hazed with a "dry fog," it was impossible to know the future beyond each hideous, rolling wave. A few attributed that summer's bizarre weather phenomena to volcanoes in Iceland, but most read the rusted sunlight and sulfuric wind as ill omens. Even after eight years of her life at war, Angelica would call the Atlantic "my great enemy."

Six weeks later, the ship reached France, where they were greeted first by the seaport's stench: fish, pitch, sewage, and humanity. Then John, Angelica, and Phil, along with Jeremiah Wadsworth and his son Daniel, were all speeding through woods of black poplars festooned with mistletoe. Their carriages carried them past castellated villages, past towering haystacks, past fresh-cut buckwheat harvest drying in shocks, past fields of golden millet dotted by the round backs of the peasants who reaped it, one sickle swing at a time. The scenery was at once foreign and familiar. Angelica had grown up among tenant farms. Even in France, she could recognize a poor crop when she saw one. After the summer's rank air and acid rain, many crops were stunted and sparse. For many of the French, the coming winter would be marked by hunger.

In Paris, however, it was the *annus mirabilis*, the year of awe, and the month of September held the most amazement. On the nineteenth, the court at Versailles had witnessed the Montgolfier brothers' sky-blue cotton-canvas balloon of inflammable air lift off from the palace courtyard with the world's first aeronauts aboard—a duck, a cockerel, and a sheep. Meanwhile, at the Louvre, the Salon of Paris exhibition was underway.

The Carters moved into the Hôtel d'Angleterre, on the rue Jacob, just a few doors down from the Hôtel d'York, where the most remarkable event of September 1783 had occurred just days earlier: There, the American Peace Commissioners Benjamin Franklin, John Adams, and John Jay had signed the Treaty of Paris, formally ending the American Revolutionary War. The United States was now a sovereign, independent nation, recognized by all, and at peace—at least with Europe.

As soon as they were settled, Angelica and John Carter made calls upon all the people for whom they carried letters.

To Benjamin Franklin, they carried a congratulatory letter from Angelica's father: "America is so much indebted to your exertions, on these important occasions, that I am persuaded every one of her honest citizens is pervaded with those sentiments of Gratitude, regard and esteem which I have the happiness intimately to feel."

The Carters also carried a package of letters to John Jay and his wife, Sarah Livingston Jay, each a cousin to Angelica through a different grandmother. Summoned from his post as minister to Spain to serve on the Peace Commission, John Jay had long been an ally to Philip Schuyler, a fellow New Yorker, even during what Angelica's father now called "the days of my distress when It was criminal in the eyes of a misguided multitude to be my friend."

The third American delegate on the Peace Commission was John Adams. After the fall of Fort Ticonderoga, he had remarked, "I think We shall never defend a Post, until We shoot a General." Angelica Carter carried no packages for him.

Angelica needed no letters to present herself at the Hôtel de Lafayette, but the Marquis de Lafayette was away—sitting with a dying friend. He hurried back to Paris as soon as his friend was past harm. Their reunion gave them all "Unexpressible Satisfaction," and soon the

Carters and the Wadsworths were regulars at the weekly dinner the Lafayettes gave for Americans at their home on the rue de Bourbon. By "Americans," the Lafayettes meant veterans of the American war, ideological *américains*, as well as actual American citizens.

In France, Angelica Carter met not only her friends but also, at last, the wives she'd heard so much about from lonely soldiers very far from home. Among these French ladies was Adrienne Noailles de Lafayette, whose husband and brother had run away together to join the American war. And John Carter's colleague Dominique Éthis de Corny had recently married a glamorous widow. Marguerite de Corny soon took Angelica—whom she called "Angélique"—under her wing, escorting her to salons, whose hostesses—*salonnières*—conducted conversation as if it were a symphony. Art, theater, education, and fashion—not just clothing, but general aesthetics—all of it interested Madame de Corny, who possessed a "brilliant wit."

With female friends, Angelica Carter could access another side of Paris. At dinners, gentlemen may have quipped about the female artists now displaying work at the Louvre (some said that Madame Élisabeth Vigée Le Brun's paintings had to be the handiwork of a lover), but their wives were impressed. And at that year's Paris Salon, women who had recently worn whalebone corsets and paniers so wide they had to turn sideways to pass through a doorway now studied paintings that lauded more "natural" women, such as the breastfeeding lady in the large, luminous pastel portrait at that year's Salon by Adélaïde Labille-Guiard. The works presented by the queen's favorite, Madame Le Brun, included a portrait of Marie-Antoinette in elegant *déshabillé*—a white muslin chemise cinched with gold-ribboned gauze. Some sneered that the queen's wide straw hat was meant to cover the hair loss caused by her pregnancy with the *dauphin*. Some were offended to see their queen painted in what looked to them like underwear or, worse, peasant garb. But others recognized the young queen's rejection of highly formal clothing as an expression of France's enthusiasm for the revolutionary ideas associated with the American war. If Angelica Carter had imagined what a young French queen might wear, the young French queen may likewise have imagined the attire of a free and simple American lady, like the "young and pretty Madame Carter," described in the manuscript the Marquis de Chastellux now circulated among his friends.

When Angelica managed to pull her gaze away from the marvels of Paris, she called upon her friends in the American diplomatic corps. At seventy-seven, Benjamin Franklin was suffering severely from gout and "gravel," and he complained to all that these kidney stones forced him to urinate lying down. As much as he loved Paris, he wanted to go home.

The last time Angelica had seen the eminent Dr. Franklin had probably been when he stayed at The Pastures on his return from Quebec with only a marten-skin hat to show for his efforts. Six months after that, Dr. Franklin had sailed for France, where some credited that hat with his successes: the 1778 Treaty of Amity that initiated the alliance between France and the United States; General Rochambeau's expedition providing military support to the Continental Army; a series of large monetary loans and gifts; and now, his crowning achievement, the 1783 Treaty of Paris, whereby the world would recognize the independent, unified country he'd been inventing in his mind for decades.

The Jays also rented a neat little house on the outskirts of Paris, near the Franklins. John Jay left for the health spas of Bath in England almost as soon as the treaty ink had dried, to recover from the strain of the negotiations, but Sarah continued hosting a weekly tea for Americans that Angelica attended. As two American ladies of the same age, cousins with many friends in common, they had a great deal to talk about. Sarah was hungry for news of home, of the war, and of the people she knew. Angelica had to be curious to know the stories of Sarah's four years as a diplomat's wife. Since they'd arrived in France, Sarah had given birth to two little girls, including her "little Nursling" Anne, born only that summer. Sometimes she went to the theater. People visited. She looked in on Benjamin Franklin and his grandson. But before France, Sarah had had a hard time.

Sarah, her husband, her brother Brockholst (previously an aide to General Schuyler), their nephew Peter Munro, and an enslaved maid called Abbe (probably on loan from her parents) had left New Jersey for Spain, only to be caught in a violent storm at sea that dismasted their ship. In the weeks it took the crew to muscle the ship into port in Martinique, Sarah had one comfort: She had left her toddler back at her family's home, Liberty Hall, in New Jersey. By the time they reached Spain, she was suffering from a difficult pregnancy. John Jay was frequently gone from home, trailing after the royal court, and Brockholst sailed back to the United States, only to be captured at sea. Most of the time, Sarah and Abbe were alone together. When the new baby was born, things brightened temporarily, but then the baby caught a fever that caused such unrelenting convulsions that, on the last day of the infant's life, her eyelids would not close.

In both Spain and France, as the wife of a minister plenipotentiary, Sarah had an official diplomatic role—hosting, receiving, and attending official functions, with or without her husband. When Angelica arrived, Sarah was the only American woman in France in an official capacity.

Angelica had no such official role. John Carter was vying for contracts to supply France with American goods—ideally, tobacco—but he was not an American official. Yet, unlike Sarah, who had been in Paris more than a year but did not like to call upon people who did not call upon her first, Angelica had a literal army of friends, and when an American representative was called for, she was on the list. By October, Sarah and Angelica were two of the *only* Americans in Paris. When the new peace treaty granted amnesty to Americans for fighting in the war against Britain (as opposed to calling them traitors, as before), many Americans in Paris—including John Adams, John Jay, and John Carter—rushed across the channel to England. Likewise, Englishmen came to France, including a delegation of political gentlemen who wanted to meet the famous "American" general, the Marquis de Lafayette.

Among them was William Pitt, who at twenty-five was already a rising member of Parliament and all but predestined to follow his father and become prime minister. The Marquis de Lafayette had fought bravely in the American war, but he was distraught at the idea of giving a dinner to Englishmen. The marquis's ancestors had been warriors since the days of Joan of Arc, and all that while, England was their enemy. His own father had been killed by a British cannonball at the famous Battle of Minden, in Prussia. As much as he professed to love liberty, part of him had joined the American war for the love of an ancient hatred. The marquis admitted: "The humiliation of the war before last and their insolence during the peacetime gave me a feeling of aversion toward them that only grew with the horrors with which they defiled America." After centuries of war, how could he make peace? But France *had* made peace. And making peace meant performing normal peacetime actions, like dinners.

The marquis summoned American friends to his dinner with William Pitt and his friends. Most of all, he wanted Benjamin Franklin to come. "You are the Center Upon Which Moves the Whole Party," he pleaded, knowing full well that Dr. Franklin was all but bedridden and would need powerful, yet delicate persuasion. Likely it was Sarah Jay and Angelica Carter—themselves persons of interest—who helped cajole Dr. Franklin to the Hôtel de Lafayette, for the marquis boasted that the Americans had superior force at table that evening: "Mr. Pitt had the support of five Englishmen, and there were a dozen rebels including the ladies."

To the amazement of the marquis, the evening was a great success. The marquis liked William Pitt, who left him "very satisfied with his intellect, his modesty, his nobility, and a character as interesting as the role for which his position destines him." He especially liked how he himself had behaved: "Had our Revolution Miscarried, I could not have met a Briton But What I would Have Quarrelled with Him. But in the Way it Went, I think We May Be at our Ease with them," he wrote afterward to Jeremiah Wadsworth. Then he added a maxim that echoed the distinctive cadence of their "amiable friend" Angelica: "Since it Becomes American Soldiers to be kind to the Conquered."

"Perhaps you had better appear ignorant of this affair till you hear more," John Jay wrote to Sarah from England in October. He had caught wind of startling news about John Carter, and he wanted her to share it with Benjamin Franklin. "It turns out that Mr. Carter was driven by

Bankruptcy to America. His true name was *Church*, which (the better to conceal himself) he changed for *Carter*. The Fortune he has made enables him to settle with his Creditors, and assume his former name. I hear he has done both."

This was no longer a secret: The London papers had reprinted the bankruptcy announcement from a decade earlier for "John Barker Church, Mark-lane, London, grocer." That first time the summons ran, in 1774, no young grocer had appeared to face his creditors, but now, in 1783, a smartly dressed gentleman in his mid-thirties presented himself at the Guild Hall and satisfied each and all. Once his debts were paid, he called upon his uncle, John Barker, of Goodman Square. After he reconciled with the man for whom he was named, he was no longer "John Carter."

While resting in Bath, John Jay found this gossip titillating, but Sarah was too busy with her own secret to care. During her husband's absence, their maid, Abbe, had run away. Abbe, with her toothaches and her rheumatism. Abbe, an enslaved Black woman Sarah had likely known her whole life, but never known. Granted, in Paris, "run away" was not an apt phrase: Abbe was not a child, or a wife, or chattel, but a woman who was legally free to leave if she chose. And Abbe had simply opted to take another job with a laundress—a job that paid a salary. For Sarah, this was unthinkable, and she asked the Franklins to help her. Either Temple Franklin or his grandfather summoned the Paris police, who went to the laundress's house and arrested Abbe. Dr. Franklin himself advised Sarah to leave Abbe in "the house of confinement" for a few weeks to bring her to her senses.

Sarah knew exactly what she'd done to offend Abbe. She had hired a French nurse named Louisson to look after the new baby. Abbe had probably been born into her position with the Livingston family, and being enslaved did not preclude her from her own pride of place. Caring for the baby, Abbe believed, was her rightful role. When Sarah denied Abbe this entitlement, a bond was broken that had little to do with Abbe's actual bondage. Abbe already knew that it was her legal right to leave. Now she acted on these rights and separated from the Jays. Unfortunately, laws were of little use to a woman without means or friends,

particularly when that woman was a Black American in a foreign country who had never known any life but enslavement.

Sarah was uncomfortable with the Franklins' recommendation that
she leave Abbe in jail. The weather—still erratic—had turned unusually
cold. But she had decided she would not see Abbe until Abbe apolo-
gized. Instead, she sent her teenage nephew Peter Munro to visit the jail.
Peter advised Abbe to ask her mistress for forgiveness and permission to
come home. But Abbe told Peter that she would remain where she was
until she could be sent to America, rather than "returning home to be
laughed at and work too." If Sarah was homesick, Abbe, who could not
or did not write letters or receive messages, must have been much more
so. She wasn't only enslaved; she was trapped, and now, imprisoned.

Three years earlier, after her infant died seizing, Sarah had written to her
mother that: "The attention and proofs of fidelity which we have receiv'd
from Abbe demand & ever shall have my acknowledgements." Sarah loved
Abbe, her one female companion from home. Abbe likely loved the Jay
family too—when Peter visited her, she asked him how they were. Bondage
complicated these bonds of affection, but Sarah could not see it, and she
wasn't unique. The house Sarah and Abbe had lived in back in New Jersey
was called Liberty Hall. That summer, Sarah had sent her sister Kitty Livingston a list of the toasts her husband had given at their Independence
Day dinner—the thirteenth and final toast was to "Liberty & Happiness to
all Mankind." The Revolutionary War had since ended, freeing the United
States from an oppressive system of government. But even in the Jays' own
house, the highest aims of the revolution had yet to be realized.

John Jay sent instructions from Bath: "I think with the Doct^r [Frank-
lin], that it would be best to suspend all attention to her for some
Time—I hope she is separated from Wine and improper Company, and
that, without being indulged in the Conveniencies, she has all the Nec-
essaries of Life—if so Sobriety, Solitude & want of Employment will render her Temper more obedient to Reason."

At La Muette, near the Bois de Boulogne, the umbilical rope that rooted
a manned balloon to earth was cut, and the orb rose three thousand feet

in the air (by Sarah Jay's estimation), then began to descend too quickly. Onlookers gasped in horror, but the aeronauts fed the furnace more straw and sailed over Paris, finally descending near the Boulevards. A week after that, a hydrogen balloon—made of taffeta and covered with elastic-gum—dazzled the public once more. Then, on December 7, at a hotel on the rue Jacob, just doors away from where Britain and the United States had signed the Treaty of Paris, Angelica gave birth to the daughter she and her husband had conceived in Philadelphia, in the elation of the war's end. In a letter in which Sarah Jay reported that "Mrs. Carter" had delivered a daughter and both were well, she announced to her husband that Abbe had finally begged to return to the Jay home.

"I granted her request & am glad to find her penitent & desirous to efface by her future Conduct the reproach her late mis-step has merited," Sarah crowed. But if Sarah imagined she had conquered Abbe's rebellion, she was wrong. It was Abbe herself who had been broken. Days after Abbe left jail, she fell ill with a violent cold.

That month, the Seine froze, and Abbe died.

More snow than anyone had seen in years fell on Paris and clogged the city. Then it began to rain. The river rose three meters above its normal level and Parisians began to fear for the bridges.

Although food and fuel supplies were dwindling, Champagne still flowed in parts of Paris.

Angelica, who had entered her time of confinement as Madame Carter and emerged as Madame Church, finished lying-in just in time to raise a glass to the new Society of the Cincinnati. In Paris, there were two ceremonies in which the veteran officers of the American Revolution were inducted into the order. The highest-ranking French officers of the American War of Independence gathered at General Rochambeau's house on the rue du Cherche-Midi, while those who'd served in the American Army met at the Hôtel de Lafayette. At both events, officers were presented with gold eagle medals. Angelica wrote home to Betsy about it. "Is your lord a Knight of Cincinnati?" she asked her sister. "It has made a most wonderful noise here."

As a noncombatant, John Barker Church was not a Knight of the Cincinnati, though he coveted the gold eagle medal. But he was open to consolation prizes—for instance, a contract to supply France with some particular import from the United States like the tobacco contract Robert Morris had managed to poach from him. The United States was now independent from British regulation and taxation, but sea trade had been one of the drivers of the War of Independence. Once the war was won, merchants were eager to see what economic structure and trade models would replace the colonial model. John hoped the military friendship between France and the United States would now prove fruitful in trade, but there were many impediments. Silk was the first product he had attempted to export to the United States, but he was charged a fee by each nobleman's territory that cargo crossed, so the profit whittled down to nothing worth his while. Now he wanted to ship forty thousand bottles of Champagne, but, again, logistics were proving prohibitive.

"England is decreasing the duties on articles exported to America," he observed to his friend the Marquis de Lafayette, who in turn told the reform-minded Controller General of Finance: "If France were to do as much, for example, on mirrors and that whole branch of glassware, it would have an advantage over British manufactures."

Reforms would take time, and John Barker Church had waited nearly seven years to show off his wife and children to his mother and sisters. So, in early March 1784, John and his family boarded a packet ship at Calais and sailed "home" to England.

CHAPTER 16

Social Fabric

"Home" for John Barker Church meant both the North Sea port town of Great Yarmouth and the smaller fishing village of Lowestoft, nine miles down the coast.

Great Yarmouth smelled perpetually of the smoking fish for which it was famous, and the rows of ancient houses were so narrow—some barely three feet wide—that not even a cart could pass through the town's alleyways. Instead, goods had to be wheeled about in narrow-gauge "troll" carts. As for the local view of the recent war, one lurid example still dangled from a gibbet above the breakers on the North Denes. A privateer was entitled to prisoner-of-war status, but the Englishman whose corpse now rotted in the wind was captured off a French letter of marque and executed as a pirate.

John Barker Church had not taken up arms against England, and, even if he had, the amnesty guaranteed by the peace treaty absolved him of treason. As to his other transgressions—skipping out on debts and absconding with funds—money had resolved those wrongs. His widowed mother's forgiveness, however, was another matter. He was her only living son, and he had been gone ten years.

In the seven decades she had lived near the North Sea, Elizabeth Church had known of many men who had disappeared. North Sea gales and floods ravished the region's ships and drowned its mariners. Press gangs and pirates carried off others, often for years of service at sea. Some bodies washed back up on the stony beaches, bloated and battered, to be buried in the solid earth. Other men were simply gone, with no gravestone beside the parish church to mark the full-stop of their lives. Elizabeth Church's own husband, Richard, was a man without a churchyard stone. Yet, every once in a while, someone lost to the gray horizon sailed home again. This had happened to her brother, John Barker, who had been captured off a trading ship in the Mediterranean by Barbary corsairs and enslaved for years to the Emperor of Morocco, until Britain sent an emissary to Fez to ransom several such captives. John Barker had returned to England, and, by the time his namesake nephew was born, he had already made his first fortune as a merchant adventurer and his second in maritime insurance. Then he turned to philanthropy, governing Trinity House, a charity that supported the families of other sailors who were lost or disabled at sea.

When her youngest son had disappeared—lost not at sea but to the London coffeehouses where the sugar merchants played for high stakes—Elizabeth Church had at least known John was alive. Word had trickled back to England that someone had seen John in Le Havre, France. But a year later, the war began, and her son's name was not mentioned publicly anywhere for a very long time. Had she known his nom de guerre, John Carter, she would not have been reassured. In the history of Great Yarmouth, it was John Carter, the town bailiff, who had supposedly hosted the 1648 meeting of Oliver Cromwell's Parliamentarians at his house on Quay Street where the decision was made to execute King Charles I. Elizabeth Church had named her son for her brother, who had come back. He'd replaced that name with the moniker of a regicide.

The Churches, the newest Mrs. Church was learning, were textile merchants. John's father had been a linen draper; his uncle John Barker was a merchant adventurer in the Ottoman and Russian Empires (import routes for Persian silk and other textiles); and the elder of her

two daughters, Matilda Church, had served her girlhood apprenticeship to a Norwich seamstress. Typically, merchant men traveled and
traded, while merchant women managed the business of the shop, so
it's probable that Elizabeth Church ran the commercial side of the
family enterprise, before and after her husband's death. And "the business of the shop" had come to represent England itself, now that the
economist Adam Smith had called the country "a nation of shopkeepers" in his 1776 treatise on *The Wealth of Nations*. Outside England's rar-
efied nobility, English wives and daughters worked in all trades, but
when it came to the manufacture and trade of women's clothes in particular, women were in trade independent of their male relatives. The
mantua-maker—who crafted not just those blowsy overgowns but also
nightgowns, petticoats, and *robes de chambre*—was called "sister to the
tailor." The mercer and the milliner, trading in embellishments and
accessories such as the fans, gloves, headpieces, ribbons, and feathers
that elevated attire to fashion, were nearly as likely to be women as were
their customers.

Trading in cloth and clothing, the three Church women were not so
removed from the thrum of world events. It wasn't just fish that crossed
the Great Yarmouth Quay—the Yare River was also the outlet to world
markets for East Anglian textiles—colorful, lightweight double-worsted
"Norwich stuffs," and black "Norwich crape" and heavy bombazine—
its warp silk and its weft worsted—that had replaced the white veil for
widows' wear. And when the tide ran the other way, ships came in from
the ports of Holland, where English wool was traded for Dutch linen.
Likewise, cloth and clothing signified social rank almost as specifically
as a military uniform, and as England's middle class expanded, so did
the demand for finer fabrics, and, going further, for that "fashion."
Camlet for riding, glossy lutestring for evening, ribbons and fringe and
lace for embellishing, and the right cut and drape of a dress—getting a
look right meant cracking the code on class. Once, sumptuary laws had
restricted the purchase of luxury items to members of the nobility, but
now, widows of the lower classes were no longer fined when they wore
bombazine and Norwich crape when they mourned.

Nor was class the only political aspect of the cloth trade. Clothing demarcated politics: from the working-class pragmatism of a sturdy linsey-woolsey to the provocative romance of the muslin chemise of a French queen. Angelica Church understood the relationship of cloth to politics—how many years had she scorned English cloth to prove herself a Patriot?

The textile industry had in fact been a staging ground for some of the very conditions that gave rise to the American Revolution. When Elizabeth Church of Great Yarmouth was still Miss Elizabeth Barker of nearby Lowestoft, English women wearing imported calico or chintz in public risked being doused with ink or *aqua fortis*—the skin-burning nitric acid used in yellow dyes—or having the inexpensive cotton cloth torn from their bodies. Meanwhile, wearing made-in-Britain worsteds and wool-silk blends called "stuffs" was seen as patriotic. In response to these protests, Parliament enacted a compromise between international trade—the British East India Company—and the domestic cloth manufactory. A series of Calico Acts banned "the Use and Wear of all Printed, Painted, Stained or Dyed Callicoes in Apparel, Household Stuff, Furniture, or otherwise," to "Preserve and Encourage the Woollen and Silk Manufactures of this Kingdom." In subsequent years, in its effort to control commerce between the home country and the colonies, Parliament instituted the Molasses Act, the Hat Act, the Iron Act, and the Sugar Act, imposing duties and restrictions to ensure that England remained the hub through which all colonial trade passed: a closed loop, with raw materials—from beaver fur to iron ore—coming in, and manufactured products going out.

Now, men like John Barker Church and thinkers like Adam Smith were advocating for freer trade.

As Mrs. Church and her daughters appraised the newest Mrs. Church and the two children she'd brought with her, Angelica took their measure in return. Matilda Church was particularly hard to read. She had old-fashioned habits—still riding a horse on a pillion behind her servant, as was done a century earlier, for instance—and in town she had a reputation as an eccentric. As many in Great Yarmouth and Lowestoft remembered (in that way that small towns remember across generations), the Church sisters descended from another pair of peculiar sisters. Their great-grandmother, Deborah Pacy, and her older sister, Elizabeth, were nine and eleven when they began to suffer swooning fits and then lost, in turn, their capacity to stand or hear or see or speak. The sisters had reportedly regurgitated crooked pins and, once, a two-penny nail. Their Puritan father testified before the circuit court at Bury St. Edmunds that these symptoms were the result of witchcraft, and two Lowestoft widows were hanged. A generation later, in Salem, Massachusetts, the case of the Pacy sisters was invoked as precedent in the trials of American "witches."

The law carrying the death sentence for witchery was repealed the year Matilda Church was born. But Great Yarmouth children still avoided Kittywitches Row, the narrowest of the town's narrow alleys. And an egg seller might wonder by what force her basket of eggs should happen to fall just as the peculiar Matilda Church passed by. Despite never marrying, Angelica's sister-in-law was called "Mrs. Church" in public spaces and on legal documents. Indeed, she was mistress of herself: She had her own profession, her own large house on King Street, and her own money in the Bank of England. But her sister, Miss Elizabeth Church, twelve years younger, was stuck in the role of an unwed youngest daughter, bound by duty in perpetual service to her elders. Her life might have been quite different if her brother had not absconded with the family's respectability and possibly her own social prospects.

John and Angelica did what they could to repair the rent fabric of the Church family. Angelica asked Miss Elizabeth to come and live as her sister in London. Now John could provide a dowry for his sister and, if she wanted, she could marry. Then, just as Angelica had named her children Philip and Catharine to help heal the breach with her parents over her elopement, the couple now invited John's mother, Elizabeth Church, to stand as godmother to their new baby when, in an ancient church on a bluff above the North Sea, she was christened Elizabeth Matilda Church.

John likely hoped these gestures were sufficient, that his honor in the family had been restored. Now perhaps their lives could move forward as if no ocean or war had ever come between them. Now they would bury the dead, shake hands, and live on. But beyond the church where they celebrated the christening still hung the remains of that pirate-traitor in his gibbet. A permanent peace between the parent and the offspring states would require still more work, on both sides.

CHAPTER 17

A Separate Peace

1784–1785

Angelica Church was twenty-eight the year she moved to the greatest city in the world. Ten times the size of New York, double the population of Paris, London was the hub of global commerce and finance, shipping, and, of course, shopping. Everywhere she looked, there were shops: silk shops, fan stores, porcelain shops, glass shops, watchmakers, gin shops, confectioners, fruiterers, lamp shops, linen shops, cutlers, map sellers, gold- and silversmiths, vintners, portmanteau sellers, haberdashers, perfumers, cane makers, musical instrument shops, stationers, and on and on. John had leased a house for them on Sackville Street, near Piccadilly's St. James Church. This neighborhood was known especially for having the best booksellers on earth.

Once a broad West End avenue that had grown from a country road dotted with handsome estates where the most fortunate Londoners retreated from the urban stench while being conveniently close to the Court of St. James, Piccadilly had become a perpetual throng of thundering carriage wheels. Sackville Street was quieter, and the houses on the west side of the street overlooked the formal gardens of Melbourne House.

Angelica's rowhouse was three stories tall and had five window bays across the front, nearly as many as The Pastures in Albany. It had Baroque modeled plasterwork on the ceilings—laurel leaves and arabesques—and a fireplace made of white and multicolored marble. As spacious as it was for a London townhouse, in Piccadilly, where royals and nobles lived and houses skewed palatial, the Churches' new Sackville Street house was—almost—modest. Nearby were "houses" like Buckingham House, where Queen Charlotte had recently delivered her fourteenth child, Princess Amelia; and Devonshire House, where the spirited Duchess of Devonshire, Georgiana Cavendish, who was Angelica's age, had just given birth to her first. Then there was Burlington House, where the Duchess of Portland, subdued by chronic illness, raised her six living children. And at Melbourne House, just beyond the Churches' back-garden wall, lived the Viscountess Melbourne, Elizabeth Lamb, one of the most prominent liberal-Whig political hostesses in all of London.

Angelica was impressed, but after John sailed back to France to continue working with the Marquis de Lafayette on freeing up trade, what she most wanted to do was to see her friends. She wanted to see Margaret Gage, the wife of Commander Thomas Gage, who had sailed from Boston with her children and those soldiers who had been wounded in the Battle of Bunker Hill. Then, too, she wanted to see Margarita Low, also a cousin, whose husband had sat in the Continental Congress until the Declaration of Independence changed the war's direction to one he would not follow. And the Loyalist refugees wanted to see her too, their former differences dulled by hunger for news of home and the foreigner's longing for the familiar.

Then her old friend John Trumbull arrived. He had also spent part of the war in London, but the son of Connecticut's governor wasn't a Loyalist. He was simply pursuing his dream of being a great painter. Back when Angelica was living in Boston with two babies and her husband was running his shop on Long Wharf, Jack Trumbull used to come take tea with her and her sister Peggy, and to bounce her daughter Kitty on his knee (Jack was Kitty's godfather). Back then, when Jack talked about going to England despite the war, to find the American painters who'd already moved to London—the great Benjamin West and John Singleton Copley—and to try his luck, Angelica and Peggy encouraged him to write to their father for a letter of recommendation to Benjamin Franklin, which Jack had done. When Jack first came to London, he'd met with great success—no privateers seized his ship, and Mr. West was kind. After Benedict Arnold had been found out and British Major John André was hanged as a spy, however, the English had retaliated by rounding up Americans in London and charging them with high treason. After spending seven months in prison, Jack returned to Boston, where he went to work for the firm Wadsworth & Carter through the final months of the war. Now, with the amnesty, he had come back to continue his studies.

Reunited in London, Jack and Angelica resumed their friendship. He introduced her to the art world, and she engaged him to paint portraits of herself with the new baby, now called Betsy, and of her son Phil. Both paintings were studies of master works of royal subjects, but Jack and Angelica gave each an American twist. The painting of Phil imitated a painting Benjamin West had made of King George III's son Octavius. In their respective paintings, each small boy has a hat: Octavius, an honorary brevet colonel, wears a black-ribbon cockade on his, but Phil's boasts a macaroni feather, a symbol of defiance. As for props, the British prince holds a sword; the American boy holds a musket. The prince stands beside an overturned hobbyhorse. The American has one foot upon an overturned toy coach.

As for Angelica, Jack Trumbull painted the twenty-eight-year-old mother of four in a gown of rose-gold silk with a gauze fichu up to her neck and roses in her coiffed, powdered hair—all topped off by a headpiece of silk and ostrich plumes. She is poised, her nose is straight, her eyes and mouth are relaxed and soft. Angelica's health had been poor since her fever in Philadelphia—which might be why she is shown seated—but the fitted bodice of her gown, the pale ribbon around her waist, and her slender arm show she is thin and strong as she lifts her baby Betsy up to a second woman, perhaps her sister-in-law, Elizabeth Church.

Where Phil's portrait is modeled after that of a prince, Angelica's is a copy of a queen. The first portrait Élisabeth Vigée Le Brun made of Marie-Antoinette in 1783—the one in the simple chemise and straw hat—had caused such an uproar that she redid the portrait, replacing the (foreign-made) muslin chemise and simple straw hat with a French silk gown and elaborate headwear that was the height of that season's Parisian fashion. In Jack Trumbull's painting of Angelica, her hair is done like the queen's, powdered and frizzed, like a cloud of pale smoke under a strikingly similar hat. More pointedly, where Queen Marie-Antoinette stands alone, Angelica is set amid a triumvirate of sister, mother, daughter.

In August, John returned from France and the Church family set off to see Great Yarmouth in its summer glory. The town was trying hard to attract spa-goers. It offered sea-bathing—which, like the town's famous smoked herring, was widely touted for treating stiffness and joint pain—either in one of the bathhouses that pumped seawater into bathing tubs or in one of the elaborate carts that were driven out beyond the breaking waves so that women could enter and exit the water discreetly. John boasted in a letter to his brother-in-law Alexander that, after Angelica's six weeks of sea-bathing, "her health is much mended."

A year into their travels, John and Angelica were still tourists, glutting themselves on art and music and theater and shopping as if these honeyed months would have to last them all their lives.

"I think we shall go to Paris about the end of next month and stay there two or three months, and the Beginning of April take our passage to America," John had written to Alexander. But that isn't what happened.

Instead, Elizabeth Church, John's mother, intervened: She was not, in fact, satisfied by a few brief visits, whatever gifts her long-lost son had brought, and a namesake godchild she would never see again. Recalled to his duty (by guilt or by promise of an inheritance), John put on hold all plans to return to America. With this decision, Angelica's postwar Grand Tour metamorphosed into real life.

Only John sailed to New York in the spring of 1785. Only John embraced Angelica's parents, her sisters, her new brothers-in-law. Only John met the new babies—Peggy's Kitty, Betsy's Angelica, Cornelia Livingston's Harriet. Only John drank so much French Champagne with her father that Philip Schuyler pledged never to touch the stuff again. Only John went to dine in the country with Henry and Lucy Knox and their friends from the war.

Between social engagements, John tied up loose ends in the United States. He ended his business partnership with Jeremiah Wadsworth, parting as friends. He granted his brother-in-law Alexander Hamilton his power-of-attorney and asked him to sell both his lot on Broadway and his land on the North River. He was cutting ties, one by one, with the country he and Angelica and their friends had worked so hard to bring into being. It took only weeks. Then John boarded the ship *Greyhound* with his two small children, Kitty and little John, and their nursemaid, Molly, and they left New York.

John seemed happier than ever on his voyage back to England. "We have winds as good as Heart could wish, except that last Thursday just as we got over the Banks of Newfoundland, at 9 in the evening, it blew a most violent Gale," he wrote to Jeremiah Wadsworth. He wrote on and on: "My dear little ones are well and in high spirits they have never been sick except the first day for about half an Hour and their maid Molly has been equally well. Little John backs his stern just as Phil used to do, but in the Gale he was very angry why I did not leave him at New York and not bring him in this rolling ship, and Kate was very angry with the Captain that he would not tie the ship up." A few pages on, he boasted, "We caught 10 Cod and a Halibut on the Bank, and we have plenty of stores. . . . Our cow gives us a Syllabub every Evening."

It was Sunday night, the third of September 1785, when the carriage from Falmouth pulled up at the house on Sackville Street, and Angelica rushed down to greet the babies she'd left on the other side of the ocean two years earlier.

With four children living at Sackville Street, plus John's sister Elizabeth, the nursemaid Molly, and the servants, the new house didn't feel so large. Phil was seven, Kitty almost six, John four, and Betsy not yet two. Soon, Phil would leave to begin the school year at Eton College, but Angelica worried about that, too. Boys at Eton were subject to their own fierce hierarchy. The daily fare of mutton, bread, and beer went first to the older students. Junior students like Phil, if they had no relative in town, were sent each morning to a "dame's house," where they were made to wash their face and were fed breakfast. Even at seven, Phil would not be among the school's youngest students, but as an American, so soon after the war, he would surely meet with animosity from his British peers.

Then, in the *Morning Post*, an advertisement for a freehold villa "suitable for a noble family" presented a solution. Down Place sat on the banks of the River Thames, a few miles upstream from Eton. The house was large and white and looked a little like a castle, but, more important, it had large kitchen gardens, a menagerie, and an orchard. Here, the children could run free, fish in the river, and ride their ponies, as Angelica had done growing up on New York's North River between the wars. Here, half a day's journey by carriage from London, her friends could come for visits that were not as formal or routinized as a city "rout." They would play games of tric-trac or whist or loo or plan expeditions to Windsor Castle or the observatory belonging to their neighbors, the sibling astronomers Friedrich and Caroline Herschel, to look at stars and planets. Best of all, Phil—and soon his little brother John, too, when his turn came to attend Eton—could come home for wholesome Sunday dinners.

"Jack is grown a fine Boy," John Barker Church reported to Alexander Hamilton the following spring, after Phil had entered Eton. "He is now at a pleasant Villa which I have purchas'd on the Banks of Thames three miles from Windsor where we shall soon Repair to pass the Summer." John and Alexander were still doing business together. John was shipping goods to the United States—turpentine and rosin—and his brother-in-law handled the money. But their letters always touched on the personal relationship upon which their mutual trust was founded. "Mrs. Church is well; in about two Months she will give me another Boy or Girl," John confided.

Similar news crossed ways at sea: Betsy Hamilton and Peggy van Rensselaer were also both expecting. But, unlike their husbands, whose business crisscrossed the ocean, Angelica and Betsy could not share across such a distance the work and anxiety of mothering small children. Angelica had not met her godchild and namesake, Angelica Hamilton, who was already a toddler. Nor had Betsy met little Elizabeth Church, whom Angelica of course called Betsy. "I would write you an account of fashion, but I hear American ladies are at the head of everything that is elegant," Angelica had written glumly to her sister Betsy a few weeks earlier. "Give my love to Alexander, and tell him that some day when I am in a very gay and witty humour I will write to him." American ladies were now at the head of everything elegant, except for one American lady who might have reigned over New York society were she there. Living as a neighbor to King George III and Queen Charlotte whenever the royal family came to Windsor Castle was not a life to complain about—but how far she had come in an unexpected direction!

In the spring, Angelica gave birth to her third son; in August, he was christened Richard in an old stone parish church by the vicar of Bray.

In the bedlam stage of motherhood—with five young children and two large houses to run—and far away from her homeland—still very much in revolution, if not war—Angelica might have disappeared into the depths of her private life. For a while, she did.

CHAPTER 18

A "Charming Coterie"

1786–1787

The Churches built an English life. When he wasn't trading, John Barker Church played cards at gentlemen's clubs and went to the races; when she wasn't mothering, Angelica Church went to the theater and attended musical parties. The couple gave dinners on Sackville Street and had guests out to Down Place for extended country gatherings they called *fêtes champêtres*. Gradually, their circle of friends widened and deepened, not for any cause save the pleasure of the society of friends and interesting people. The war was over—now they meant to live.

Even as she increasingly lived as an English gentlewoman, Angelica saw herself as an American patriot and de facto representative of the United States. In public, in England as in France, she was performing what it was to be an American. Also concerned about how other Americans were perceived, she helped where she could.

Angelica made a particular effort with the American diplomats John and Abigail Adams and two of their adult children—John Quincy and Abigail, called Nabby—who had moved from Paris to London that year and taken a house on Grosvenor Square, not far from the Churches. John Adams was now minister plenipotentiary to both Britain and the Dutch Republic, so he and John Quincy were often abroad, but Abigail Adams and Nabby remained in London, where Angelica was uniquely positioned to help them get their bearings in society.

Two autumns earlier, when Abigail Adams had first arrived in Paris, she had dismissed Angelica as "a delicate little woman," and of John Barker Church, she had written: "As to him, his character is enough known in America." When she gave a large dinner for Americans in Paris, she did not invite the Churches. But Angelica was said to please in all company—and, in time, she pleased even the opinionated Abigail Adams of Braintree, Massachusetts. Now and then, the Adamses invited Angelica to dine at their house on Grosvenor Square and in turn Angelica took Nabby to see plays at the Drury Lane Theatre. The Adamses even came to look forward to visits from John Barker Church—who would present himself at Grosvenor Square with letters and packages and news from America whenever one of his ships came in.

Socially fluid, John and Angelica could make themselves agreeable at Grosvenor Square one day, and the next they would attend a musical soirée given by their increasingly close friends, Maria and Richard Cosway. Richard Cosway was a prominent portrait painter whose miniatures were "fashion itself." Twenty-four-year-old Maria Cosway's work was exhibited at the Royal Academy; Angelica likely met her through Jack Trumbull. In addition to painting, Maria was multilingual, an accomplished musician and singer, and striking to look at, and Maria and Angelica came together as if by those magnetic forces all the fashionable devotees of the German mystic Dr. Franz Mesmer were now espousing so passionately. Maria described their friendship simply: "She Colls me her Sister. I coll her My dearest Sister."

Not everyone loved Maria as much as Angelica did. One London wit described the Cosways' circle of friends as "Charon's boat"—the mythic vessel to the underworld. The critic was referring specifically to Maria's celebrity husband, especially his penchant for wearing shoes with pink heels, dressing up in period clothes, and speaking what was dubbed "glibity." And then there was the Cosways' friend Mademoiselle la Chevalière d'Éon, who lived as a woman but fenced as the man she was raised to be. ("Her hands and arms," a friend remarked dryly after dining with the mademoiselle at the Cosways' home, "seemed not to have participated of the change of sexes, but are fitter to carry a chair than a fan.") Maria's own nonconformity with proscribed gender roles was just as transgressive. In England, women might paint for pleasure—ideally, landscapes and flower arrangements—but not professionally: "Staring in men's faces, is very indelicate in a female," explained the famous Dr. Samuel Johnson. In Italy, where she'd grown up and been inducted into the Academy of Florence as a teenager, she had been something of a prodigy. In England, where her family had arrived after her father's death so that she might marry another source of support for them all, Maria opted not to understand the English language and English people when she didn't like what they said, and she continued painting ambitious allegories and histories, even portraits.

Nabby Adams described Maria Cosway to her brother as "one of those soft gentle pretty Women, whose Compliance with the request of the company would please more than her Airs could possibly give her importance," and someone who "plays and sings well, but has nevertheless, the foibles, which attend these accomplishments."

Angelica didn't care. Maria was her friend. And they both needed friends.

Maria especially needed a friend in October 1786. After an extended working holiday in Paris, she and her husband had crossed the Narrow Sea from France and ridden through the night from Dover to London. On their heels came a letter to Maria—a sheaf of paper, really—twelve painstaking pages in a distorted hand. With the excuse that he did not know the lady's address, Thomas Jefferson had sent the letter within another to Jack Trumbull, asking him to place it directly into the lady's hands.

The letter went on and on, but Thomas Jefferson hewed to one theme: "Let the gloomy Monk, sequestered from the world, seek unsocial pleasures in the bottom of his cell! Let the sublimated philosopher grasp visionary happiness while pursuing phantoms dressed in the garb of truth! Their supreme wisdom is supreme folly: and they mistake for happiness the mere absence of pain," the letter gushed. "Had they ever felt the solid pleasure of one generous spasm of the heart, they would exchange for it all the frigid speculations of their lives."

No sooner had she received this bewildering testament than Maria went to see Angelica at Down Place.

Angelica did not know the American minister plenipotentiary to France, but she had read his writing before. As a congressman, Thomas Jefferson had joined her cousin Robert Livingston on the committee that composed the Declaration of Independence. As the governor of Virginia, he had written *Notes on the State of Virginia*, which was published the year she lived in Williamsburg. If Angelica had not read the book then, a new edition had been printed in Europe to coincide with its author's new role as a diplomat. This letter was an altogether different text.

If Maria was not forthcoming with the details of the "paroxysm" that occurred between her and the American diplomat, then Jack Trumbull, who'd introduced them, filled in the gaps for Angelica. In Paris, Jack had taken Thomas Jefferson along to meet his artist friends for an excursion to the Halle aux Blés et Farines, a round stone building celebrated for its large wood-and-glass dome. That a modest grain market should be made so glorious was an architectural innovation far beyond a mere building—it was a structuring of values, culture, and commerce, and it was precisely the sort of thing the American diplomat loved. In the light-filled Halle aux Blés, that September day, Thomas Jefferson encountered what he called the "most superb thing on earth," but for once it was not structure and social architecture he was describing: "The *Halle aux Bleds* might have rotted down," he confessed afterward to Maria. All he'd seen that day was her. Jack Trumbull would tactfully "lose" the pages from his diary from the weeks that followed, when Richard Cosway was off painting the children of the Duke of Orleans and when Thomas Jefferson, forty-three and four years a widower, and Maria Cosway, twenty-six and five years married, spent a few ecstatic weeks exploring Paris together.

Then Mr. Jefferson had fallen and broken his right wrist. The pain of the injury, or the mortification it caused him, seemed to clear his mind, if not his heart. Angelica, as an American, perhaps comprehended the problem better than her cosmopolitan friend. Maria Cosway was Champagne and Chantilly lace to the nostalgic Virginian's spring water and flax linen, Sèvres porcelain to his salt-glazed stoneware. In her excellence, Maria Cosway was the aspiration manifested, but Thomas Jefferson preferred the pursuit of happiness to its realization. When Maria was gone, he had written the letter—all four thousand words—with his left hand. Then, like a man dangling from the tether of the Montgolfier balloon, he had let go and returned to Earth. This new letter, then, was not an escalation or continuation of their romance, but a postmortem spasm.

Maria's confusion was reasonable: The letter was a dialogue between the head and the heart; ostensibly, neither side won the argument.

"It is an excess which Must tear to pieces a human Mind when felt," she wrote in reply after she returned to London from Down Place. A month later, Maria wrote again to France: "*Cosa vuol dir questo silenzio?*" What means this silence?

Thomas Jefferson could not resist the vacuum: "I am always thinking of you," he wrote in one of several gallant letters he sent her over the following months. "If I cannot be with you in reality, I will in imagination."

Convinced that Thomas Jefferson wished to be with her in reality, Maria Cosway made tentative plans to return to Paris in the spring, but then it was Angelica who needed a friend. Her baby Richard was not yet a year old when he was carried back to the parish church to be buried. It was the first time Angelica had lost a child. In England, mourning was not observed for very young children—no period of seclusion, no proscribed clothing. But the loss was no less felt for the absence of black crape and bombazine. Angelica's sisters each had a new baby—but she had neither baby nor sisters nearby to console her. But she did have friends.

Maria postponed her Paris travel plans and took her own mother and sister to Down Place to keep Angelica company. And Jack Trumbull came, of course. Even the De Cornys came, all the way from France, to visit their friend. They were not family in the sense that her mother favored—a web of bloodlines and marriage bonds—or her father's understory of subordinates. This gathering, ostensibly a summer holiday, was more like what happened back in Albany when the river ice cracked: A lateral friendship spread widely enough to support and balance one another.

Gradually, Angelica's friends brought back her happiness, but the loss of Richard changed her in one permanent way. Now that she had laid her child to rest in English dirt, and no matter where she might pass her life thereafter, part of her would always remain in England.

The next person to seek help from this coterie of friends turned out to be Thomas Jefferson, who had written from Paris to each of the women he knew in London, seeking assistance with his daughter, Polly. This included Maria Cosway, Marguerite de Corny on her holiday, and Abigail Adams—but not Angelica, whom he did not know.

Polly Jefferson was eight when she arrived in London from Virginia, having crossed the Atlantic with only an enslaved adolescent girl named Sally Hemings to look after her. Abigail Adams was summoned to bring the two children off the ship. A mother of four living children and one new grandbaby—Nabby had recently married her father's secretary—Abigail Adams had plenty of experience with children. But she was not prepared for Polly, who arrived "rough as a sailor" and had to be "decoyed" off the ship, or for Sally, who was "wholy incapable of looking properly after her" and "wants more care than the child." The prim New Englander found the state of the children's belongings equally appalling. Polly lacked for frocks and stockings, for a hat, for a comb and a toothbrush, and for books; Sally, whom Abigail Adams suggested sending home on the ship's return voyage, needed calico gowns and coats, aprons, and stockings. While she shopped for these necessities, Abigail Adams sent Jack Trumbull running about London to find someone heading to Paris who might carry her letters quickly.

Maria Cosway also received word of Polly's arrival but wrote regretfully to the girl's father that she had not seen Polly because she was not known to Abigail Adams. This wasn't precisely true: Abigail Adams and Nabby, now Abigail Smith, had socialized with Maria Cosway. What Maria likely meant was that the Adamses were among the many people—men and women—who gawked at her as a "singular Character" but did not choose to know her.

A letter from the American minister also arrived at Down Place for Marguerite de Corny. "If I had had confidence in your speedy return, I should have embarrassed you in earnest with my little daughter," the minister wrote, perhaps with some hope she'd take charge of his daughter without costing him embarrassment. But the De Cornys had taken an excursion to see the English countryside, and the letter languished unopened for a week. Now it was Marguerite who was embarrassed—she also had not called on Abigail Adams. "If I had known that your child was at her house, I wouldn't have put off going to see her for a moment. I regret that you have deprived me of a means of being useful to yourself."

Of them all, Polly's father may have been the most fearful of facing Abigail Adams. As none of the women he knew volunteered to accompany the children to Paris, he sent his French valet to collect them. Conscience drove Abigail Adams to reply to this new plan that she wished she had not told the minister his daughter had come, and she refused to force the sensitive Polly to do anything further against her will.

In the end, however, Mrs. Adams deferred to Polly's father's wishes, and the girls were sent to France.

After Polly and Sally left for Paris with the valet, questions lingered about their visit, especially about Thomas Jefferson's plan to enroll Polly in the convent school that his older daughter Patsy already attended.

As supporters of the American Revolution, all of Angelica's friends had strong thoughts about education. Abigail Adams favored keeping a daughter home, if possible: "I hope she will not lose her fine spirits within the walls of a convent, to which I own I have many, perhaps false prejudices," she lamented of Thomas Jefferson's school plans for Polly.

Maria Cosway—who had loved her own convent school so much that part of her still longed for the cloistered life—would have supported the idea, as did Marguerite, who had recommended the school to Thomas Jefferson in the first place: The most enlightened families she knew in Paris all sent their daughters to the Abbaye de Penthemont. Even Jack Trumbull, once briefly a teacher himself, had a perspective on the matter. He recalled his sister Faith's boarding school almost with envy—while he had learned Greek and Latin, she had learned to paint in oils.

Such conversations were more than chitchat. From the Stoics to Plato, John Locke to Jean-Jacques Rousseau, on through Dr. Samuel Johnson, among so many others, the matter of educating children had been a core tenet of philosophical discourse. An education was power—and who got one and who didn't was critical to shaping not just individual minds but society. Now, books by women were joining the conversation. New in Piccadilly's bookstores that year was the treatise *Thoughts on the Education of Daughters* by a young English lady named Mary Wollstonecraft, and *Letters on Education*, a meditation by the historian Catharine Macaulay Graham that argued for a public education system. In Paris, Marguerite de Corny was a neighbor of the pedagogue Madame de Genlis, author of *Adèle et Théodore: Lettres sur l'éducation*, which posited that education was the key to female emancipation.

Based on her parenting choices and her own upbringing, Angelica Church likely shared Mary Wollstonecraft's views on instructing children on the beauty of the natural world, on encouraging judicious reading as a deterrent for dissipation and an enervated mind, and on cultivating their talents for making music and art. And Angelica and Mary Wollstonecraft both held a distaste for vapid conversation. Likewise, Angelica shared Catharine Macaulay's opinion that "Milk, fruit, eggs, and almost every kind of vegetable aliment ought to be the principal part of the nourishment of children." But she did not agree with Mary Wollstonecraft's argument that, for girls, a domestic education was superior, and more liberal, than that which could be had in a school. A mother's instruction would be fine, if she had not wanted her children to excel beyond her own reach, but Angelica had higher goals for her children. England insisted on people staying in their place, a place usually inherited. A gardener's child would become a gardener, a duke's child would become a duke. But Angelica's parents had sent her to school to learn what they had not learned, to give their child opportunities beyond their own. She expected school to raise her children up, to help them belong in worlds that were not accessible to her, just as she had been sent to school to access realms beyond her parents' reach. Perhaps this was vanity or hubris—on a par with posing as a copy of a queen. English culture certainly scorned the "climber," but Enlightenment principles centered on ideas of self-improvement and the pursuit of knowledge and espoused education as crucial to individual and societal improvement.

Of course, it was easier to educate boys. If one had the money for fine schools, there were many highly reputable options. But Kitty Church was seven that summer, and there was no Eton College for her. Much as her mother had been, Kitty was a precocious child and had affected a ladylike elegance very early on. She spoke Dutch and some French. She lived in houses full of books and her mother had started her on the pianoforte. As for art, Kitty was surrounded by Royal Academicians: her neighbor Anne Seymour Damer (whose sculptures sometimes stood in Sackville Street like ghosts in the London fog), the Cosways, and her godfather, Jack Trumbull. Kitty had the advantage of all of that, but Angelica wanted more for her little girl—especially once she learned that the American minister to France was sending his daughters to what she understood to be the finest school for girls in France.

In France, women did not leave the room when talk turned to politics. Instead, *salonnières* such as Marguerite de Corny arranged and conducted conversations as if they were symphonies of expression, of thought and ideas. Maria Cosway had experienced the same—in France, she was a working artist; in England, a work of art. Nor was women's participation in French art and culture new among the upper classes in France: The Marquis de Lafayette's novelist great-grandmother had been a literary light in her time. France was not perfect—all the proliferating rumors of Queen Marie-Antoinette's boudoir malfeasance was proof of that—but the French people Angelica Church knew had treated her not as a table decoration but as a valued, intelligent person—a valid source of information and opinion. Meanwhile, in England, the accomplished women she knew—Maria Cosway, Anne Damer, even her sister-in-law Matilda Church—were treated with suspicion, as if each had a whiff of witchery about her.

So, it was decided: At the end of the summer, Maria Cosway and the De Cornys would sail to France in time to see the exhibition of the Paris Salon (after all, Maria had unresolved business with the American minister). Then Angelica Church and Jack Trumbull would follow in December, bringing Kitty with them. After the holidays, Kitty would enter the Abbaye de Penthemont, and her mother would remain for a while in Paris and have a happy winter among her friends.

Thus, in December 1787, Jack Trumbull, Angelica Church, and eight-year-old Kitty set off for Paris, looking forward to seeing both Maria and the De Cornys. But when they arrived, Maria was gone. She had come to see that year's Salon, of course, but she'd expected to see Thomas Jefferson also, and perhaps resume whatever it was that had happened between the two of them. But while Maria was in Paris, the minister made himself scarce until it became evident that she had mis-read his intent. Stung, Maria retreated home.

"Have you seen yet the lovely Mrs. Church?" she wrote to Thomas Jefferson on Christmas Day from the gray safety of London. She was putting on a brave face. "If I did not love her so Much I should fear her rivalship."

"I never saw her before," replied Thomas Jefferson.

But that was about to change.

CHAPTER 19

Constitutional Convention

Paris, 1788

When "Angélique" returned to Paris, expecting a happy reunion with old friends in the dazzling city of white stone and intellectuals, she found herself in a very different city from the one she'd first explored in the *annus mirabilis*, the year of awe. Even if she tried to show Kitty the novelties of Paris—the artists' ateliers at the Louvre, or the Palais-Royal newly renovated by the Duke of Orleans as an entertainment and shopping complex—it was impossible to overlook the fact that the economic situation in France had taken a dangerous turn.

The red skies and rank, sulphuric fog through which the Churches had sailed in the summer of 1783 had caused crop failures across Europe. The American debt remained unpaid. To make up the deficit, the Crown raised taxes. In the rising crisis, Queen Marie-Antoinette had become a target of public vitriol. Pamphlets distributed in Paris depicted *"l'orgie royale."* They said she slept with her brother-in-law. They said she slept with women. The queen fought back with her own propaganda. In the official portrait displayed at that year's Paris Salon, Élisabeth Vigée Le Brun had painted the queen in regal red velvet, a child on her lap, two at her knee, and, beside her, curtained in black, her dead baby's empty cradle. As the painting asserted, even if she was a queen, Marie-Antoinette was still a woman and a mother. She wore no diamonds, but a jewelry case stands behind the empty cradle, evoking to viewers that iconic story of the Roman lady Cornelia, who allegedly had said her children were her jewels. The portrait was stunning as a work of art, but the painting had not quelled the rising anger any more than increased taxes and devaluing the *livre* had reversed inflation.

"The internal Situation of France is Very Extraordinary," Angelica's friend the Marquis de Lafayette explained. "The dispositions of the people . . . are working themselves into a Great degree of fermentation." But the marquis was hopeful that this foment caused by "deranged finances" would lead to progress in France. He did not wish the queen any ill, but he did want the monarchs to submit to a constitution.

Only in the finest neighborhoods could anyone ignore the rising poverty plaguing France. The De Cornys, with whom Angelica stayed that winter, lived in just such a neighborhood—in the ninth arrondissement, on the rue de la Chaussée-d'Antin. Louis-Dominique Éthis de Corny was now *Procureur du Roi et la Ville*, supplier to the king and the city. Nearby lived Jacques Necker, a Swiss banker and former minister of finance who now lobbied for a national bank as a means to stabilize France's economy. As for Marguerite de Corny's female neighbors, they too were leaders of French society. Madame Necker was an active *salonnière* and founder of a charity hospital, and her twenty-two-year-old daughter, Madame Germaine de Staël, was already an accomplished playwright and author. And diagonally across from the De Cornys' elegant home was Madame Montesson's mansion, which included a private five-hundred-seat theater that often featured the plays penned by her niece, Madame de Genlis, the renowned writer and educator.

After her long retreat, Angelica likely took in Parisian high life—a feverish whirling sphere of flirtation,, glamour, and intoxication—floating on bubbles of Champagne until the high wore off and the glaring light of day revealed what rouge and powder could only mask so long. Paris was still grand—for those who could afford it—but that grandeur was cracking. Everyone blamed the queen.

The condemnation of Marie-Antoinette was complicated for women like Angelica. "Engeltje" had been born the same winter as the Austrian Duchess "Maria Antonia." In 1778, they both had become first-time mothers. In 1786, the previous spring, they both had lost a child for the first time. This shared timeline was reinforced by mutual friends. During the war, French officers had regaled Angelica with descriptions of their vivacious young queen, whom some of them knew well and loved. They described her parties, her clothes, and her pleasure house, the Petit Trianon. Like many Americans, Angelica still felt a deep debt of gratitude to the king and queen of France—for the money loaned to Congress, for General Rochambeau's army, and for the naval squadron that had arrived in the Chesapeake just in time to prevent the British from retreating instead of surrendering at Yorktown. But this gratitude also had a personal side: Few had profited so extensively from French largesse than her husband, John "Carter"—supplier and, briefly, financier to the French Army.

As Angelica visited her friends, she could not help but see how the years had worn on them all. Those young men she had traveled with during the war—dancing for their health and spirits and toasting liberty like they all knew what it was—were careworn by families, their flagging fortunes, and the strain of French politics.

The Marquis de Chastellux, now in his fifties, had married, but his two-volume book, *Voyages de M. le Marquis de Chastellux dans l'Amérique*, which Angelica had helped him research, had been harshly criticized since its publication. The marquis had tried to be as honest as he could in relaying his impressions, but not everyone appreciated his unflattering interpretations. Many people who appeared on his pages, including her own parents, felt they deserved better treatment.

As for the Lafayettes, they were divided between the cares of raising children and the cares of their constituents. In addition to their three living children—Georges Washington, who was Kitty's age, and his younger sisters, Anastasie and Virginie—the Lafayettes were raising George Washington Greene, since his father, General Nathanael Greene, had died of heatstroke trying to farm his way out of the debt he had incurred buying clothing for his soldiers. Caty Greene had resisted sending the boy abroad, but even with Jeremiah Wadsworth's close assistance (which came with compromising strings attached), Caty was struggling to keep her family afloat financially. The marquis and Angelica exchanged what news each of them possessed. Nearly a decade had passed since they had been "howlowing" together in Boston.

Now Angelica easily dusted off these old friendships. Only time and a little distance had come between them. The bonds were still strong between France and America—as they had been after Yorktown—save for the matter of those unpaid debts.

Between social engagements and helping Marguerite de Corny care for her sick husband, Angelica Church finally met Thomas Jefferson.

"I have seen too little of her, as I did of you," Thomas Jefferson wrote to Maria Cosway. This was not quite true. Angelica's Paris shopping was already piling up at the minister's Hôtel de Langeac—she had an entire trunk of French caps that she had tasked him with shipping to her brother-in-law in New York. But he did admit what Maria knew would be true—her "Angélique" had made an impression on the American diplomat: "I find in her all the good the world has given her credit for. I do not wonder at your fondness for each other."

"I give you free permission to love her with all your heart," Maria replied, releasing him as he had her. "I shall feel happy if I think you keep me in a little corner of it, when you admit her even to reigning Queen."

Perhaps embarrassed by his rudeness, Thomas Jefferson made excuses. "It was not my fault," he wrote to Maria. "Unless it be a fault to love my friends so dearly as to wish to enjoy their company in the only way it yields enjoiment, that is, en petit comité. You make every body love you."

Even as he idealized those years of his life that he had been a married man, Thomas Jefferson, had become accustomed to absolute rule of his own household. He had avoided Maria Cosway's attractions in nearly the same way he had avoided Abigail Adams's assistance parenting his daughters. But Maria was a painter—she looked into men's faces—and she likely guessed how easily her American friend would slip into the hollow space of the homesick widower's nostalgia.

Thomas Jefferson seemed to have convinced himself that he had no use for any queen. He had even derided the king himself for depending on his: That past spring, the American minister had reported to the United States that the king "has no mistress loves his queen and is too much governed by her." And he hoped that his home country would never run the risk of letting women step beyond the bounds of domesticity. But for all he said, Thomas Jefferson was clearly susceptible to women. Maria Cosway, Abigail Adams, Marguerite de Corny—he wrote to them all, confided in them, and exchanged favors. (He even bought stockings for Mrs. Adams, who was one year older than he was.) But where Maria had been like a muse out of old Greek stories, Angelica was an American. She was familiar. She knew his friends. She knew his books. She shared his love of country—she had even seen his Virginia. She was, like him, a veteran of the American Revolution, though neither had donned a uniform or captured a redoubt or slept on the frozen ground at Valley Forge. She even shared his admiration for France, even as she longed, as he did, for home. And, at thirty-one, she was near the age his wife had been when she died.

Perhaps Angelica's tastes ran a little high and a little French for Thomas Jefferson (she admitted freely to her enjoyment of luxuries). Perhaps her political savvy overstepped the bounds of what he felt was suitable for her gender (she read books on finance and was versed in the political situations in three countries). But for that winter in Paris, the first year that Thomas Jefferson had both of his living daughters with him since their mother's death, a mother had appeared in his family milieu. Perhaps they ate Sunday dinners *en famille* at the Hôtel de Langeac and afterward Angelica and the girls took turns playing songs on the new harpsichord. Perhaps the two parents took all of their girls— Kitty, Polly, and Patsy, who was fifteen, and maybe even Sally, who was Patsy's age—on a carriage ride through the frosted Bois de Boulogne. From a distance, they could have been mistaken for Thomas Jefferson's ideal American family.

He would recall this interlude in Paris with Angelica and what he deemed their "charming coterie" as "those scenes for which alone my heart was made."

After the holidays, Kitty and the Jefferson girls were all ensconced in their convent school, and Parisian hosts resumed their dinners and open houses. At these soirées, the economy, the American debt, and the queen's alleged lewdness were common topics of debate. But at the Hôtel de Lafayette, another matter vied for the center of conversation: The new US Constitution—not yet ratified—had reached France. Both Thomas Jefferson and the Marquis de Lafayette had received copies of the document that would replace the Articles of Confederation and frame the government of the United States going forward—that is, if enough of the states would ratify it. The Marquis de Lafayette reported to the United States that the Americans in Paris were "debating in a Convention of our own as Earnestly as if we were to decide upon it."

Thomas Jefferson was the least enthusiastic in his support for the document that only distance had prevented him from helping to craft. The former Virginia governor said that he would have preferred to append a guarantee of rights to the "venerable fabrick" of the Articles of Confederation, with its guarantee of sovereignty to the states. Absent that option, he felt strongly that there ought to be an explicit Bill of Rights, like the one the English had.

Among the Americans in France that winter was the man they called "Common Sense." Anonymous no longer, the pamphleteer Thomas Paine was the most democratic of the party. He opposed monarchy, aristocracy, and class distinctions. "It is wrong to say God made rich and poor," he contended. "He made only male and female." The corsetmaker-turned-political-theorist was in Paris that winter seeking financial support for an iron bridge he had invented, so the equilibrium of arches was much on his mind as he contemplated the three branches of government and the bicameral congress mapped out by the new Constitution.

So long as it was for the people and accountable to the people, Thomas Paine supported a strong central government. Even in the tract that had earned him his nickname, he had written: "The continental belt is too loosely buckled." Likewise, his most recent tract argued in favor of the Bank of North America, which John "Carter" had helped launch and in which he remained a shareholder, even as Pennsylvanians sought to revoke its charter.

"Ingratitude has a short memory," wrote Thomas Paine of the bank, to the surprise of many whose antiauthoritarian views were less nuanced. "It was on the failure of the Government, to support the Public Cause, that the Bank originated. It stept in as a support when some of the persons then in the Government, and who now oppose the Bank, were apparently on the point of abandoning the cause, not from disaffection, but from despair." Thomas Paine believed that the security of gold and silver in the bank and consolidated law would achieve more liberty, more prosperity, and less oppression for more people.

As for the Marquis de Lafayette's position, he read the new US Constitution through the lens of his hopes for France. He longed for a constitution to impose checks and balances upon his country's absolute monarchy. From this vantage point, his critique of the new US Constitution was that it gave too much power to the executive branch.

Angelica Church's opinions were not noted. Of course she had them, and likely she expressed them: "The eloquence of silence is not a common attribute of hers," Alexander Hamilton would say of his sister-in-law. But as a woman who had been taught from girlhood how to behave in political circles, she had learned a second layer of diplomacy—how to speak as a woman in a room full of men who considered it entirely "natural" that a woman would have no vote or public say. If Angelica held back any of her own views on the matter of the Constitution, she did not hesitate to make Thomas Jefferson a gift of a leatherbound volume of the *Federalist Papers*, made up largely of essays that her brother-in-law Alexander Hamilton had written in support of that document.

Thomas Jefferson was firmly in the camp of men who felt women had no place in politics. "French ladies miscalculate much their own happiness when they wander from the true field of their influence into that of politicks," he remarked to Angelica. He had long held the opinion that women's happiness ought to be pursued through marriage, motherhood, and domestic occupations. Such limitations were not oppressive, he reasoned, but rather liberating and equalizing: "It is civilization alone which replaces women in the enjoyment of their natural equality," he had written in *Notes on the State of Virginia*. The housewife was neither slave nor whore nor queen. She was "natural," according to his standards. France had only deepened his convictions on the matter. Since coming to Paris, where men and women behaved so differently from the way they did back in Virginia, the diplomat had had a lot to say about gender roles.

Angelica had been raised in the same ideological world as the American minister—a world in which a woman's realm was her family. But here their thinking likely diverged. Where Thomas Jefferson might have imagined the ideal family as that of individual men, fair and equal, like a row of uniform Virginia tobacco plants, to be grown and harvested in a single generation, Angelica Church's concept was more like a stand of northern oak, roots and branches intermingled and supportive, sheltering an understory for centuries.

Even now, through her daughter Kitty, who would remain in Paris to attend the Abbaye de Penthemont for the school year, Angelica was forming a family bond when she prevailed upon Thomas Jefferson to look after her eight-year-old daughter as his ward. This act flattered him as a father, whereas Abigail Adams had challenged him when she offered to have his daughters live with her. Granted, Kitty might rely also upon the De Cornys, the Lafayettes, and her godfather, who came regularly to Paris, but the favor Angelica asked of the minister was the sort that gave more than it asked. She had entrusted him with her jewel. And, in return for the privilege of doing her this favor, Angelica had a second, even more delicate request.

Jack and Angelica had carried letters from London to Paris, including one from Abigail Adams. They already knew the contents: Congress had accepted John Adams's resignation as the minister plenipotentiary. A diplomatic position would soon be vacant, and Angelica wanted it— not for herself, of course, because that was impossible—but she knew people who would be suitable—her cousin Robert R. Livingston or her brother-in-law Alexander Hamilton, for example. But, above all, she would choose her father. Philip Schuyler had many skills pertinent to a diplomatic posting, but he also had her. As the adult daughter of a minister plenipotentiary—especially if her mother remained in New York to manage their estate—she would have official claim to a role she knew she could play as well as anyone.

Thomas Jefferson loathed petitions from women. Personal solicitations, petitions, memorials—those were for kings, who bestowed favors whimsically. He saw women's petitions as the corruption that most threatened France's efforts at reform. He wrote that year to George Washington that, "In my opinion a kind of influence, which none of their plans of reform take into account, will elude them all, I mean the influence of women in the government. The manners of the nation allow them to visit, alone, all persons in office, to sollicit the affairs of the husband, family, or friends, and their sollicitations bid defiance to laws and regulations." A republic had laws, due process, and justice. Under such a system, all (white) men might be equal. But women, who had no right to vote or speak for themselves in court, still had no legal channels save appealing to men to speak on their behalf.

Angelica knew better than to press the matter far, but she did speak of her father: "I am very certain that you would please each other," she would remark. And the diplomat replied that he hoped "to become acquainted with your father who must be good, because you are so. The fruit is a specimen of the tree."

Angelica Church spent two months settling Kitty at the convent, visiting friends, and debating the new US Constitution, while Jack Trumbull was creating portraits of French officers for a painting he planned of the surrender at Yorktown. Then the two American friends left Paris to return to London. In Luzarches, twenty miles north of Paris, the rear carriage wheel broke. They found smiths to clamp the wheel back together, but it was a temporary repair, and the accident to one wheel revealed that two others were barely any better. Even after unloading Angelica's trunk of books to lighten the load, and depositing it at a post office to be sent back to Thomas Jefferson's house, they traveled the next sixty miles to lodgings in Amiens, "in continual apprehensions of being let down in the mud." Traveling so slowly, they worried they would miss their ship. But they arrived at the ancient walled town of Boulogne-sur-Mer to find warm firesides and their packet ship still in port. Nonetheless, their bad luck persisted. "We cross'd the channel in beautiful weather and in four or five hours, but our unpropitious Genius would not let us escape even on such a day without mishap," Jack Trumbull reported of their ill-fated journey. "In going out of the harbor we ran foul of a post which marks the channel, damag'd the vessell and frighten'd us." Fortunately, the travelers, though shaken, were not shipwrecked—if anything, they were pleased with themselves for still being the adventurous people they had been back in the wilds of their homeland.

But the real upheaval lay just beyond the placid horizon. As the ship's crew righted matters, Angelica looked back a little longer at the country she loved second to her own: It would be her last look at France at peace.

CHAPTER 20

Summer in New York

1789

One year later, at the English port of Falmouth, Angelica Church waited out a March squall. As soon as the winds permitted, she and her traveling entourage—which did *not* include her husband or any of her children—boarded the packet ship *Tankerville* and sailed away from England. Angelica hated the sea. But she missed her family, and she would not miss out on the summer of 1789 in New York.

The voyage from the British Isles to the island town of New York took the *Tankerville* fifty-six days. Given the equinox, March was a bad month for sailing, Thomas Jefferson had warned her, urging Angelica to wait a month or two and travel home to the United States with him. Instead, Angelica made the trip with her brother Phil Schuyler, who had dropped out of Columbia College, as New York's King's College was now called. If Angelica felt any bitterness toward her brother, the first in her family to attend any college, her family would say the fault was hers: He had just become the third of Catharina Schuyler's children to elope. Also aboard the *Tankerville* was the twenty-nine-year-old Dutch minister just appointed to the United States, Franco van Berckel: "gaudy as a peacock," but amusing.

As Angelica crossed the Atlantic, a parade of events took place on either side. In England, a state procession celebrated King George III's recovery from the mysterious bout of madness that Angelica had kept abreast of all winter through the doctor the Church family shared with the royal household, and reported upon to the American minister, her friend Thomas Jefferson. The Prince of Wales, whose regency John Barker Church had hoped for, would have to wait to reign. In France, a very different procession marched from the medieval Notre-Dame Cathedral to the church of Saint-Louis with candles in hand. These twelve hundred deputies represented the three "estates" of France: the clergy, the nobility, and the commoners. Several of them had once marched (or sailed) on behalf of the American Revolution. King Louis XVI had summoned the Estates-General for the first time in more than a century to address the escalating financial crisis. Also that month, in New York, fifty-seven-year-old George Washington climbed into a carriage and rode through streets thronged with well-wishers. To meet the Estates-General, Louis XVI had donned an overcoat of golden fabric and the kingdom's largest diamond upon his hat. For his thanksgiving promenade, George III had sported his navy-and-scarlet Windsor uniform, heavily embellished with gold braid. To his inauguration as the first US president, George Washington had worn a brown suit made of broadcloth from Jeremiah Wadsworth's new woolen company, embellished with only plain metal buttons and a sword. When he descended from the carriage before New York's Federal Hall, George Washington passed through two files of troops before entering the building. Fourteen years since the shots fired in Lexington and Concord had ignited the American Revolution, and six years since the signing of the peace with Britain, the government framed by the new US Constitution was just taking its seat. Now, the man who had led the Continental Army returned to public view on the balcony of Federal Hall. Before the crowds of well-wishers in the street below and up on the surrounding rooftops, the general set his hand upon an open Bible and in a soft voice repeated the words after New York's chancellor, Robert R. Livingston.

Once the first presidential oath had been sworn, Chancellor Livingston turned to the crowd and announced, "It is done."

Two days after the first president was inaugurated, as she stood on the deck of the *Tankerville,* Angelica Church had her first view of New York since before the American Revolution began. Between the ravishment of the war and its recovery, the town was nearly unrecognizable. Fort George, once that prominent landmark whose ramparts she had explored as a girl with Susanna Moore, was being demolished, its debris dumped in the river to shore up the bank. Trinity Church, along with most of the buildings between Broadway and the North River, had been burned in the fire of 1776, after the British had captured the town. But for all that had been ruined, much had been improved. Streets had been cobbled, with footpaths on either side. A new road to the village of Greenwich was being built along the river.

Once she disembarked, Angelica was surrounded by the familiar— Catharina Schuyler had sailed from Albany just in time to meet Angelica's packet, and with her was Betsy Hamilton, now a mature thirty-one-year-old woman, pregnant and flanked by children—Phil, Angelica, Alexander, James, and Fanny. Perhaps it was at their reunion that Angelica realized her little sister was no longer a "Betsy," a nickname that now more aptly suited her daughter. And henceforth, except for the occasional condescending slip, Angelica would call her sister "Elizabeth," "Eliza," or, most coolly, "Mrs. Hamilton."

As for Alexander Hamilton, Angelica had heard that lawyering had made him soft. "Col. Beckwith tells me that our dear Hamilton writes too much and takes no exercise, and grows too fat," she had admonished Elizabeth in a letter earlier that year. "I hate both the word and the thing, and I desire you will take care of his health and his good looks, why I shall find him on my return a dull, heavy fellow. He will be as unable to flirt as Robert Morris; pray, Betsey, make him walk, ride and be amused." But her brother-in-law, for all the fame he now claimed, was still an active, even frenetic little man. Best of all, there was nothing dull or heavy in his repartee. As to whether he could still dance as well as he talked—Angelica would see for herself.

The first inaugural ball took place at Assembly Hall on Broadway, just days after Angelica landed in New York. The fact that there were three hundred people in attendance solved the problem of how she might see her old friends at once, without slighting anyone. While President Washington walked through the figures of a minuet or a cotillion with her sister, Angelica could survey the room. New York's ladies were resplendent: There were gowns of celestial blue and white and yellow satin, of striped Indian taffeta, embellished with rosettes, silk fringe, ribbons, Italian gauze. And on their dressed and powdered heads were hats plumed in the Spanish style or cockaded, and an abundance of "borrowed hair." One woman wore a pouf of gauze in the form of a globe. Another wore a double-winged headpiece made of crenellated white satin, wreathed with artificial roses.

From behind the French fans painted with George Washington's face that each lady received as a party favor, New York eyed Angelica in return. By thirty-three, most women were well past their bloom and precious of their remaining teeth, but sea-bathing and Down Place had restored Angelica's "slender health," and the best dressmakers and milliners in Paris and London had supplied her wardrobe. She must have been incandescent with happiness at her homecoming and, as the evening unfolded, at the distinct pleasure of being the center of attention. For all the spectacle of the inaugural celebrations, one lady wrote of Mrs. Church's homecoming, "next to Genl. Washington, she was the object of Public Curiosity and attention."

So many women had helped bring about that evening, though none had been elected to a seat in either of the chambers of government in the newly renovated Federal Hall. As to voting, if any women had managed to cast a ballot, the new federal government would soon eliminate that irregularity. But when it came time for the toasts, it became evident that the "brilliant collection of Ladies" would not be excluded entirely from the decision-making process. That first week in the new bicameral legislative body, the most heated topic of debate had been how the president ought to be addressed. Vice President John Adams argued that the leader of the United States ought to be elevated, and he favored the term "Your Highness." This shocked his more egalitarian colleagues, but then again John Adams had spent most of that decade as a diplomat, referring to "His Most Christian Majesty" of France and "Their High and Mightinesses" for all the lords of the States-General of the Dutch Republic. The House had rejected this proposal in favor of the unadorned "George Washington, President of the United States." At the ball, however, John Adams thought he might get his wish after all, though he was displeased about how, "at Supper the Ladies would not drink to "the President"—they all drank to "his Highness," as he related to a friend. "The Ladies probably must settle the dispute.— and thus Accident, feeling Caprice, always; and never Reason, decides the fate of nations."

The second inaugural ball was given by the Count de Moustier, the French minister plenipotentiary to the United States, at the house on Broadway that he shared with his sister-in-law, the Marquise de Bréhan. Thomas Jefferson had initially described the marquise (or marchioness) in glowing terms: "I rejoice in the character of the lady who accompanies the Count de Moustier to America," he had written to Abigail Adams. "Simple beyond example in her dress, tho neat, hating parade & etiquette, affable, engaging, placid, & withal beautiful, I cannot help hoping a good effect from her example." More recently, when Angelica asked the diplomat to write a letter of introduction to this lady, he felt compelled to add a warning: "I send you, my dear Madam, the letter to the lady you desired, and leave you at liberty to use it or not, as you find most agreeable when you shall be at New York. You are not a stranger to the distance which has been established between her and the societies of that place."

New York's fierce rejection of the diplomats from France was man-ifested in its conviction that the minister and his sister-in-law lived as man and wife. It was the most damning of insults—a man in the sway of a perverse woman. In code, John Jay had explained the situation to

Thomas Jefferson: "Appearances (whether well or ill founded is not important) have created and diffused an Opinion that an improper Connection subsists between him and the Marchioness." Jefferson had begun working to have the Count de Moustier recalled to France. But the scandal was a symptom of a larger problem: The "amity" between France and the United States was fading.

"If France had wished to destroy the little remembrance that is left of her and her exertions in our behalf," snipped one congressman, "she would have sent just such a minister: distant, haughty, penurius, and entirely governed by the caprices of a little singular, whimsical, hysterical old woman."

None of this slander deterred Angelica. Possibly, she had become inured to extramarital intrigues, living in France and England where liberty and libertinage were entwined. More likely, she cared little about relations between the count and the marquise, and she cared a great deal about the fraying relations between France and the United States. Given her history of bridging the differences between the allies, she would not shun France's diplomats. Nor would President Washington.

Besides, the French ball was splendid. The evening featured a choreographed dance performed by eight men—four in French uniforms, four in the Continental Army's buff and blue—and eight women wearing white ribbons and garlands of flowers that matched the uniforms.

Aided by the support of those prominent attendees, the French ball helped turn the tide of public opinion. A subsequent coded dispatch to France reported: "Madam Bréhan is every day recovering from the disesteem and neglect into which reports had thrown her and ... Moustier is also becoming more and more acceptable or at least less and less otherwise." As interpersonal relations improved, so did diplomacy: "His commercial ideas are probably neither illiberal nor unfriendly to this country. The contrary has been supposed. When the truth is ascertained and known unfavorable impressions will be still more removed."

Still, the US's unpaid debt to France remained an open wound.

In the weeks that followed, New York ladies gave levees, teas, and dinners. In June, Sarah Jay gave birth to a son and John Livingston, Phil Church's godfather, got married. Then came Independence Day, and a party given by the Society of the Cincinnati. The memorial began as a solemn event, eulogizing members who had died since the war, including General Greene. Then the society members moved to the City Tavern to quaff patriotic toasts and make speeches, before proceeding to dinner and entertainment. President Washington was recovering from an infection and was not among the company, but Martha Washington had arrived in New York, and she attended in the president's stead. The vice president's wife, Abigail Adams, had also arrived in New York since the inauguration, and she too joined the party. So did many old friends of Angelica: her father's faithful aides-de-camp Brockholst Livingston and Richard Varick, both now married; and her uncle John Cochran, who was no longer doctoring and now hoped for an appointment in the new government.

As joyful as each reunion was—as occurs with so many travelers returned to their homes—after the initial embrace Angelica felt as distant from her friends as when she had been in England. She had missed everyone, but she had also missed so much that it was hard to find the thread of those old friendships. Everyone's lives had gone on without her. Six years living abroad had made her a stranger.

As soon as she was finished lying-in, Peggy van Rensselaer traveled to New York—both to see her sister and, perhaps, to see the new "republican court" presided over by a reluctant Martha Washington. But their brother Phil Schuyler had returned to his bride Sarah and the baby she'd delivered while he was traveling, and their brother Johnny Schuyler could not leave farming at that time of year. Even their father remained in Albany, prevented from traveling by "Gouty swellings" and kidney stones, which Philip Schuyler described in full detail to Alexander Hamilton in hopes that his son-in-law would herd his children home to him. But Alexander was out of town on legal business.

While her friends' lives churned on, Angelica found herself most at home among other foreigners. She was a favorite guest that summer of Baron Friedrich von Steuben, a Prussian-trained officer who had joined the American Revolution in January 1778—quite possibly after attending the revelry at Angelica's house on Frog Lane, the day before it burned. People said it was he who had trained the Continental Army to do more with a bayonet than roast meat on a fire. That summer, Angelica Church called him "my Baron," and although he was older than her father, her baron played the besotted rake and called her "la petite Church."

"Yes, Madame, I love you seriously," the sixty-year-old baron would profess to her in French. "I love you and there is nothing extraordinary in that a young man such as myself is easily captivated by a woman as lovable as you."

Their wordplay was risqué, even if few others understood them. "Here I am at this moment writing to you before this small candlestick," the baron teased. "I will make this light the Sacred Flame of a Vestal Virgin, and if my bathrobe were not so soiled, I could easily resemble a Vestal Virgin myself. What do you think of that?" This "saucy" banter between the bachelor baron and Angelica raised few eyebrows among the Cincinnati: Since the general's banishment from the army of Frederick the Great for "indiscretions" had sent him to America, his likely homosexuality had been fiercely shielded by his friends.

In July, Angelica and her sisters planned to go to Albany, as their father had asked them to do. But, on the eve of their departure, Philip Schuyler traveled to New York after all. He had been elected to serve as one of New York's first US senators.

When the senator arrived in town, he and Rufus King, the other senator elected, first drew lots to determine who would take the two-year term and who would take the six, to stagger future elections. Philip Schuyler drew the short straw, which was fine with him, as he wrote home to his family: "I believe I shall be heartily tired of the business before my time expires."

After a week's visit with their father in New York, Angelica and Peggy and Peggy's baby boarded Captain Bogart's sloop upriver. Alexander had gone ahead; Elizabeth would follow. Their brother Johnny would travel down from the Saratoga farm that he now managed with his new bride. (Like all his siblings save one, he'd sought forgiveness rather than permission to marry.) On the way, Angelica would disembark at Rhinebeck to collect her brother Phil and his wife Sarah and their baby. Only Philip Schuyler would miss the reunion, his only comfort being the use of Mrs. Church's carriage while she was gone. But he sent home with his daughters a cargo of chicken, ducks, pears, and citrus.

All eight of Catharina Schuyler's living children returned home to The Pastures that August. This time, no bands of British rangers attacked them in their home, and no soldiers guarded the doors. The only invaders that had threatened northern New York that year were the summer mosquitoes and the Hessian flies that had devoured the previous year's wheat crop. These golden hours did not last long. To young parents with children and farms and careers to tend, "domestic ease" seemed a myth soldiers invented in places like Valley Forge while dining on salt beef cooked on a bayonet. With Congress in session, Alexander could not be kept from New York. Johnny and Phil had farms to manage. Life plowed forward for the Schuyler clan.

At the beginning of September, President Washington appointed Alexander Hamilton secretary of the treasury. On his second day on the job, Alexander met with the Count de Moustier to discuss the American debt to France. The French minister recorded that Secretary Hamilton affirmed "that Congress should no longer seek to evade or postpone the payment of public debts, the King would be reimbursed purely and simply under the terms of the Contract by means of sums borrowed in Holland and which could be paid into the Royal Treasury." The key to this plan was Franco van Berckel, Angelica's Dutch friend from the *Tankerville*: "If new lenders are persuaded by the beautiful pictures that will be presented to them of the present and future resources of the United States, it will be very fortunate for the old creditors," the Count de Moustier remarked, clearly relieved that the biggest diplomatic problem facing the two nations might find a resolution on his watch.

Thirteen days later, on the second page of New York's *Daily Gazette*, a short report from France relayed that, on July 16, the Bastille in Paris—a medieval fortress that the regime used as a state prison—had been seized by the citizens. "No less than three hundred persons are employed in demolishing that once beautiful fortress," the newspaper reported. With this symbolic dismantling of a structure that had come to signify tyranny—it seemed then—France had accomplished its own revolution. People deemed the affair in France "remarkable for its mildness." One commentator marveled that "The principal destruction produced in the late wonderful Revolution arose from the ardour of the people themselves."

The Count de Moustier was about to see the situation in Paris for himself: He had received permission to return to France and attend to his health and private business. Thomas Jefferson had received the same permission from his own government—but the homesick diplomat would learn—after he, Patsy, Polly, and Sally landed in Williamsburg—that he had been appointed to replace John Jay as secretary of foreign affairs. His respite at Monticello would be brief—the longer he stayed, the longer Secretary Hamilton would act in his stead. The Dutch plan for the French debt was already in motion.

At the end of September, Angelica received a letter from her husband with the news that their children were ill. Her brother-in-law immediately bought her a passage back to England. Three days later, Angelica and her three servants boarded His Britannic Majesty's ship *Sandwich*, bound for England.

For a day, the packet stood out to sea, making final preparations and waiting for the wind, the late autumn hills of her homeland still in view. Via the pilot who guided the ship out of New York Harbor, Angelica sent a letter back to shore for Alexander: "Let neither politics nor ambition drive your Angelica from your affections," she pleaded in her farewell. "A thousand embraces to my dear Betsy, she will not have so bad a night as the last, *but poor Angelica*."

She closed her farewell: "My best affectionate wishes to my Baron. Same to Van Berckel and L'Enfant." After six years living as a foreigner in France and England, she'd returned to the US to find herself most at home in the company of a Prussian military tactician, a Dutch diplomat, and a French architect.

To soothe her distress, Angelica's baron sent a ridiculous letter to her aboard the *Sandwich*: "If Church were an Italian, this opening would be sufficient to close the gap between the use of a Dagger, Poison and all these means of destruction in the hands of a jealous man," the baron gushed in French. "Since he is a good Englishman, give him a good beefsteak, a bottle of Port, tire him during the day, call him 'my dear husband'.... and I am going to continue my declaration of love in all forms."

To Alexander she complained, "My Baron desires me to write *beaucoup de petits folies* but I am not much disposed for gaity." Then again, the baron's letter wasn't entirely funny or meant to be: "*Mais cruelle!* You have left me without a farewell kiss," the baron wrote as if to warn her. "Here the Minister flees with the sister-in-law—leaving me as the Guardian of his lamenting wife; oh, what a Situation I am in at this moment—I fear for you—I fear for Hamilton. His crying wife is distressed. The old husband of Anty is like a wolf, and that little devil, Phill, who does his best to cry louder than all the Company." Between the lines, the baron seemed to be making light of dark truth. In playing the cicisbeo, he was the clown at the bullfight, performing antics to distract attention from what he, a gay man, was particularly able to recognize: an illicit attraction so dangerous it might get people killed. "Me, I do not wish to regret this conversation, it would make you so proud that poor Church can no longer manage his wife," Angelica's true friend wrote. "But again a farewell kiss—oh, that goes to my head."

Her sister Elizabeth sent a farewell letter, too, but it failed to reach the *Sandwich* before the wind came and the packet put to sea, carrying away her "Very Dear beloved Angelica" for what could well be forever.

CHAPTER 21

Head Full of Politicks

1790–1792

"I am impatient to hear in what manner your Budget has been received," Angelica Church wrote to Alexander Hamilton after she had reached England and recovered her composure. She promised the secretary of the treasury that she would send the best books she could find on finance via the fastest ships. But from her vantage point across the sea, the American budget was likely too little too late for France. America had forgotten her friendship with France as Angelica felt herself forgotten. "I sometimes think you have now forgot me and that having seen me is like a dream which you can scarcely believe," she pouted to her brother-in-law.

The storming of the Bastille may have been second-page news in New York, but for Angelica's friends in Paris, the fourteenth of July, 1789, had been a disconcerting day, especially for Dominique Éthis de Corny, who arrived home at the rue de la Chaussée d'Antin to find the American minister waiting there with Madame de Corny to hear the details of that day's strange work. The "paroxysm"— again, Thomas Jefferson's word—began when Minister of Finance Jacques Necker was dismissed and the French military began amassing near Paris. In response, a new *Garde Bourgeoise* was proposed—a national guard—and the Marquis de Lafayette was elected its leader. To arm this new guard, Dominique Éthis de Corny and a few other representatives from the City Committee were sent to seize the weapons that the French military stored at the Hôtel des Invalides and the Bastille Prison.

When the committee members called at the Hôtel des Invalides, their request was denied, until a mob gathered and compelled the governor to comply. When they reached the Bastille, a mob was already there. Someone was playing "Yankee Doodle." The deputies planted a flag of truce in the yard and the prison answered in kind from the parapet. Before the parley could occur, Monsieur de Corny and the representatives of the City Committee prevailed upon the people to fall back a little. But when the governor of the Bastille emerged from the fortress, the crowd surged forward and the prison guards opened fire, killing four of the agitators. With blood on the street, a peaceful transfer of the weapons from the military to the national guard ceased to be possible. In what seemed only an instant to members of the City Committee, the mob was inside the fortification. The agitators seized the weapons, released the prisoners, and dragged the bodies of the governor and his lieutenant to the Place de Grève, the public execution site, where their heads were cut off, put on pikes, and paraded through the city to the Palais Royal.

Monsieur de Corny was conflicted. On one hand, the City Committee had achieved its objectives. The military in Paris had been disarmed, but the mob violence he had witnessed that day rattled him. At Versailles, King Louis XVI was shielded from the full story at first, but the following morning, the Duke of Liancourt, a friend of the Marquis de Lafayette, exercised his hereditary right to enter the king's bedchamber and clarified the situation. Memory reduced their exchange to two sentences:

"*C'est une grande révolte?*" the king was said to have asked.

"*Non, sire,*" the Duke of Liancourt replied. "*C'est une grande révolution.*"

At this, the king agreed to go to Paris in a carriage flanked by two files of the Estates General and protected by the *Garde Bourgeoise*. People lined the streets by the tens of thousands, some armed with muskets obtained from the Bastille, others with pikes or scythes. When the procession reached the Hôtel de Ville, the king agreed to yield to the discretion of the Estates General.

The Marquis de Lafayette would have his constitution, but Thomas Jefferson wrote to London: "A more dangerous scene of war I never saw in America, than what Paris has presented for 5. days past."

Angelica's own political fortunes had shifted during her absence from England. She returned to learn that, in her absence, her husband had purchased the "pocket"—or "rotten"—Borough of Wendover, a property that guaranteed him a seat in Parliament's House of Commons.

Wendover was not John Barker Church's first foray into politics. He had run for Parliament three years earlier, standing for the vacant seat at Maldon, and had lost, 211 votes to 13. He shrugged off the loss as worthwhile: "to spend a few hundreds" to prepare his way for a future bid. At the time, Angelica had confided in Alexander that "Church's head is full of Politicks, he is so desirous of making once in the British house of Commons, and where I should be happy to see him if he possessed your Eloquence."

Never one to bet small, John had next attempted to stand for Windsor, where King George III had his favorite home. In response, the radical commentator Charles Pigott wrote, "This man, who had acted as commissary to the old and open enemies of his country, who ought to have shunned infamy in obscurity had not only the assurance to fix his residence close to that of the sovereign, against whom he had taken so active a part, but carried his wanton insolence to the height of declaring his intention of offering himself as representative for the borough of Windsor." Even King George weighed in, writing to Prime Minister William Pitt that "Mr. Church, who was Commissionary to the French in North America, means to stand; his principles are so avowedly enemical that his political conduct may easily be judged. . . . I desire you will without delay direct some other name to be mentioned as the candidate." Stymied by the king, but not deterred, John sought another route to his objective. If it wasn't entirely honorable to obtain a seat in

Parliament by way of a "rotten" borough, a district in which no eligible voters resided, it was done. Even Prime Minister Pitt had first arrived in Parliament that way.

If John thought his wife, who so openly admired her politician friends, would be happy to hear his news, he was disappointed. She was too depressed about leaving the United States. "You are happy my dear friend to find consolation in 'words and thoughts.' I cannot be so easily satisfied. I regret America, I regret the separation from my friends and I lament the loss of your society," she wrote to Alexander. "I am so unreasonable as to prefer our charming family parties to all the gaieties of London, I cannot now relish the gay world, an irresistible apathy has taken possession of my mind, and banished those innocent sallies of a lively Imagination that once afforded pleasure to myself and friends—but do not let me pain your affectionate heart, all will be well and perhaps I may return to America." As much as Parliament might interest her, the deeper John Barker Church dug in, the farther away Angelica was from the country she loved.

Fortunately for Angelica's low spirits, spring arrived early in England in 1790. The orchards at Down Place were in full bloom by late March and the fields of rapeseed along the route from London turned sunny yellow. The arrival that spring of a family friend from New York might have helped also, but Angelica was slow to warm to Gouverneur Morris when he presented himself at her London house.

Angelica likely assumed he had come only to see her husband, whom he had already approached about selling bank shares. Gouverneur Morris was not related to the Philadelphia financier Robert Morris, but he did work for him. John Barker Church was not inclined to sell, but he and Gouverneur Morris had sat down together in the gambling houses and kept their options open.

Another reason for Angelica's unusual chilliness toward Gouverneur Morris may have been self-protection. Irreverent, loose in his connections, free in his thinking, he had never married; he insisted that a bachelor as old as he—thirty-eight—would not make a good husband.

But he wrote poetry for many women and probably started the rumor himself that he had lost his leg from injuries he'd sustained from jumping out of a lover's bedroom window—when in fact he'd caught his leg in a carriage wheel.

At dinner, he managed to keep his eyes off the Church girls' governess long enough for Mrs. Church to ask him whether Mr. Bingham would be appointed to a foreign office—she had heard he had been offered the ambassadorship to Holland.

Mr. Morris did not think so.

Mrs. Church said vaguely that she wished *someone* would be appointed minister to Britain.

Mr. Morris understood immediately that she didn't mean *any* someone. He had no objection to discussing politics directly with a woman, but he cut her short with the plain truth: He did not think Britain wanted an American diplomat. Nor did he expect her simply to take his word for it. Two nights later, back again for dinner, Gouverneur Morris put Angelica's question to Charles James Fox—the British opposition leader known for his advocacy of civil liberties, support for the American and French Revolutions, and opposition to the slave trade, as well as for his slovenly dress—who was a fixture at the Churches' table. Mr. Fox answered that Mr. Pitt had no plan in place for formal diplomatic relations, and, though relatively friendly toward the United States, he was unlikely to take any trouble on that matter.

Conversation moved on. There was speculation about a "Monster" inciting terror throughout London by cutting fashionable women in the backside with a rapier; some women, thinking themselves fashionable, contrived armor to wear beneath their petticoats; others carried pocket pistols. There was the seemingly endless trial of the ex-governor of Bengal, Warren Hastings, which was becoming an inquest into the very nature of empire. There was news of a motion against General Lafayette in France's National Assembly. Nothing had come of it, but internal division clearly threatened the revolutionary work underway in that country. There was also debate over Secretary Hamilton's plan for the United States debt to France.

Gradually, Mrs. Church and Mr. Morris got the measure of each other. They disagreed on issues. Angelica wholly supported her friend General Lafayette and his revolution in France. Gouverneur Morris, who had witnessed the storming of the Bastille and the Women's March on Versailles, was more skeptical. Over that spring, Angelica came to appreciate that Gouverneur Morris did not scorn "the tender breasts of women" concerning themselves with politics like Thomas Jefferson or speak in risqué *petites folies* like her Baron von Steuben. She could get used to his occasional spontaneous poems. More crucially, he actively pursued her friendship—not for favors or bank shares but because he always seemed to want to know what women thought. He knew her family and her friends and the world in which she had grown up, so he was not at all surprised that she was intelligent and well informed, and he sought to know her opinion. Meanwhile, he sought out others' opinions of her to understand the nature of her role and influence.

One Loyalist refugee from New York, Margarita Low, complained to him that "Mrs. Church, in her Efforts to get into High Life, neglects her old Friends." When he drew the lady out, he learned that Mrs. Low had warned Angelica against associating with Maria Cosway. Then he understood why Mrs. Church had snubbed Mrs. Low.

As to Angelica's "efforts to get into High Life," Gouverneur Morris witnessed her success the night he attended his first ball at Sackville Street. The Churches' guests were a glittering mix of Americans, French, and Britons, all known for liberal politics. There were bluestockings, artists and actors, Whig members of Parliament and enlightened members of the French and British aristocracy, and then there were men like him, a one-legged New Yorker who'd helped write the US Constitution.

For her party, Angelica Church had not only broken down the walls separating American patriots from the American Loyalists who still lived as refugees in England, and between the French and English, she had arranged with her neighbors, Lord and Lady Melbourne, to take down the wall between their two gardens in order to create a dancing pavilion. She had learned long ago that dancing was good for morale.

Among these dancers was the Prince of Wales, the presumptive heir to the British throne, and his secret wife, the twice-widowed Maria Fitzherbert, who was forbidden to marry him by the Royal Marriages

Act. Mrs. Fitzherbert was the same age as Angelica Church, and the prince, six years younger than them both, was zealous in all he did—from love and politics to eating, drinking, and gambling. Also among the royals at Angelica's party were France's "princes of the blood": the Duke of Orleans and his brothers. Like the Prince of Wales, the Duke of Orleans espoused reforms for his country, but his proximity to the throne made his motivations somewhat suspect.

Since the departure of John and Abigail Adams two years earlier, there had been no diplomat representing the United States at the Court of St. James. Nor had a new minister replaced Thomas Jefferson since his departure from France the previous fall, leaving his young *chargé d'affaires* to manage alone in an unraveling country. But the Churches' ball revealed to Gouverneur Morris and the other Americans present that evening that American interests had a home in London, and that home was on Sackville Street. He was impressed: "On the whole the Manner of these Persons is very well, considering the haughty Coldness of the Nation and that I am an American," he wrote of Angelica's party.

Alas for Angelica, the reports that reached across the Atlantic were less flattering than Gouverneur Morris's. "I am sorry to inform you that by accounts by the packet from England Mr. Church continues to games," Senator Schuyler wrote home to Angelica's mother. "Altho he and another person have lately won Eighty thousand Guinies from Charles Fox and another, and the money paid,—I would much rather he had lost ten thousand, upon Condition that he never more gamed.—for in fact a gamester's estate is but a precarious thing."

Angelica studied her new friend Gouverneur in return. She may have known, or guessed, that he had been proposed as a replacement for Thomas Jefferson as minister to France. The idea had been put to rest, however, by James Madison, a congressman from Virginia, who had objected on the grounds that Mr. Morris's manners were "oftentimes disgusting—and from that, and immoral & loose expressions had created opinions of himself that were not favourable."

The bachelor's reputation for enjoying the company of women was not all that offended Mr. Madison. Two summers earlier, Gouverneur Morris had served as a delegate to the 1787 Constitutional Convention in Philadelphia, where he had been a vocal critic of enshrining slavery in the new US framework via the three-fifths clause that would allow slave states to claim their enslaved populations toward representation: "Are they men? Then make them Citizens & let them vote," Gouverneur Morris had argued before the assembly when debating the clause. "Are they property? Why then is no other property included? The houses in this city are worth more than all the wretched slaves which cover the rice swamps of South Carolina." The Constitutional Convention was not the first political body to which Gouverneur Morris had addressed the hypocrisy of slavery in a liberal society wherein "a regard to the rights of human nature and the principles of our holy religion, loudly call upon us to dispense the blessings of freedom to all mankind." A decade earlier, when drafting the New York State Constitution, Gouverneur Morris had proposed language calling for the abolition of domestic slavery, "so that every human who breathes the air of this State, shall enjoy the privileges of a freeman."

Not one single delegate to the Constitutional Convention had proposed that women be extended the right to vote, or the "privileges of a freeman," but free women, regardless of race, were at least represented as full, five-fifths persons.

Gouverneur spent one spring afternoon at Maria Cosway's house on Pall Mall with Angelica and her neighbor, the sculptor Anne Seymour Damer. The three women were known for erudition, wit, and a splash of radicalism. Easy in their skins, their elegance so ingrained it was as natural as reflex, Maria and Angelica were partial to diaphanous, high-waisted, corset-free gowns that were conveniently the height of both style and comfort. Anne Damer, a widow several years older than her companions, sometimes opted for the ease of men's clothing. On this day, however, fashion was far from their minds.

After a difficult pregnancy and a traumatic birth, Maria Cosway had become a mother. The new baby, Louisa Paolina Angelica, was healthy, but the new mother was struggling to nurse her. Now, as friends sat with her, and someone else held her baby, Maria sketched compulsively.

Gouverneur read the room and took a seat. Each sat with a first-hand understanding of adversity. Famously, Anne Damer's husband had died by suicide—he had been so determined that when he realized he had the wrong-size lead balls for his pistol, he had carefully pared them down to size so he could shoot himself. His family had blamed Anne for his death, forcing her to support herself, which she now did—currently she was creating a sculpture of the king. Tragedy had shaped Maria Cosway, too. She was the first of her Hadfield siblings not to be murdered by a nurse trying to save the babies' souls from Protestantism. (Maria arrived at Catholicism by way of the nuns at her convent school, not through her English-born parents.) As for Gouverneur, he had his wooden leg. By comparison, Angelica's childhood growing up amid almost constant war seemed a happy one.

To lighten the mood, Gouverneur asked to see Maria's drawing. She was designing an emblem for the ceiling of a garden temple at Down Place. It was a letter A, for Angelica, which the Three Graces were festooning with flowers. Friendship sat within the A, and winged Love hovered overhead, holding in each outstretched hand the head and the tail of the snake that encircles the scene—an emblem of eternity, Maria explained.

To contribute, Gouverneur concocted one of his spontaneous poems—

> Here Friendship adorn'd by the Graces we see
> Maria, design'd by thy Art.
> Yet the Emblem was sure not invented by thee
> But found in Angelica's Heart.

Despite her friends' efforts to cheer her, Maria got worse and not better. Puerperal Melancholia was a known malady—it was not only the body that risked damage in childbirth. Rest and air and light were the best-known remedies, and there was precious little of these in London. The doctors, according to Maria, feared for her life. Certainly, she feared for it. All she wanted was to go home. To Italy. And her husband encouraged her to go with her brother, an architect who had been granted a fellowship from the Royal Academy to study in Rome. Richard Cosway, the artist everyone dismissed as a "macaroni" and a fop, would care for the child while Maria tried to recover from her melancholia in the country of her birth. He even bought a new coach for them so they might travel more comfortably.

Society had never been generous or gentle toward Maria, and now it condemned her actions as further proof of her depravity. Londoners quipped that "Mrs. Cosway ran madding all over Europe . . . leaving her husband & new-born Baby at home here."

In June, the so-called Monster who had been stabbing women in the streets was caught. It was said he was a member of "some unnatural Society, who hold Females in Abhorrence."

If Angelica went to France for the *Fête de la Fédération* on the anniversary of the storming of the Bastille, as her father assumed, Gouverneur Morris said nothing of it, but Madame de Corny did mention that Angélique and Kitty were well when she wrote to Thomas Jefferson about the *Fête*. So perhaps she did cross the Channel from Dover to see the grand event on the Champs de Mars, where General Lafayette received the oath of King Louis XVI to the new French Constitution.

William Short, the American *chargé d'affaires* in France, wrote to Gouverneur Morris that the "spectacle was really sublime & magnificent. . . . The Marquis de la Fayette seemed to have taken full possession of the *fédérés* [delegates]—his popular manners pleased them beyond measure & of course they approved his principles. . . . the moment may be regarded as the zenith of his influence—he made no use of it, except to prevent ill."

It rained during the ceremony. Queen Marie-Antoinette had stood with her little *dauphin* fussing in her arms, and her red, white, and blue plumage drooping, and promised for herself and on behalf of her son also to uphold the Constitution. Then the sodden crowd shouted, *"Vive le roi, vive la reine, vive Monsieur le dauphin!"*—and it was done.

For Angelica Church's old friend from the rowdy, "howlowing" days of the American Revolution, this formal transition from absolute to constitutional monarchy completed France's own glorious revolution. In a fraction of the time it had taken America to achieve this, France had become a country with individual rights and checks on their government. But not everyone was as convinced by the day's spectacle. After receiving the oath, General Lafayette stepped down from the Altar of the Fatherland to make way for the bishop, Charles-Maurice de Talleyrand, to say Mass. As Monseigneur Talleyrand limped past the marquis, he hissed, *"Par pitié, ne me faites pas rire"*—For pity's sake, don't make me laugh.

Gouverneur Morris also had doubts. "A Frenchman loves his King as he loves his Mistress to Madness, because he thinks it is great and noble to be mad," he replied to William Short. "Then he abandons both the one and the other most ignobly because he cannot bear the continued Action of the Sentiment he has persuaded himself to feel."

Gouverneur Morris was no more a formal operative than Angelica was, but President Washington had commissioned him to "sound the disposition" of the British government on a few points that were sensitive to the United States, such as the frontier posts in North America that the British Army still occupied, in violation of the 1783 Treaty of Paris, and the matter of a commerce treaty that John Barker Church and Alexander Hamilton both hoped to attain. And, yes, the matter of formal diplomatic ties. Angelica wasn't the only person who wished for an American minister to be posted to Britain, but President Washington did not want to be too forward. After all, England had no representative to the United States, and this irked the president. He had written Gouverneur Morris that "their omitting to send a Minister here, when the United States sent one to London, did not make an agreeable impression on this Country."

Likewise, President Washington's last letter to Angelica Church had hedged on the question—"Madam," the president replied to her inquiry about appointing an American minister to Britain, "As the letter . . . relates to an event of public import, yet to be determined, and on which the decision may be governed by circumstances not yet considered, I can only do myself the honor to acknowledge the receipt of it—and to express the respectful consideration with which I am Madam Your most Obedt Servt."

Alexander seconded the president: "There is as yet no certainly here of the mission from England; which must precede one from this Country." As to whether his father-in-law Philip Schuyler would be considered for the post, he wrote: "There is no proof of my affection which I would not willingly give you. How far it will be practicable to accomplish your wish respecting your father is however very uncertain—Our republican ideas stand much in the way of accumulating offices in one family—Indeed I doubt much whether your father could be prevailed upon to accept."

Clearly Angelica hoped to have a formal role representing the US interests, and having her father in the post of United States ambassador to Britain would put her as close as a woman could hope to be.

From Philadelphia, Thomas Jefferson suggested an alternative role for her: "I wish Mr. Church could think our Congress as agreeable a field of service as that he has chosen where no efforts can prevail against the money of the government," he wrote to Angelica in London. "From the estimate I am able to make of the sum of happiness enjoyed in this country and in any one of Europe, I think it preponderates here greatly. His habits of friendship indeed have been formed there; but he is not without them here: yours, of the most tender kind, are all here, and that this is a better country for one's children to be fixed in."

The US Congress may have appealed to Angelica, but with John seated in Parliament, the Church family was more "fixed" in England than ever. Still, as the months went by and no minister was named, Angelica remained the most prominent person connected to the new American government who was then present in London. In this unofficial capacity, she mingled with diplomats. The Genoese ambassador visited Down Place. So did the French minister, her old friend Monsieur

La Luzerne, who had helped save her life when she and Peggy fell ill on the march northward from Williamsburg.

Angelica Church's expanding reach in Europe did not go unnoticed in the United States. "You hurt my republican nerves by your intimacy with *'amiable'* Princes," Alexander wrote to her. "I cannot endure that you should be giving such folks dinners, while I at the distance of 3000 miles can only console myself by *thinking* of you. But I pray you dont let your Vanity make you forget that such folks are but men and that it is very possible that they may not be half as worthy of the good will of a fine woman as a parliament man or a Secretary of the Treasury."

Angelica had not forgotten. In her 1792 New Year letter, she wrote to her sister, "What are Kings and Queens to an American who has seen a Washington!"

In February 1792, the London papers announced: "Yesterday morning, the Lady of John Barker Church, Esq, of a son, at his house in Sackville-street." Those same papers reported the defection of French military officers and advised that "numbers of pikes" had been manufactured and distributed to the public "on pretext of arming them against the enemy of the public liberty."

In April, John Barker Church and Gouverneur Morris picked their way down Sackville Street. They went slowly over the cobblestones. One carried an infant; one had a wooden leg. Directly across Piccadilly was St. James Church, where the baby was christened Alexander Hamilton Church. In that spring of 1792 that he became godfather to Angelica Church's newborn son, Gouverneur Morris also received word that he had been formally commissioned as the American minister plenipotentiary to revolutionary France, his "disgusting" manners evidently no longer a cause for concern. No relative of Angelica Church had been appointed to a diplomatic post. Instead, she had made the minister plenipotentiary a member of her family.

Gouverneur Morris presented his credentials to the French government the same week France first used the guillotine.

CHAPTER 22

The House on Sackville Street

1793–1796

T he exodus of émigrés from France to England and Switzerland and elsewhere had begun as a slow leak. Some were Royalists, others had backed the French Revolution until they splintered off from the fracturing movement. Some, such as the Duke of Orleans, left the country, bided their time, and then returned. Others, like the De Cornys, remained, committed to cause and country. Mob violence was escalating.

An American minister plenipotentiary to Britain had arrived in the final days of 1792, but Thomas Pinckney from South Carolina would need some time—and some help—to get his bearings. In the meantime, the French who could claim friendship with the United States knew where to go. One of the first to arrive at Sackville Street was Louis-Marie de Noailles, who had fought in the Battle of Yorktown and represented France in the surrender negotiations. Angelica knew him as the man who danced all night at Minister de La Luzerne's ball in Philadelphia and, in Paris, as a regular at those heady Monday-night American dinners at the Hôtel de Lafayette—Adrienne de Lafayette was his sister. Since then, he had helped draft the French Constitution and presided over the National Assembly as it abolished feudalism and compulsory servitude. In April 1792, the former vicomte had resigned his military commission and left France for England.

Next to arrive at Sackville Street, likely bearing a letter from their mutual friend Marguerite de Corny, was Charles-Maurice de Talley-rand. The highborn former bishop had come to London ostensibly to reestablish diplomatic ties after Minister de La Luzerne had suffered a severe attack of paralyzing palsy and died. Recently famous for his advocacy of state-funded universal secular education in France, and somewhat infamous for his work to secularize the state, he had met Angelica previously in France. Though he had not fought in the American war—due to his club foot—she had known his younger brother, an aide-de-camp to the late General Chastellux. Whereas the younger Talleyrand brother had fought in the American Revo-lution with an earnest enthusiasm (despite his status, he marched with the foot soldiers), Angelica would also appreciate the sardonic humor of the intellectual, whist-playing elder brother, especially since Charles-Maurice de Talleyrand immediately complimented her eleven-year-old Kitty, whom he had known during the days of her Paris education.

One social reformer (and ex-nobleman), François-Alexandre-Frédéric de Liancourt—who had explained to the king in his bedroom that the storming of the Bastille was not a revolt but a revolution—crossed the Narrow Sea that the French called *La Manche*, or "the Sleeve," hid-den beneath a pile of firewood, after his valet had put a pistol to the head of the terrified boatman and forced him to sail. Frédéric de Lian-court had, according to one Englishwoman, "the air of a man who would wish to lord over men, but to cast himself at the feet of women." Perhaps the ex-duke cast himself at the feet of Angelica Church, but more likely he presented adequate credentials.

Many women remained in France to hold their property, but Rosa-lie Duthé of the rue de la Chaussée d'Antin took no chances. A former dancer at the Royal Opera, she was now in her forties, but she had a public reputation as a courtesan to royals. A full-length nude portrait of Mademoiselle Duthé hung in Louis XVI's brother's pleasure house, the Bagatelle. She could only guess what special atrocities a mob might visit upon her once-spectacular person. The reputation that prodded her to cross the Narrow Sea crossed with her. According to the social critic Charles Pigott, the Whig MP John Barker Church "supported in the most splendid style a practiced courtesan, whose meretricious skill once extorted the praise of superiority."

On the tenth of August in 1793, the Tuileries Palace was stormed, ending the reign of Louis XVI and, with it, General Lafayette's constitution. After that, the exodus from France became a flood. England worried that some had come to foment revolution.

With the arrival of old friends, and the nonarrival of other friends, the energy at Sackville Street changed.

Angelica, energized by purpose, took care of her friends, but she was cautious. "The French are mad," she wrote in her 1793 New Year letter to her sister Elizabeth. "But I have great curiosity to be well informed in what light they are regarded by the majority of America and what is the opinion of the discerning few. You have intelligence at hand."

John Barker Church joined the Friends of Liberty, who convened on the anniversary of the storming of the Bastille at the Crown and Anchor Tavern to celebrate the "Anniversary of the late glorious Revolution in France, by which so many millions have been restored to their rights as men and as citizens." But even as the Churches supported the moderate revolutionaries who had arrived from France, they were concerned. Now that men had traversed the Narrow Sea in a balloon, violence in France seemed too near for comfort. John began selling off his French funds. Down Place was listed for sale by Mr. Christie.

Angelica's main concern—even as she helped her French friends—was the United States. As the Pinckneys settled into their new house at 1 Great Cumberland Place, across from Hyde Park, Angelica made the new diplomats welcome. American Minister Plenipotentiary Thomas Pinckney had been educated in England, and his wife, Elizabeth Pinckney, was a young mother with many children. The king had received the new American minister coldly, but Angelica wrote to Elizabeth Hamilton that she and Mrs. Pinckney were already sisters.

Angelica's enthusiasm suggests that all her prodding for a minister was not solely about her father or herself, but rather a genuine interest in having her country properly represented. And now it was. And just in time. By Angelica's next New Year letter, war between France and Britain seemed imminent, but what that would mean for the United States was less clear. The Franco-American alliance established by the Treaty of Amity, such happy news in 1778, now threatened to entangle the United States in new conflict. "My heart beats with anxiety and fear the Americans here speak of war between this country and one a thousand fold dearer to me which Heaven avert in consequence of an order from the British Court to take all ships heading to France or her Colonies," Angelica wrote to her sister. "Show this to Hamilton and bid him write to me for he is too silent."

There was no time to wait for Alexander Hamilton's reply.

The British had welcomed the French initially, but the tolerance for finicky guests had worn thin. Louis-Marie de Noailles thought he might feel more welcome in the United States, where he was a war hero, not just a dependent refugee.

When Louis XVI was put to death later that month, Britain's anxiety turned to panic. In February 1793, Parliament passed the Aliens Act and issued a catalogue of "highly dangerous" émigrés, including several of Mrs. Church's friends. When the English expelled France's new minister, France declared war on Britain.

As Angelica watched the third war of her lifetime drum into action, she handed off her baby Alexander to his nurse and began writing. She reopened her lapsed correspondence with Secretary of State Thomas Jefferson, announcing that: "I plead guilty to the charge of Idleness only; for when my friends require my assistance few are more willing than myself and there is no occasion in which I take more pleasure than in warmly recommending to your attention the Count de Noailles."

When the British ordered Charles-Maurice de Talleyrand's immediate expulsion, she solicited aid from Hannah and Samuel Breck, recalling "the Hospitality with which they received me when a stranger at Boston"; from her father in Albany; and from her sister in New York. "I commit these interesting Strangers, they are a loan I make you, till I return to America, not to reclaim my friends entirely but to share their society with you and dear Alexander the amiable," Angelica wrote to Elizabeth, unsure whether her sister, who spoke no French, would be able or willing to help. As a further signal, when Monsieur de Talleyrand sailed, he carried not only letters but hand-kerchiefs that Angelica had embroidered as tokens of her gratitude and affection—a system of credit and currency exchange as complex as John Barker Church's bank shares. "The kindness with which I am been treated by all the considerable people here—it is to you, uniquely, that I owe it," Charles-Maurice de Talleyrand wrote to her from the United States, confirming that her credit was still good. "It happens to me at any time, that I pronounce your name, I am shown benevo-lence and consideration."

Delighted to hear her friends had been so well received, Angelica heaped gratitude and praise upon her sister:

> I have a letter my dear Eliz[a] from my worthy friend M. de Tall-
> eyrand who expresses to me his gratitude for an introduction to
> you and my Amiable, by my Amiable you know that I mean your
> Husband, for I love him very much and if you were as generous
> as the old Romans, you would lend him to me for a little while,
> but do not be jealous, my dear Eliza, since I am more solicitous
> to promote his laudable ambition, than any person in the world,
> and there is no summit of true glory which I do not desire he may
> attain; provided always he pleases to give me a little chit-chat, and
> sometimes to say I wish our dear Angelica were here.

Letter by letter, often between women, émigrés were funneled from France to America. The conduits included the Princess de Henin (Gen-eral Lafayette's aunt) and Angelica Church in London; Elizabeth and Alexander Hamilton in New York; Hannah and Samuel Breck in Bos-ton; Anne and Thomas Bingham in Philadelphia; and former diplo-mats the Jays and the Adamses (but not Benjamin Franklin, who had died in 1790 at the age of eighty-four). All were French speakers who had formed friendships with the French Army during or since the American war. Now, they guided and received émigrés.

Angelica believed that aiding the French who had served in the American Revolution—either on the battlefield or at court—was American patriotism. She urged her sisters to "Make our Country agreeable to them as far as it is in your power (and your influence is very extensive) console them by your Hospitality, and the Image of your Domestic happiness and virtues."

Soon, Peggy van Rensselaer, though confined to her armchair by a recurring stomach ailment, dusted off her rusty French to discuss the new revolution with the daughter of one of the French officers she'd once marched with during the war. Lucie de la Tour had cut off her long hair during the voyage, sold her court dresses when her ship docked, and was now mourning her guillotined relatives in a rented log cabin outside Albany and learning how to milk a cow.

Despite expressions and actions of goodwill, it was not a happy time.

"If I remain here another year, I shall die," Charles-Maurice de Talleyrand wrote to Madame de Staël.

"Expatriation from one's *patrie* is a torture that one hides more or less badly, the more or less time one suffers, but whose pain is always felt," Frédéric de Liancourt wrote to his wife.

This complaint may have failed to evoke much sympathy from Madame de Liancourt, who was living through the Reign of Terror, but Angelica would have understood his meaning. "I wish they would oblige me to go to America," Angelica quipped of England's expulsion of her French friends.

Meanwhile, France seethed blood.

General Rochambeau, leader of the *Expédition Particulière* in North America, and his son, who had been disciplined during the American war for attempting to smuggle slaves out of Virginia to freedom, were both imprisoned.

General Vioménil, one of the brothers who had given a dinner in honor of Angelica Carter and Caty Greene in Newport, was mortally wounded defending the Tuileries and died in hiding.

General Lauzun, whose legionnaires' bravery at Yorktown earned him the honor of carrying the news of the surrender of General Cornwallis to France, was guillotined.

General D'Estaing, who commanded the first French squadron to join the American war and fought in the Battle of Newport, was guillotined.

To Thomas Jefferson, Angelica Church reported: "Madame de Corney is a widow with a very limited fortune, and retired to Rouen; Mrs. Cosway gone into a convent at Genoa; Monsieur de Condorcet under accusation, but fortunately escaped or concealed in France, Custine *à l'abbaye* a sacrifice for the fall of Valenciennes; and the Queen of France at the conciergerie, and taking her Tryal." Before Angelica's letter reached the United States, Marie-Antoinette had been guillotined.

General Lafayette, whose good intentions had helped spark the inferno in France, was still alive—or at least no one had heard of his death. The general had renounced his army commission and crossed the lines of Austrian and Prussian forces that had amassed along the French border to prevent the revolution from spilling out of France. He had hoped to reach The Hague and seek passage to the United States, but he was recognized and captured. In Paris, rumors spread among the revolutionaries that he had turned coat. A mob ransacked the Hôtel de Lafayette. Adrienne de Lafayette was now in prison.

When Angelica heard of her friends' predicament, she wrote to Secretary of State Thomas Jefferson: "La Fayette is in prison at Magdebourg; and enclosed is the extract of a letter he has been so fortunate as to find means of conveying to a friend and relation, who has sought an Asylum in this country; His Love of Liberty has rendered him culpable in the eyes of a Despot: and you Sir cannot read the recital of his sufferings without tears. General Washington's interference is the only hope left to him and his family."

Secretary Jefferson responded promptly that "my heart has been constantly bleeding" for their friend. But no more could be done. "The influence of the United States has been put into action, as far as it could be either with decency or effect. But I fear that distance and difference of principle give little hold to Genl. Washington on the jailors of La Fayette."

Thomas Pinckney thought an appeal to Vienna would be appropriate and right, but Gouverneur Morris, struggling to preserve American neutrality in the open war between England and France, disagreed: "The less we meddle in the great quarrel which agitates Europe the better will it be for us," he argued. "Although the private feelings of friendship or humanity might properly sway us as private men, we have in our public character higher duties to fulfil." Then Gouverneur Morris was recalled to the United States and replaced by James and Elizabeth Monroe. Elizabeth Monroe took over visiting Adrienne Lafayette in prison, but hers was the strongest gesture of support the Americans dared make. Even Angelica's father referenced "Prudential reasons added to political ones" that prevented the United States from intervening. As for the British, Parliament debated aiding General Lafayette but decided against it—the alliance with Prussia and Austria was too critical to hazard. Having come to the end of political channels, Angelica realized she would have to go it alone if she wanted to help the old friend to whom she felt her country owed so much. But, by this time, no one knew where the ex-general was.

In the spring of 1794, a young doctor named Erich Bollmann set off from London to make a tour of the Prussian and Austrian dominions. In addition to sightseeing and observing different hospitals, the doctor was looking for the lost general. From his travels, Dr. Bollmann sent Angelica reports sprinkled with exclamation marks about dancing, romantic vales, and baths where ladies and gentlemen bathed together in the same room. Buried in these notes was intelligence. Dr. Bollmann was unable to tour the fortress at Aldenberg, but at Glatz he learned that two Frenchmen who had been captured with General Lafayette were held there, until they had been caught passing messages in soup.

At Brünn, he toured a hospital and a fortress, learning from his guide about one French prisoner kept there, known to the public only because he had hurt his leg in an escape attempt. Then, finally, he found what he was looking for. "By chance I have been informed that Mr. Lafayette, Mr. Bournouville, and Mr. La Tour and several others," he reported, "really are living at Olmitz [Olmütz] where they are very narrowly enclosed." Dr. Bollmann would backtrack to Olmütz—"Olmitz is as fine a place as ever a town can be, which is neither commercial nor manufacturing. I saw the works of the fortress, the Cathedral, the civil and military Hospitals, and made some very agreeable acquaintances! The Jesuits formerly occupied several very large and handsome buildings in Olmitz which now are destined for several purposes! In one of them the military hospital is established, in the other they keep the French prisoners of war!"

Angelica did not hear again from the wandering Dr. Bollmann until after he was released from the Austrian labor camp where he was imprisoned after he was captured attempting to flee the country with Monsieur de Lafayette.

Indebted to the doctor for his efforts, if disappointed in his results, she helped him emigrate to the United States. When he arrived and told of the failed prison break, Secretary Hamilton recognized his sister-in-law's fingerprints all over the project, and he told President Washington that he believed the Churches "had a chief agency in promoting his undertaking."

At least their old friend had been located. Adrienne de Lafayette, once she herself was freed from prison in France, could travel to Austria with their two teenage daughters, to petition the emperor for his release. Denied this (the emperor was Marie-Antoinette's brother), the general's wife and daughters would join him in his prison cell.

In 1794, two British ships were seized by the French, taken to the West Indies, and destroyed. The ships carried thirty shares of the Bank of the United States, all of which had been issued to John Barker Church.

The shares would be reissued, but the war in France had become a risk to business.

Now that Britain and France were at war, US relations with both nations—particularly maritime ones—were upended. By the 1778 Treaty of Amity, the United States and France were formal allies. Now Congress wanted to treat with Britain, and the flow of letters asking favors reversed directions.

"I took leave of Mr. [John] Jay who is to embark this morning. He goes with the wishes of a whole people that he may return with the olive-branch," Philip Schuyler wrote to his "beloved Angelica." Even Charles-Maurice de Talleyrand wrote to Angelica Church that "All reasonable people hope that Mr. Jay will succeed in restoring harmony between America and England."

The American delegation arrived in July 1794. With John Jay were his teenage son, Peter Augustus, and his secretary, Jack Trumbull—a happy return. Angelica reported of their arrival: "Mr. Jay has been perfectly received at Court and by the Ministers, as yet no material business is done. The people are anxious for a peace with America, and the allied armies are beat out of Flanders and on the Rhine. These circumstances may determine the minister to be just and wise." To facilitate the treaty, John Barker Church invited his friend Charles James Fox to dinner.

John Jay also reported on his reception at Sackville Street: "We are much indebted to their Civilities and friendly attentions. She looks as well as when you saw her, and thinks as much about America and her Friends in it as ever. She certainly is an amiable agreable Woman."

John Jay engaged in a series of one-on-one meetings with his British counterpart to discuss the points of the treaty fully, without committing anything to writing. Thomas Pinckney, the minister plenipotentiary, assisted where he could, but in August, his wife Elizabeth died, and the now-widower father of five was inconsolable.

Angelica Church, though she also grieved for the ambassador's wife, kept close to the treaty process. Peter Jay wrote to his mother, Sarah, that "M^r. & M^{rs}. Church have been profuse in their civility, we are to

dine with them today for the fourth time since our arrival." The Jays—
John and his son Peter—would dine with her six times in their first
month in London, and then at least monthly after that, in addition to
outings to the theater, invitations to Kitty Church's birthday party, and
an excursion to purchase trees.

At the end of November, the treaty negotiations were completed.
"My Task is done—," John Jay wrote to Alexander Hamilton via the
packet that carried the treaty to New York. "Whether *Finis coronat opus*,
the President Senate and Public will decide."

The public decided it did not view the work favorably. Many Americans felt the "Jay Treaty" gave too much for too little. Virginians were
angry that there would be no indemnity for the enslaved people "carried off" by the British during the war. Rhode Islanders were angry that
there were no guarantees of protection for Americans being impressed
into service by British ships.

By the time the Jays reached home, effigies of John Jay were being
burned in protest. When Alexander Hamilton attempted to explain
the treaty to a crowd of protesters, they threw stones at him. Nonetheless, Congress ratified it. And it was effective in its chief aim:
As the war between France and Britain devolved, the United States
remained neutral.

In September 1796, one year after Congress ratified the Jay Treaty,
George Washington announced that he was stepping down as president, and John Adams and Thomas Jefferson vied to replace him.

Likewise, the bereaved Thomas Pinckney resigned as minister plenipotentiary, and Alexander Hamilton wrote to Angelica in London with
news of his replacement: "I wrote you last by Mr. King who sailed a few
days since for London as our new Minister Plenipotentiary. You must
not think the less well of him for not being a Jacobin—for he is a very
clever fellow and will do credit to your Country. He will not give me the
trouble of defending any Treaty of his making—for to be sure of every-
body's approbation he is instructed to do nothing but after a previous
consultation with you."

Angelica replied via her sister that she would be happy to "fit" Mrs. King for court and to give her "the necessary advice how to be well served and not *too much* imposed on." A little wistful to be leaving the role that had never actually been hers, she remarked, "I hope she is well made and peaceful, that she may represent well."

Angelica's tour was finally over. She was going home.

Part 4

THE NEW
"UNITED" STATES

What have I, as a woman, to do with politics? . . .
Lawmakers thought as little of comprehending us in
their code of liberty, as if we were pigs, or sheep.

—*Mrs. Carter*, Alcuin, *Charles Brockton Brown, 1798*

We differ as friends should do.

—*Thomas Jefferson*

CHAPTER 23

The *Fair American*

1796–1799

"There is something independent and agreeable in living where one was born," homesick Angelica Church had written to her brother Johnny from England. Not that Angelica had much experience: She had seen Albany only once since the War of Independence ended.

Now, Down Place and the "rotten" Borough of Wendover had both been sold. An auction preview was advertised on Sackville Street which touted a "fine-ton'd Piano Forte by Garcka," an eight-day clock, a drawing-room suite in chairs and sofas, a four-poster bed and goose featherbeds, card and dining tables. Angelica was saying goodbye to her pier glasses and girandoles, her Wilton and Scotch carpets, even her bedchamber chairs. After fourteen years of missing her home, it was surprisingly difficult to leave England.

As the Church family shed houses and furniture, John attempted to collect outstanding debts. Charles James Fox, who owed him a small fortune, protested that he had "no command of ready money." Instead, the MP promised to send Angelica some partridges from his upcoming hunting trip.

"Mrs. Church intends to go out to America," the young diplomat John Quincy Adams wrote home to his mother, Abigail, from London. "Her Husband is to follow her the next year, proposing to make their final settlement there. As he has only seven or eight thousand Sterling a year income, he says he cannot afford to live in England." This was wry commentary—seven thousand pounds was three and half times the salary of a US minister plenipotentiary.

But months slipped past, and the Churches did not sail. Instead, Angelica began voicing reservations. Days before her fortieth birthday, she wrote to Alexander, "If friendship is only a name, for what do I exchange ease and taste, by going to the New World, where politics excludes all society, and agreeable intercourse."

Alexander replied, "Your Countrymen are zealous but they are not mad. All will go well here."

But in the spring, Angelica fell ill. By August, it was clear that she would not be able to sail that year. "I cannot now leave England, altho' some better prepared to meet the sea, my great enemy, I have yet been," she promised. "In the spring my dear Eliza it will be my turn to show you how much I love you since not even the French nor Algerians shall prevent me sailing in April or March." Perhaps it was not illness nor corsairs nor even the very clear and present danger of the French that caused her anxiety, but events in the United States. The same month that George Washington had made his farewell address to Congress, newspapers reported conflagrations in Savannah, Baltimore, and New York. It wasn't clear what was causing these fires, but American enslavers had long feared the ignition of a slave revolution like that which had liberated the West Indian colony of Saint-Domingue from France. Only two years earlier, in 1794, Angelica's hometown of Albany had charged and hanged three enslaved teenagers—Bet, Dinah, and Pompey—for starting a fire in a barn. Angelica wrote: "The accounts we hear from America are not flattering, and I dread the effect on my children."

At this final hour, she seemed to doubt herself. Were the rough-hewn United States really the best choice for her children or had her patriotism become a form of disloyalty to her family? Now that the clarity of her convictions had weathered with age, like the skin on her face, perhaps she would spare her children the experience of war, if she could only see the conflagration coming.

No fresh revolution began in 1796 in North America, but in

February of 1797, French revolutionary forces did fight on English soil. Militarily, the Battle of Fishguard was only a two-day skirmish, but it exacerbated England's ancient fears of a French invasion, be it military or ideological. This fear sparked a run on the Bank of England but John Barker Church had already withdrawn his savings in gold, in anticipation of soon sailing to New York, when the bank suspended payments.

Watching the cliffs of England from the deck of their chartered ship, the *Fair American*, the Churches had to feel some peace, even as they faced weeks at sea and the risk of being harassed by French privateers.

Six weeks into the new Adams administration, New York's papers announced the *Fair American*'s arrival in New York and John B. and Angelica Church's intention to live at Government House. Standing at the prow of Manhattan, this enormous, pillared brick house had been built for President Washington. But the federal government had relocated to Philadelphia before construction was complete. The mansion had served instead as New York's governor's residence, until the state government also relocated: Governor John Jay and his wife, Sarah, and their young children now lived in Albany. By occupying such a prominent address—if only temporarily, while their own house was finished and furnished—the Churches broadcast their intentions (or pretensions) of assuming prominent roles in that city.

As to what role Angelica Church would play, one suggestion arrived almost immediately from Vice President Jefferson. "Dear Madam," her old friend wrote. "I learn through the newspapers your arrival at New York and hasten to welcome you to the bosom of your friends and native country.... Your affections, I am persuaded, will spread themselves over the whole family of the good, without enquiring by what hard names they are politically called. You will preserve, from temper and inclination, the happy privilege of the ladies, to leave to the rougher sex, and to the newspapers, their party squabbles and reproaches."

"Party squabbles" between (and among) Democratic-Republicans and Federalists now plagued the nascent country, and Thomas Jefferson and Angelica's brother-in-law were on opposite sides of the gaping partisan divide. Throughout President Washington's administration, Alexander Hamilton, then secretary of the treasury, and Thomas Jefferson, then secretary of state, had been like two high-strung horses trying to pull the same carriage in separate directions. Worse, now that John Adams was president, both Alexander Hamilton (who had campaigned against him) and Thomas Jefferson (who had run against him) were opposition figures.

Thomas Jefferson's note implied that Angelica Church might have it in her power to soothe the political mood. Angelica was well apprised of his views on a woman's place in the social order (and that what he said—that women should not get involved in politics—and what he did—talk about politics with women—were not the same). But the vice president and Angelica had both seen where party "spirit" had taken France.

Of the Church children, only Philip, who had turned nineteen at sea, and Kitty, seventeen, could remember the United States at all. The country of their birth may have been made mythic to them by their mother, but the reality was now before them. To them, a town of fifty thousand inhabitants was a mere village when compared to London's one million. Unlike Piccadilly, where gilt carriages had to be dodged at the risk of one's life, New York swarmed with oxcarts, goat carts, and dogcarts. Even in paintings of New York's proudest house, Guernsey cows lounged in the drive. One young lady they would come to know—Jack Trumbull's niece—described New York as a "great hencoop of a city." Most of Angelica's children had never met their Aunt and Uncle Hamilton or their Grandmother Schuyler. Betsy Church, thirteen, did not know Phil Hamilton, fifteen: the cousin her mother half-teased that she'd marry one day. But New York and their New York cousins would not stay unknown to the Church children for long. Jack Church and Phil Hamilton were only months apart. Betsy Church and Angelica Hamilton were within a year of each other, as were Alexander Hamilton Church, five, and John Church Hamilton, four.

John and Angelica's family included more than just their children. They arrived from Europe with staff—a French cook, an English maid, and an Italian valet. (The governess Mademoiselle Félicité had opted to marry a marquis instead of emigrating with her employers.) To supplement this salaried staff, Alexander had purchased for them a "negro woman & child," evidence that fourteen years living in France and England, where domestic chattel slavery was largely prohibited, hadn't made the Churches entirely averse to owning other humans. As for Ben, there had been no word of him in years, since Peggy had tried to retrieve him, but his temporary owner refused to relinquish him to anyone but Mrs. Church herself. Most likely, since no other record exists, Ben had died. Perhaps he was one of the thousands of unnamed Philadelphians who died in the 1793 yellow-fever epidemic.

Of course, recognizing nothing now before them, Angelica's children could not see what was absent. They would not gaze upon the seawall promenade along the battery and marvel that an ancient bastion of colonial power—Fort George—was entirely gone. They did not mourn their mother's brother Johnny Schuyler, who had died at Saratoga of a putrid fever, or "her" Baron von Steuben. But they were not spared sharing in the grief for their thirteen-year-old cousin Catharine van Rensselaer, who had died while her cousins were at sea, because their Aunt Peggy arrived at Government House shattered and ill. Angelica had put her sister immediately to bed.

"When I can get to Your fireside," Angelica had promised her sisters before she'd come to New York, "all our children, and our respectable and truly amiable parents, all awake may go to sleep for me."

Angelica understood it to be her duty to spread her affections "over the whole family of the good." First, however, she had to put her own family's house in order.

The joyous reunion of the large Schuyler–Church–Hamilton–Van Rensselaer clan that Angelica had long imagined was inevitably more complicated than she had anticipated.

At first, Angelica fussed over Peggy, who suffered intermittently with

what her father described as "gout of the vitals." Then a public letter
to Alexander Hamilton printed in the newspapers forced Angelica to
turn her attention also to her sister Elizabeth. The letter referenced
an "alleged connection" to a "Mrs. Reynolds," and a "confused and
absurd story about her," which the writer accused Alexander of using
as a cover-up for financial wrongdoings. "Pardon me for adding that
Mr. Wolcott and the other gentlemen must have found it hard to help
laughing in each other's faces," the letter taunted, "when you told them
the penitential tale of your depravity."

Alexander was in Philadelphia the day the letter ran, but John
Barker Church hurried to the Hamiltons' house to check on pregnant
Elizabeth. "I am this Instant Return'd from your House," John wrote
to his brother-in-law. "Eliza is well she Put into my Hand the Newspaper with James Thomson Callender's Letter to you, but it makes not
the least Impression on her, only that she considers the whole Knot of
those opposed to you to be Scoundrels." Elizabeth seemed impervious,
but Alexander was irate. With his brother-in-law by his side, he called
on James Monroe and accused him of breaking his word of honor.

Years earlier, when he was secretary of the treasury, Alexander had
apparently had an affair with a married woman named Maria Reynolds. When her husband discovered them, Alexander began to pay
him hush money, but the off-book payments by the man then charged
with safeguarding American finances came to the attention of others
in government. When his colleagues confronted him with their suspi-
cions of financial malfeasance, Alexander confessed to his extramarital affair. Since his colleagues did not think these crimes pertained
to government, they agreed to keep the confession to themselves, but
now, five tumultuous years later, the story had leaked.

James Monroe denied being the source. Then, according to one witness, Colonel Hamilton accused Colonel Monroe of false representation, and Colonel Monroe called Colonel Hamilton a scoundrel. Before
it came to pistols, John interceded, but Alexander would not let the
matter go. That August, as Elizabeth was lying-in from the birth of
their newest son, her husband took his grievances to the newspapers, as
John "Carter" had done during his conflict with Tadeusz Kosciuszko a

decade earlier. "My real crime," Alexander announced to all who read newspapers, "is an amorous connection."

Elizabeth sailed to Albany with her new baby and her daughter Angelica, leaving her other children with their Aunt Angelica, while their Uncle John worked to clean up the mess.

"Tranquillize your kind and good heart, my dear Eliza," Angelica wrote to her. "I have the most positive assurance from Mr. Church that the dirty fellow who has caused us all some uneasiness and wounded your feelings, my dear love, is effectually silenced. . . . All this you would not have suffered if you had married into a family less near the sun."

No sooner had the uproar over the Hamiltons begun to subside when Angelica's attention turned to two other siblings. In a letter seeking his "dearly beloved" Angelica's help, Philip Schuyler complained of "the imprudence of one child and the criminality of another." Cornelia Schuyler, who was twenty-two, had taken a jaunt to Stockbridge, Massachusetts, with her sweetheart, to call upon the same official who had married the "Carters" twenty years earlier. She was now the wife of George Washington Morton, a tall, promising New York lawyer. Rensselaer Schuyler, on the other hand, had a gambling problem. Philip Schuyler informed Angelica that he was seeking an act of bankruptcy on Rensselaer's behalf, to prevent him from taking on any more debt. Then he would settle his son on a farm and leave him to live within his means. As to which offense was imprudent and which was criminal, Philip Schuyler assumed Angelica knew, and he expected her to take care of them.

All this while, John Barker Church was calling in outstanding debts small and large. Peggy van Rensselaer owed him £59 for duties and freight on articles Angelica had sent her sister. Robert Morris owed him money for the bank shares he had purchased on credit years earlier, through Gouverneur Morris. The terms of this deal had been renegotiated several times already, by Alexander Hamilton, but now John was determined to have the debt settled. Robert Morris hoped he would accept the land that he mortgaged to secure this debt—100,000 acres of timber stands and arable river flats on New York's new and expanding western boundary. When Philip Schuyler had registered this mortgage for the Churches, he wrote to them that, "such is the rapid increase of settlement in that country that I believe the property sufficient to cover the debt." Now, however, the price of land was plummeting, and Robert Morris pleaded for more time. "If he were pressed by Necessity I could not think hard of his pressure," he wrote to Alexander Hamilton, believing John Barker Church to be a man with the means to be patient. "But as that is not the case and I am willing to pay for indulgence I hope he will grant it."

John kept his cards to himself, regarding the degree of his necessity, but he refused to grant indulgence. The financial panic in England had spread to the United States, tightening credit and forcing fore-closures on land speculations, causing prices to drop. Somehow, he knew that Robert Morris was out over the precipice, and this time, there was no saving him. Robert Morris was an old friend; his son had been a visitor at Down Place. But if Angelica Church liked to joke that Robert Morris was too big to flirt, he was not too big to fail. And when he fell, the entire economy felt the shock.

Even the Churches felt it. In addition to calling in debts, they cur-tailed expenses and even charity. "My good Mrs. Church had infinite care for me," the widowed Marguerite de Corny confided in Thomas Jefferson. "I do not blush to confess that she kept me going for a long time. She has since been thwarted by her husband, but admire this per-fect friend with me."

Angelica gave a Twelfth Night ball, but even she could not dazzle everyone. All one critic had to say about her ball was that Mrs. Church was one of those among whom "A late abominable fashion prevails, from England, of Ladies like washer-women with their sleeves above their bare elbows."

In April 1798, Angelica gave birth to her seventh baby—a son who was named Richard, after the child she'd lost in England. As she was lying-in, whatever fragile, fraying bond of peace remained between the United States and France finally snapped, and France began seizing American ships engaging in trade with Britain.

To negotiate a resolution, President John Adams sent a diplomatic envoy, but the new foreign minister for the Directory of France was not interested. Charles-Maurice de Talleyrand, the diplomat whom Angelica Church had helped escape to the United States, had been assisted in returning from his exile by the writer Germaine de Staël, whom Angelica remembered from the rue de la Chaussée d'Antin. Why he scorned the Americans' efforts to reach a peace was mysterious. Perhaps after his years in Philadelphia, he felt no love for the United States. Or perhaps—to avoid risking future exile or worse—he felt an imperative to prove his loyalty to France.

When diplomacy failed, New York merchants began subscribing investors and arming their ships. Just in case it became necessary to declare war, George Washington was summoned from his retirement, and Colonel Alexander Hamilton was made—at last—a general, superseding his old friend Henry Knox. Philip Church, who was twenty, was commissioned a captain of infantry and became his uncle's aide-de-camp.

In his youth, John Barker Church might have fitted out a privateer himself, in the anticipation of war being formally declared, but now he saw a different opportunity. Three hundred American ships had been captured by French privateers the previous year, or six percent of that year's shipping. By a gambler-banker's calculation, a six-percent loss was not terrible, especially when those seizures were illegal, according to the rules of war. So he partnered with another Englishman, John Delafield, and their firm Delafield & Church began selling maritime insurance. But as the so-called Quasi-War intensified, the odds worsened. In April, the schooner *Dorchester* was captured. In May, the brig *Hiram* was taken. Both were insured by Delafield & Church.

As tensions and the temperature rose, even though their father harangued them to come north, Angelica and her sister Elizabeth and their young children retreated to a rented country house in Harlem. Angelica likely hoped it would feel like Down Place, but the magic was hard to re-create. If they were bored, at least they were safe. That summer, it was yellow fever, not France, that attacked New York. Elizabeth and Alexander had survived the miasmic plague once, but their households were not immune. "A negro boy of John Barker Church" and "a black man of Alexander Hamilton" were counted among New York City's two thousand dead of the disease.

"His time hangs heavy on his hands," Alexander wrote to the secretary of war that summer, inquiring, in confidence, whether his brother-in-law might be a candidate for a position as a naval agent. He described John Barker Church as a man "of strong mind, very exact very active & very much a man of business. He is about fifty but of uncommon strength of constitution."

Another ship, the brigantine *Eagle*, had been captured. John Delafield cut his losses, and the insurance firm dissolved, but John Barker Church doubled down. French privateers had captured American merchant ships without formally declaring war. The seizures, therefore, were illegal. When he paid a claim on a cargo, he became the owner of the lost goods. When this war ended, compensation would assuredly be paid. Confident that the law was on his side, John even began buying spoliation claims from other insurers—at a deep discount—and waited.

Alexander may not have shared John's optimism about the French spoliations, but his brother-in-law could not be dissuaded. A bureaucratic sinecure was not to John Barker Church's taste; his days as an agent were done. Instead, he agreed to join the board of directors of a new enterprise called the Manhattan Company, led by their friend Aaron Burr.

John and Alexander had known Aaron Burr since the war, when the three men had orbited the Schuylers' house in Albany. They had political differences—Aaron Burr had joined the Democratic-Republicans and he had briefly unseated Philip Schuyler from the US Senate—but political differences did not prevent them from socializing and working together. Aaron Burr's daughter Theodosia was close with the Church–Hamilton cousins—Theodosia Burr and Kitty Church were two of the best educated girls in New York. Recently, though, Aaron Burr had suffered several setbacks. His wife had died; Philip Schuyler had taken back the US Senate seat; and the collapse of land prices had nearly bankrupted him. To fend off ruin, Aaron Burr had sold his furniture and mortgaged his empty house. Then he proposed establishing the Manhattan Company.

Ostensibly a water company, the Manhattan Company was a response to the latest yellow-fever outbreak, which doctors attributed to the growing city's poor sanitation. Especially putrid was the city's water source, a spring-fed pond north of the city into which drained the filth from water-intensive industries located nearby—including several tanneries and a slaughterhouse. The private company would provide New York with "pure and wholesome Water" funded by shares sold to investors.

New York's mayor, Richard Varick, backed a draft proposal for a private utility company, funded by shareholders rather than taxes. So did Alexander Hamilton. Particularly appealing to New York politicians was the fact that this private company would pay for itself by being more than just a utility company—which would have taken years of planning, development, and investment to turn a profit. The Manhattan Company would also function as a bank, using surplus capital as the company saw fit.

John Barker Church knew no more than Aaron Burr about drinking water, but he did know about banks.

Then, at a dinner given by Angelica's cousin, Chancellor Robert Livingston (also a Democratic–Republican), John made a case that implied Aaron Burr had been financially rewarded by a foreign company for his work in the state legislature. When word of this conversation got back to Aaron Burr, however, he demanded an apology. John was willing to concede that he had made the statement without sufficient authority, but unless it could be proved false, he would not apologize. Aaron Burr would not dignify the accusation by proving it false.

On the first of September in 1799, the Manhattan Company launched. The next morning, a Monday, it opened its doors at 40 Wall Street and began taking deposits and issuing loans. That evening, Aaron Burr and John Barker Church crossed the North River to the dueling ground at Hoebuck, New Jersey. As the challenged party, John had the choice of weapons, and he had brought with him an elegant pair of dueling pistols: English made, stocks carved of lovely dark wood, weighted bronze, and, at .54 caliber, using larger and more dangerous ammunition than typical dueling pistols.

When his second struggled to ram the ball into this unfamiliar gun, Aaron Burr became impatient and took the pistol as it was. Shots were exchanged. John's pistol ball pierced the skirt of Aaron Burr's coat, but Aaron Burr's gun misfired. Then, according to protocol, each man consulted his second, the seconds parleyed, and all agreed that the matter was adequately settled. Then the two duelists "amicably shook hands" and returned to Manhattan, where they had a bank to run.

If John Barker Church and Aaron Burr saw the dispute between them settled by that quick trip across the river with a pair of pistols, New York did not. "Party spirit" burned hot.

During the war, they had imagined that civic life would be "domestic ease." The Cincinnati would all go home and plow their fields. Instead, civic life looked increasingly like taking up that plow to strike one's neighbor with it. The specter of the guillotine hung over New York.

As Thomas Jefferson had put it to Angelica in his welcome-home letter: "We have not yet learnt to give every thing to [its] proper place, discord to our senates, love and friendship to society." This was one notion of order. It depended upon individual "Republican virtue," with everyone playing their roles properly, like dancers who know all the steps of the minuet. Meanwhile, France had gone a different way: In November of that year, a coup replaced the Directory of France with the Consulate and named the thirty-year-old Corsican general, Napoleon Bonaparte, as first consul. A strong executive would dictate behavior.

Back in 1776, *Common Sense* had shown society and government as intertwined and interdependent. "Society is produced by our wants, and government by our wickedness," Thomas Paine had written then. "The former promotes our happiness positively by uniting our affections, the latter negatively by restraining our vices."

Since declaring independence, the white men in their state houses and in Philadelphia's Congress Hall had been crafting and revising a new American government, but American society was also taking shape in the streets and shops and social gatherings. This work, too, had its dominant figures and its partisans. Society was the whole point—not a diversion.

Alexander Hamilton and Thomas Jefferson had vied publicly for a decade in their power struggle over the nation's direction. But all through their rivalry, these two adversaries shared one thing in common: They both loved and confided in the same woman. "Your letter . . . has served to recall to my mind remembrances which are very dear to it, and which often furnish a delicious resort from the dry and oppressive scenes of business," Thomas Jefferson had written to Angelica while he was serving as secretary of state. "Never was any mortal more tired of these than I am. I thought to have been clear of them some months ago: but circumstances will retain me a little while longer, & then I hope to get back to those scenes for which alone my heart was made." Secretary of the Treasury Alexander Hamilton had written to her of nearly identical sentiments a few months later: "[H]ow oddly are all things arranged in this sublunary scene—I am just where I do not wish to be—I know how I could be much happier; but circumstances enchain me—it is however determined that I will break the spell."

For Angelica Church, every dinner, every ball, every *fête champêtre* was political. From The Pastures to Frog Lane to the rue Chaussée d'Antin to Down Place to Sackville Street, friendships were formed and maintained and discussion and debate advanced ideas. Her pursuit was not happiness—but "amiability."

It was a young French woman who'd survived the Reign of Terror who recorded Angelica's next deft move. "Do you know her?" Josephine du Pont wrote to a friend. "Certainly well by reputation, but have you ever seen her? . . . I could not be more impressed with her ease of manner, her warm politeness, the fine training of her daughters, and the excellent appearance of her home."

Not yet thirty, Josephine was closer to Kitty's age than to Angelica's, but she was impressed by the nonchalance with which Madame Church wore her fichu, shocked that Madame Church did not have a single inch of mirror in her superb salon, and, though she did not personally disapprove, noted that New York was unnerved that Madame Church would sometimes receive callers in her bedroom.

Once they arrived in New York, the Churches took the Du Ponts under their wing. Pierre du Pont de Nemours, Josephine's father-in-law, was a renowned economist—a "physiocrat"—who had served as a leader of the National Assembly during the first phase of France's revolution. And her husband had served previously in the French diplomatic corps in the United States. (Angelica might have remembered Victor du Pont from the ball given by the French delegation to celebrate George Washington's inauguration.) The family had not exactly fled France, but, now that the Quasi-War between the United States and France had ended, some of them planned to establish themselves as merchants of French goods in New York.

"What I like of your politics is that *savoir vivre* unites [people], not in their opinions but socially," Josephine wrote to an American friend. "Mdme Ch . . . seems to make a point of treating the chiefs of the party opposite to her own with the greatest distinction."

Savoir vivre—knowing how to live—was not about laws and policies or even virtues. It was a form of grace. When the Du Ponts gave a party at their house on Liberty Street, Madame Church arrived on the arm of Aaron Burr—who was not only a known political rival of her father and brother-in-law but also, save for a misfire, might have killed her husband in their duel. Such a public action made a statement as loud as any speech or newspaper opinion. Once again, Angelica was dancing with the enemy. Partisanship was going to tear the new country apart. She would not risk their still-turning revolution on a grudge and a bloodless duel.

Despite her poor English, Josephine du Pont understood her point as perfectly as anyone present and concluded, "I find such politics greatly to my liking."

CHAPTER 24

Mother/Country

When Angelica's firstborn son, Phil Church, turned twenty-one, his name appeared in the papers. "The son of Mr. C. is about to marry the daughter of Mr. Bingham of Philadelphia, the federal Senator. Thus are our advocates for war cemented together," announced a letter published in the Connecticut *Bee*.

The future that the revolutionary generation had fought for was not turning out as expected—nor could it have, since those expectations had never been unified or uniform. Some felt that the rigid hierarchy of aristocrat and peasant persisted, that the new nation was failing to deliver on the promise of "all men are created equal." Indeed, the former senator Philip Schuyler had been an institution in New York politics for a quarter of a century. Now the offspring of his three eldest daughters—the Church–Hamilton–Van Rensselaer children—were arriving at adulthood well positioned to don the mantles of social, economic, and political power, as if by right of inheritance.

The news that a Church was betrothed to a Bingham of Philadelphia was false. The two Bingham girls were already married—the elder to a British baronet, the younger to a (former) French count, although her parents were seeking to extricate their sixteen-year-old from that midnight union. Angelica had dined with Anne Bingham and her daughters during a recent trip to Philadelphia and was not impressed: "Madame de Tilly is quite *a la francaise*, rouge and short petticoats," she remarked

after the dinner. "Poor young creature she has been the victim of a neg-
ligent education. I have seen enough of Philadelphia." This wry derision
was a tone Angelica adopted more often, now that she had returned to
New York. Like the writer of the widely reprinted letter in the *Bee*, she
was likely feeling some disappointment. If so, she wasn't alone. American women were grappling with a rising sense of irrelevance.

Throughout the 1790s, a preponderance of literature had espoused
liberation for women. American works such as Judith Sargent Murray's
essays in *The Gleaner* and Charles Brockden Brown's *Alcuin: A Dialogue*
joined Britain's Mary Wollstonecraft's *Vindication of the Rights of Woman*
and France's Olympe de Gouges's *Declaration of the Rights of Woman and
of the Female Citizen*. All argued that equality for women was consistent
with the ideals proclaimed by the revolutions in both the United States
and France. But by the dawn of the new century, it was clear to American women that the War of Independence had in no meaningful way
altered their legal status as permanent dependents. If anything, greater
"equality" had replaced the former class structure with one made of
gender and race. Now, no free white man need suffer to be outranked
by a woman.

Without a vote or individual rights, "republican motherhood" became
American women's primary political estate. If women's scope was limited,
their zeal was not: Republican motherhood took on mythic proportions.
Women modeled themselves on historical and mythological mothers: Cornelia, the Roman mother who dedicated her life to her sons and espoused
education, or the Greek goddess Astrea, who, in one of Maria Cosway's
most beautiful allegorical paintings, uses the scales of justice to educate
the child-knight Arthegal.

With six children between the ages of one and twenty-one to educate
and situate, plus her interest in her siblings' children, Angelica was so
deeply immersed in the work of motherhood that she embraced this
role with her typical drive to excel. Even the article condemning her
son was proof of her success: She had raised her children to be the equal
of any aristocrat, any prince. She put her sons through Eton College

and sent Kitty to the best school for girls she could find in three countries. When war in France denied Betsy the same opportunity, she had
employed the best governess Marguerite de Corny could find in France.
She had hired tutors for her sons. She passed up social events to play
cards with her children and she invited people to her home to see the
children dance. Of course, whether motherhood was self-sacrifice or
self-aggrandizement, selflessness or selfishness, was, as ever, a matter
of opinion and perspective.

As with tightening gender roles, it was predictable in the aftermath
of war that the new generation—the offspring of "heroes"—would be
bound to underwhelm. General Hamilton's "favorable report" of his
Eton-educated nephew Phil Church had more to do with his financial
prospects as a firstborn than his character: "He is the eldest son of his
father, has had a good education is a young man of sense of genuine
spirit and worth—of considerable expectation in point of fortune," he
wrote to the secretary of war. Sixteen-year-old Phil Hamilton had not
traveled so widely as his cousin, nor had he met the Prince of Wales or
seen Montgolfier balloons rise over Paris, but he had grown up in New
York, where his grandfather and his father were among the most prominent public figures. Now, at Columbia College—where his father had
been a student before the American Revolution and where his grandfather, who had never attended any college, was a regent—everyone
weighed him against his forebears. Some considered him a "sad rake"
of little promise.

Only George Washington seemed to take a magnanimous view of
the rising generation. The general had seen many hotheaded, self-
centered youths mature into reasonably useful adults—Alexander
Hamilton chief among them—and he had hope for the future. In
December 1798, one year before his death, George Washington had
written to Angelica Church to compliment her firstborn: "From the
genteel & handsome exterior of Mr. Church (your son) and the favorable report of his merits by Genl. Hamilton, you have the most pleasing presages of his future usefulness & consequence; and as far as I
can contribute there to, consistently with my other duties, he may
freely command me."

For both Phils, and for their whole generation, the first born in an independent United States, expectations were stratospheric. This was equally true for the girls, albeit separately. Catharine (Kitty), Elizabeth (Betsy), and Angelica had been assigned their roles in the family when they were given their names. Kitty was meant to be matriarch, like her grandmother Catharina Schuyler. Betsy was meant to be good and sweet, like her aunt Elizabeth Hamilton (she was even expected to marry Phil Hamilton). Likewise, Angelica Hamilton was prodded to learn French and play the piano that her glamorous Aunt Angelica had sent her from England. But these children lived lives very different from those of their parents.

By 1800, everything they did was a matter of public interest and fuel for rumormongers. Even a family-dinner prank at the Churches' house threatened to become a public scandal. A guest had proposed a séance, claiming he could commune with the dead. To demonstrate, Alexander Hamilton was sent out and the conjurer asked the others to choose the deceased person they wished to contact. John Barker Church suggested the Baron de Vioménil. The others agreed, and John wrote the baron's name on a card.

"The Conjuror . . . proceeded to make incantation," the Churches' cousin Peter Jay relayed to his sister afterward. "Until Genl. H returned & declared that the Baron had appeared to him exactly in the Dress which he formerly wore & that a Conversation had passed between them wh. he was not at liberty to disclose."

The story was soon all over New York, that General Hamilton talked to the dead. To quell the scandal, those who were behind the stunt had to make a public statement.

Given the political climate, the question of whom the Church and Hamilton children would marry was a matter of public interest. Kitty Church, who was twenty at the turn of the century, first walked this gauntlet.

Angelica had gone to great lengths to raise her daughter to be exceptional, but society had changed little for women since Angelica was assessing her own potential husbands. Despite all of Kitty's abilities, her worth would depend upon whom she married. Her choice of spouse would likewise determine the future of the family.

Many people were involved. "I am as worried as you are not seeing here any man worthy of her," Josephine du Pont confided to a friend all the way in South Carolina. Josephine was also concerned about Kitty's taste: "[She] has not the slightest scruple about going out in the streets of NY, giving her arm to the first little Frenchman she meets, although she shows considerably more reserve towards the local man-in-the-street, whom she rather properly disdains." Kitty's predilection for French men was worse than her friend feared. In the spring of 1800, she entertained a proposal from the Chevalier Charles Colbert—who had been a lieutenant in the French Navy at Newport in 1780.

"I know too that you and Mr. Church think I am too old," Charles Colbert wrote to Alexander Hamilton, seeking an ally in his former brother-in-arms. "I see very well that you do not know the French. The warmth of their blood prolongs their youth. Away from her I love her as much as all you Americans put together, near her I love her and shall love her as at 20 . . . *Et j'aimais bien.* [And I loved well.]"

Given their own history, Angelica and John were diplomatic. They had also heard all about fifteen-year-old Maria Bingham of Philadelphia eloping with the ex-Count de Tilly, prompting her parents to bring the bride home forcibly and offer the groom a sizable cash settlement to leave the country. So they gave the chevalier hope but also pressed him to return to France first—as émigrés were doing now that France had steadied—to reclaim his property and perhaps secure a position before he entered a marriage.

While the chevalier was gone, Angelica sought out alternative alliances, and she planned a ball. The entire extended Schuyler family came to town. Friends came from New Jersey. At the last minute, the ball was canceled, but even this outcome distracted Kitty from missing her chevalier. Josephine du Pont, furious that she wouldn't get to show off the "handsome toilette" she had assembled, wrote: "Well, it happened that a ship from London brought news of the death of the fat little Cincinnatus Church's mother. Burdened perhaps with a fortune of sixty thousand pounds sterling, she left them to him after having enjoyed them up to her 95th year."

Mourning ensued. But at last, in the final weeks of 1800, Josephine reported that Kitty "was truly charming last night. . . . She had a percale dress embroidered in front with two rows of flat gold rings, the little fichu and an arm matching, with a bonnet fashioned after my 'bonnes femmes' with buckles and chains. . . . Mme. Ch. appeared with a superb diamond buckle on her negligée of point, a shawl of the same stuff originating from a lilac-lined falbala nonchalantly attached by means of a crescent of brilliants."

With the death of John's mother, the Church family was back in diamonds.

By the day of Angelica's forty-fifth birthday, in 1801, news had reached New York that Thomas Jefferson had been selected to serve as the third United States president.

Kitty Church was elated. She wrote immediately to congratulate the man who had been her guardian in France: "Did either my situation in life, my age, or (perhaps more properly) my sex, render me fit or *adequate* to be a Politician, the basis of my satisfaction might be in *public good* but as I am nothing less than that, I will only address you in the language of the heart."

This letter from a "less than" nothing girl to the new president was carried to the half-built capital by her friend Theodosia's father. Aaron Burr, though he had received the same number of electoral votes as Thomas Jefferson, had accepted second prize and would be the new vice president.

President Jefferson and Vice President Burr were inaugurated in March 1801, and soon after that, the president replied to Kitty: "The post is not enviable, as it affords little exercise for social affections. there is something within us which makes us wish to have things conducted in our own way, and which we generally fancy to be patriotism. this passion is gratified by such a position. but the heart would be happier enjoying the affections of a family fireside."

As the Federalist Party stepped down, the Church and Hamilton families went back into mourning—not for the party, but for Peggy van Rensselaer, who'd traipsed from army camp to army camp with her married sisters, who'd fascinated Frenchmen and offended other women with her great intellect before returning to Albany to marry her teenage cousin and live within earshot of the Dutch bell. Of her siblings, only Alexander, in Albany on legal business, sat with her through the final days of her long illness.

"Viewing all that she had endured for so long a time, I could not but feel a relief in the termination of the scene," Alexander wrote to New York with the news, reminding his wife to "Remember the duty of Christian Resignation."

In the months to come, "Christian Resignation" would become a refrain.

Two months after the election results ended sixteen years of Federalist rule, one month after Peggy van Rensselaer's death, John Barker Church Jr., known as Jack, was captured and imprisoned by the Portuguese *Capitanearei* of Pará, in South America. At nineteen, Jack had gone to sea as supercargo on the *Aurora*, a merchant brigantine carrying goods insured by his father for $20,000. Portugal had barred foreign traders from entering colonial ports for the purpose of commerce for more than a century, which made doing so all the more lucrative. Before the *Aurora*'s troubles began, Jack Church had secured a permit at Rio de Janeiro and sold $700 worth of his cargo there. Then, although the trade winds were right to put out for the Cape of Good Hope, the *Aurora*'s stated destination, the brig cruised north along the South American coast. Five leagues from the mouth of the Rio Pará, at a distance where land is only visible from a ship's masthead, the *Aurora* hove-to and dropped anchor. There remained one loophole in the prohibition of foreign ships coming into harbor: By the law of the sea, a ship in distress could approach land. As it happened, the *Aurora*—through accident or contrivance—was low on fresh water.

Jack Church was one of a small company that went into port on the ship's longboat, ostensibly to request permission to enter the port and hire a pilot for assistance. Certainly, he also planned to solicit a permit to trade. But the gambit failed: When the longboat reached port, all aboard were arrested and imprisoned. Soon after that, three armed ships seized the *Aurora*.

Jack Church was in prison in South America when his cousin Phil Hamilton, also nineteen, barged into a box at a theater to insult George Eacker, a young Democratic-Republican who had recently given an unflattering speech about his father. So it was Jack's older brother, Captain Phil Church, who carried their father's dueling pistols across the North River to serve as Phil Hamilton's second when he met Mr. Eacker at three o'clock on a cloudy November Monday.

Phil Hamilton's father had counseled his son not to fire, so when the signal was given, he did not raise his pistol. Neither did George Eacker. A minute passed. Finally, Phil raised his pistol, and his opponent did the same, and the sound of the shot reverberated across the river's water.

Captain Church was a strong, athletic young man, but it took more than ordinary force to haul his bleeding cousin into the boat, row across the river, and carry him home to the Churches' house on Robinson Street.

Dr. David Hosack came quickly, but the Hamiltons' newly built home was eight miles from town, near the village of Harlem. It was not difficult to see, from the extremity of Phil Hamilton's injuries, that it was his mother who was most urgently needed.

Angelica Church summoned her sister.

"Philip Hamilton linger'd of his wound till about five o'clock this morning," a friend recorded, "when he expired in the arms of his afflicted mother."

Having supported her sister and brother-in-law through that awful night, Angelica turned to the business of telling the world what had happened. In a family "so near the sun," every story had to be managed. By express, she wrote to her brother Rensselaer: "He expired this morning, with perfect resignation, and in Faith and hopes of an immortal existence," she reported, along with instructions on how to break the news to their parents carefully. "His conduct was extremely satisfactory during this Trial; I cannot write particulars now, my sister is a little composed, and the corpse will be removed from my house in an hour."

Philip Schuyler wrote to advise his grieving daughter: "Altho we may deplore the life of a beloved child yet requiring in the will of providence over grief ought not to be caused to such an extent as to injure our health." Once again, Elizabeth was reminded of her "Christian Resignation," but her father's instruction on how she ought to feel was a reminder of her duty not only as a grieving mother, but as a political wife: "You my dearly beloved Child have the most interesting and important duties to perform as the consort (of the best of men) whose happiness depends on your weal on your health on your existence."

Then the old general, now sixty-eight, reported on his own pain: "I am ... so much mended in my leg that I have been without pain, and without any aid from the fire side to the window."

Four months later, the house on Robinson Street was the site for celebrating Kitty Church's wedding to Bertram Peter Cruger, who went by Peter in New York but Pierre on the island of St. Croix, where he was born. Peter was not related to the Churches by blood, but the families were close: Before he was born, his father, Nicholas Cruger, had hired the precocious Alexander Hamilton, barely a teenager, as a clerk in his West Indies trading company.

Angelica Church wrote to President Jefferson of Kitty's marriage: "My daughter is happily married and I have no doubt but she will do for me what your daughters have done for you; yet when I am writing to you Sir, how can I believe that I may soon become a grandmother," she marveled to her old friend.

The real purpose of her letter, however, was to provide her son Jack, just released from prison in Pará, an opportunity to meet the president and plead his case. Angelica knew Thomas Jefferson hated petitions, but this was her estate: "I appeal Sir to your justice and your power as our chief magistrate and protector, and also from a persuasion that you will render me a service which will not violate your duties, when it gratifies the wishes of a Mother."

It was a low point. But even the president had those.

Angelica had yet to receive a reply from President Jefferson when James Thomson Callender, the reporter who had exposed Alexander Hamilton's affair with Maria Reynolds, published an exposé of Thomas Jefferson, alleging that the president had "kept, as his concubine"—and fathered several children by—his enslaved house-servant Sally Hemings.

Mr. Callender's exertions had derailed Alexander Hamilton's political prospects, but these accusations against Thomas Jefferson seemed to cause little more than a shrug. Possibly this was because Thomas Jefferson did not respond with a detailed confession, as Alexander Hamilton had done. Enslavers did not speak of what they did with bodies they owned. So almost no one spoke of this case. The silence was deafening. With the 1799 Gradual Emancipation Act, New York had formally begun ending slavery, albeit at a pace so glacial that it would take more than a generation to realize fully. As for the Churches, in the census of 1800, three years after they returned to the United States, they had reported no enslaved, Indian, or nonwhite members among their twenty-person household. The child Alexander Hamilton had purchased for them before their return had died of yellow fever, but there was no record of the woman, unless she was one of the four free nonwhites the Hamilton household reported that year. Angelica was among those who took a romantic view of the institution that she had been raised to think of in much the same terms as marriage—a bond of reciprocal duty that often deepened into love. Just as she would have censured a man who divorced his wife or abandoned his children, who would have little to no means to support themselves without him, she would have felt, as many New Yorkers did, that too sudden an end to slavery would allow irresponsible masters to abandon those to whom they owed a debt of care—the elderly or the infirm who were no longer "useful" or "valuable." Or that they would not adequately support freeborn children born to enslaved mothers. To her, this was a moral position.

But Angelica could have seen no moral position for Thomas Jefferson's long-term extramarital "amorous connection" with a woman he enslaved. There was simply the fact that it was done. And in Virginia, slavery was done more than elsewhere. The first two United States censuses, in 1790 and 1800, revealed that New York's enslaved population had declined over that decade from 21,324 to 20,613, while Virginia's had risen from 292,627—more than forty percent of the total number of slaves in the United States—to 345,796.

Angelica knew James Thomson Callender as a scandalmonger who had contributed to the violent "party spirit" that now divided the new nation. But she also knew, from her sister's bitter experience, that he told the truth. In Massachusetts, where there were no slaves by the time of the 1790 census, a junto was beginning to float ideas of secession.

Until this point, Angelica had been a link between these two political poles of New York and Virginia—the common ground between Alexander Hamilton and Thomas Jefferson, who had once bid her to spread her affections "over the whole family of the good, without enquiring by what hard names they are politically called." But her affection for Thomas Jefferson had waned, and she was no longer so concerned about pleasing in all company.

Angelica never wrote to the president again.

During the August of Thomas Jefferson's short-lived scandal, Angelica's twelve-year-old son, Alexander, had come down with a summer fever. Early on, she despaired of his recovery, and on the final Friday of the month, her son died.

Six months after they buried young Alexander, Angelica and Elizabeth traveled to Albany to bury their mother. At sixty-eight, Catharina van Rensselaer Schuyler had died of a stroke. Six months after that, the sisters were back in Trinity Church's graveyard to bury their infant niece. Because she was pregnant, their youngest sister Kitty had eloped while in mourning for her mother. But her child—named Catharine, of course—had died soon after her birth.

Alexander wrote to his wife, "God grant that no new disaster may befall us."

CHAPTER 25

Purchase

1802–1804

Even as they buried their dead, the Churches and the Hamiltons kept breaking ground in other ways, making right in a wilderness of grief. The Hamiltons had bought farmland in Harlem, where they planned to build a house. The Churches had purchased a tract of land on the Genesee River, which they planned to develop into farms and towns. For both families, new land meant a new start, a fresh draft, and new opportunity.

John Barker Church had never had much interest in land. Given a choice, he would prefer to place his bets on the sea. When other speculators had rushed to buy up acreage, he had usually sold land that came to him in the process of his business. His second son and namesake, Jack Church, was inclined the same way. But the Churches' firstborn child, Captain Phil Church, saw the world differently.

Now in his mid-twenties, Phil was a mix of both his upper-class education in the heart of the British Empire and his own romantic view of Philip Schuyler, the famous grandfather for whom he was named. From a distance, he had idolized his American grandfather—the major general, the senator, the developer of land and industry, the Indian negotiator, the advocate for education and canals. (Philip Schuyler also had helped create Union College, the second college in New York, which had opened in Schenectedy in 1795, and he cofounded the Western Inland

Lock Navigation Company in 1792 with the aim of engineering a navigable route from the North River to Lake Ontario). So it was with no small degree of pleasure that Phil rode west in 1800 to attend the foreclosure sale for the very same 100,000-acre tract that Robert Morris had offered to turn over to John Barker Church as payment of his debt. Now Phil aspired to be the patriot and the landed patriarch his grandfather had been.

This "new" western territory was, of course, the same land that the Continental Army had invaded in 1779, forcing the Haudenosaunee to retreat to the British fort at Niagara. Since then, Britain had relinquished its claim to the land in the 1783 Treaty of Paris, and the Haudenosaunee were compelled to do the same in the surrender negotiated in the 1784 Treaty of Fort Stanwix. Philip Schuyler had attended the Fort Stanwix treaty negotiations, but he was not a signatory. Nor were Molly or Joseph Brant, who had opposed that treaty for ceding far more territory than was just.

These treaties did not end the land disputes. Massachusetts, still bitter about its border, had vied for possession of the new territory, so a compromise granted that state the right to sell the land, which would then be incorporated politically into New York. Then came the Alien and Sedition Acts, which, among other restrictions, barred foreign nationals from owning land. (This may be why John Barker Church sent his US-born son to purchase the tract.) The legislation required the Holland Land Company, a group of Dutch investors, to purchase their holdings through the Philadelphia financier Robert Morris, who was paid for his efforts with acreage.

The convoluted process whereby territory that had long been the hunting grounds of the Seneca came into his possession did not interest Phil Church much. He simply reveled in his new role. After purchasing the land, he had made several forays to see it for himself—including climbing trees for better views. Many of the Haudenosaunee, including the Brants, had moved across the Niagara River to the neighboring British province of Upper Canada, but several communities remained. The Churches' new land tract abutted the Seneca village of Caneadea, for instance, and Phil again enacted his family's history as he introduced himself to his neighbors. Phil hired a woodsman-surveyor to help him explore the tract more precisely. They scouted the river and forests, and then, on a lark, Phil and the surveyor tramped all the way to Niagara Falls, running out of money and food and ending up trading chocolate for meals at homesteads along the route. By the time he returned to New York, Phil was "Genesee mad." So much for Eton, the law, and the army: Along that wild river, he had seen his life's work, and he was itching to begin. He was young and cocksure, and he likely could barely wait to see the future he now imagined: houses, roads, mills, businesses, canals.

His mother tried her best to mirror her son's enthusiasm for this ostensibly undeveloped wilderness. She also sought to counter Phil's visions of his own private empire with more nuanced ideas for the American microcosm they were now imagining into being. They would build a house overlooking the Genesee River, to be called Belvidere—like the house that her cousin Robert Livingston had built, only to have the British burn it in 1777, a villa like Down Place, except it would not look like a castle. They would somehow obtain merino sheep. They would plant gardens and fields using the very latest agricultural methods. They would plot a town like a miniature Paris, with a public *arrondisse-ment* at its heart. They would open a store. They would start a school.

Meanwhile, Angelica's cousin Robert R. Livingston was in Paris, serving as the current American minister plenipotentiary to the Republic of France, now under the firm hand of First Consul Napoleon Bonaparte.

He wrote to Angelica soon after he arrived there, carrying letters to her friends to solicit their friendship for him. "Your knowledge of this country affords me nothing new to offer you," he flattered her, but France had changed a great deal since Angelica Church had last been there.

From afar, the new French government sounded like a "happy" arrangement to Angelica, who long ago had listened to Thomas Jefferson, the Marquis de Lafayette, and "Common Sense" debate whether the US Constitution put too much power in the executive branch. So much had changed since then. Thomas Paine, formerly "Common

Sense," and a supporter of central banks, was now widely disdained for his critique of organized religion. The marquis—now plain "Lafayette" to Americans—was living quietly in the French countryside as Gilbert du Motier. And Thomas Jefferson, who had lauded simplicity and loved his slippers, was an ascendant political force. Perhaps a consulate was a more perfect system. Modeled on the Roman Republic, a consular government had a committee of elected officials that functioned in the executive capacity, rather than a single individual. Perhaps an elected committee—like the board of a bank whose equal stakes in that institution theoretically forestall any individual from making corrupt choices—would have more ballast than an individual president.

But what Angelica had imagined about the new regime in France and the oppressive instrument that Robert Livingston beheld when he arrived were starkly different. Under First Consul Napoleon Bonaparte, France was becoming increasingly authoritarian, and the individual rights and freedoms the revolution had sought to achieve, at such terrible cost, were now slipping away.

Robert Livingston told Angelica about a play that had recently opened in a theater in Paris. The play had been approved by the police censors, but even so, when Napoleon attended, the "Just Consul" was displeased by how members of the audience had reacted to a scene mentioning "the old family." Not only was the play canceled, but several ladies who attended that evening's production were ordered into exile.

"Alas what pain would it not have given me to have read in our papers," Robert Livingston teased his cousin, "Yesterday Madame Church was *deported* under guard to the frontiers of Canada.'"

The new minister plenipotentiary did not write to his cousin merely to continue an argument about politics. "Let me hear from you frequently," he wrote. "Speak a good [amount] of yourself, a little of the rest of my friends, but nothing of what passes here." These were not casual instructions. Knowing that France would be reading his letters, Robert Livingston hoped to receive mail that might strengthen his diplomatic position. Personal notes from Madame Church, of all people, could well aid him in the delicate work of repairing what filigree of friendship remained of the former Franco-American alliance.

His French counterpart, the French minister of foreign affairs, was Charles-Maurice de Talleyrand, a man whom England would have deported back to France if Angelica Church had not helped him emigrate to the United States. And though he had despised living in the United States, the Foreign Minister owed a debt to Angelica for the fact that he was living at all.

Since the 1794 Jay Treaty, "amity" between the United States and France had been reduced to mere threads. But Angelica happened to be one of those threads. And Robert Livingston intended to use everything at his disposal to keep the United States clear of a despot's tyranny.

Meanwhile, in Washington, Thomas Jefferson was also waking up to the new situation in France. He had just learned that, within days of the negotiated end of the Quasi-War with the United States, France had secretly negotiated a land deal with Spain that transferred the Louisiana Territory—all the land and rivers between the right bank of the Mississippi River and the Rocky Mountains—to French control.

When Victor and Josephine du Pont visited President Jefferson in February—with a letter of introduction from Kitty Church, of course—Victor explained what he had learned during a recent trip to France. Seeking to return France to its former glory, Napoleon Bonaparte had a two-pronged plan: First, France would recapture Saint-Domingue, where the Haitian Revolution had liberated both the colony from its parent state and the enslaved from the enslavers. Once that West-Indies stronghold was regained, France could regain its lost hold on North America and reclaim *Nouvelle-France*.

Shocked by this development, President Jefferson wrote Robert Livingston a private letter: "There is on the globe one single spot, the possessor of which is our natural and habitual enemy. . . . It is New Orleans."

Together, the two men had written the Declaration of Independence, severing the United States from Britain, but now, "The day that France takes possession of N. Orleans fixes the sentence," wrote one author of that document to another. "From that moment we must marry ourselves to the British fleet & nation."

Then he waited for someone brave enough to carry such a letter to Paris.

Even in New York, Angelica's friends the Du Ponts felt the pressure of Napoleon Bonaparte on their lives, and soon after Victor du Pont's visit with President Jefferson, his father, Pierre du Pont, decided to return to France to appease Napoleon and manage that end of the family enterprise. Hearing of these plans, Thomas Jefferson asked him to deliver his letter personally to Robert Livingston.

"I wish you to be possessed of the subject," Thomas Jefferson explained, "because you may be able to impress on the government of France the inevitable consequences of their taking possession of Louisiana: . . . a war which will annihilate her on the ocean."

Once "possessed of the subject," the renowned physiocrat delayed his departure for France. During that time, he wrote two long, carefully reasoned letters to President Jefferson, advising him against war and proposing an alternative. "If it is surely war you foresee," Pierre du Pont suggested, "you may prevent war's unfortunate consequences if you offer to procure what you desire, for it is always more economical."

Purchasing New Orleans was an audacious executive action of a magnitude more in line with Napoleon's autocratic rule than anything the Federalists had ever attempted. The idea contradicted President Jefferson's understanding of the Constitution, his campaign promises, and his convictions about government. And yet, averting war could be worth the sacrifice of principles: President Jefferson sent Secretary of State James Monroe to France to authorize Robert Livingston to offer to purchase New Orleans for $10 million.

Meanwhile, in France, Robert Livingston, with his signature ear trumpet, and Charles-Maurice de Talleyrand, with his signature cane, negotiated a different deal altogether. Instead of just New Orleans, France would sell the whole territory to the United States—from the Mississippi River to the Rocky Mountains, 828,000 square miles, more than half a billion acres. Instead of $10 million, they wanted $15 million, plus indemnification for illegal captures of American merchant ships during the Quasi-War—those French spoliations claims John Barker Church still owned and hoped to one day redeem but would now need to obtain from the United States, which had just spent a great deal of money.

Of course, Charles-Maurice de Talleyrand knew that spoliations were something Angelica specifically wanted: "Talleyrand called on Madame de Corny with his excuses for not doing what we wished him to do," she reported that summer to Phil Church. But, in his magnanimity toward her country, the arch-diplomat of France had repaid his debt.

When James Monroe arrived in Paris and learned of the new deal, he and Robert Livingston decided not to wait six months for permission and thus risk that France would change its—Napoleon Bonaparte's—mind.

With a few strokes of a quill, they doubled the size of the United States.

While President Jefferson fretted about the constitutionality of the half-a-billion-acre territory he had acquired by executive decree, and John Barker Church's former dueling partner James Wilkinson set out to raise the American flag over New Orleans, members of the Church family turned their attention to developing their 100,000-acre tract on the Genesee River. By the spring, First Consul Napoleon Bonaparte was declared Emperor Napoleon; at the same time, Captain Phil Church had surveyed his first town—a village composed, for now, of log houses chinked with blue clay. He named it Angelica.

Developing the land was far from easy. Phil's mother, whom Thomas Jefferson had teased long ago for being "country-mad," might have dreamed of a village in the woods, of intellectuals living simple yet luxurious lives, but Phil was more practical. He wrote to his father: "A new settlement requires poor and industrious people, rather than those settlers who will not work themselves but depend upon hiring others." He had hoped to build a "moderate sized house" to live in, but, failing to find laborers, he built himself a two-room farmhouse instead. Of course, his "poor industrious people" performed their own labor, but they had no hard money to spend. Phil's store was stocked with tobacco and pipes, knives and saws, pails, nails, needles and thimbles, gun flints and powder, tea and coffee, salt (by the peck or by the bushel) and allspice, women's shoes, shovels and hoes, candlesticks, bells, butter, lead, and sugar. But, rather than making purchases with coin, his customers preferred what was termed "paying in hair, pins and Indigo."

"In other words," Phil Church complained, "in every kind of trash."

As Phil Church was learning how to be a land baron in his two-room shack, Angelica Church was trying to stay on the good side of Napoleon Bonaparte. Angelica had never met the emperor personally, but she had met his teenage brother, Jérôme Buonaparte, who preferred the Italian spelling of the family name and had just eloped with an American woman, without the emperor's permission.

"I [went] to the beautiful party of Madame Church, where was almost the whole town, which was said to be perfectly in keeping with the idea of an English Rout," Josephine du Pont wrote of that winter's finest parties. "Mr. Jerome gained reputation as an excellent dancer he has gone very happy."

Excellent dancer or no, Jérôme was a problem for both Madame du Pont (whose husband felt compelled to lend him money, lest he offend the emperor, even as he knew that Napoleon would never honor his erstwhile brother's debts) and for Angelica Church.

"Jerome Buonaparte is unpleasantly situated his marriage not approved and his exile certain—He has been very imprudent in his conversation lately," Angelica gossiped to Phil. "I have heard from Paris that I have given him a fête."

That people in Paris still talked of her parties was something Angelica would usually have appreciated, but even as far away as New York, it was impolitic to upset Napoleon Bonaparte. Victor du Pont feared he would be bankrupted for it.

"Bonaparte dips his hands in blood," she concluded. "But he may sooner or later meet the reward of his crimes."

CHAPTER 26

Hair Triggers

1804

"Born, as I unfortunately was, in an age of revolution," President Thomas Jefferson complained to Marguerite de Corny one year into his first term as president, "my life has been wasted on the billows of revolutionary storm. the sweet sensations & affections of domestic society have been exchanged with me for the bitter & deadly feuds of party: encircled with political enemies & spies, instead of my children & friends."

Speaking of his friends, the president confessed: "I have never seen mrs Church since her return to America. we are 350 miles apart; a distance which in this country is not easily surmounted. in our party divisions too it happened that her nearest friends were my bitterest opponents; and altho' that could not affect our mutual esteem, it tended to repress the demonstrations of it. Kitty has continued to write to me from time to time."

For President Jefferson, the boundary between personal life and politics seemed as wide as the distance between himself on the Potomac and Mrs. Church on the North River—or, for that matter, Madame de Corny on the River Seine. Angelica might have wished this was her experience, but there was no sheltering from politics in her family.

As the 1804 New York gubernatorial race was turning frenzied, even though both candidates—Morgan Lewis and Aaron Burr—were from the Democratic–Republican Party, she knew she could look forward to another season of vitriol.

"The animosity between the Lewisers and the Burrers is such that it is conjectured blood will be shed on the days of the election," General Philip Schuyler predicted.

One handbill then printed in the papers was particularly problematic. In it, the author, Dr. Charles D. Cooper, reported that General Hamilton had spoken of Aaron Burr as "a dangerous man, and who ought not to be trusted." Then he speculated that, because of this statement, most Federalists would vote for Morgan Lewis, including the patroon, Stephen van Rensselaer, and his other brother-in-law, John Barker Church—"who Burr some time ago fought a duel with, and of course, must bear Burr much hatred."

Thomas Jefferson's relationship with his vice president had soured, and Aaron Burr had not only been sidelined but also removed from the 1804 presidential ticket. President Jefferson had tapped New York's former governor, George Clinton, to take his place, so the outgoing vice president was attempting to swap chairs.

Alexander Hamilton feared that Aaron Burr could ally with secessionist New Englanders and orchestrate "the dismemberment of the Union," and he had said as much in a speech. But Philip Schuyler and John Barker Church were more circumspect.

John wrote to the newspapers to correct the record, and New York's *Morning Chronicle* published a clarification: "It having been asserted in election handbills that John B. Church, Esq. of this city, is an enemy of Col. Burr, in consequence of a difference between them a few years since, which was honorably adjusted. We are requested on the part of Mr. Church, pointedly to contradict that assertion—to state that Mr. Church and Mr. Burr are on terms of friendly intercourse, and that he has *not* at the present election voted for Mr. Lewis."

On the third Tuesday in June—the same week the official tallies declared Morgan Lewis New York's next governor—the Hamilton family gave a party for their eldest daughter, Angelica.

Now nineteen, Angelica Hamilton still had not recovered from the shock of her brother Philip's death by dueling. One friend of the family described her as having "a very uncommon simplicity and modesty of deportment." But the girl's "uncommon simplicity" was a regression to a child-state. Angelica's condition was rendered more stark in comparison to the rest of her family. Her younger brothers Alexander and James had both followed Philip to Columbia College. As for her Church cousins, Phil was gone to his Genesee River, and Jack had left on a new voyage to the West Indies; but Kitty (now Mrs. Cruger) came from her new home at Bloomingdale, to show off her baby Eugene, as did Betsy, who was closest to Angelica's age. Rumor had it that Betsy was in love. Her parents disapproved of her young lawyer, Rudolph Bunner, but Aaron Burr had written to his now-married daughter Theodosia: "Bunner and Miss Church said to be mutually in love; on his part avowed, on hers not denied."

As for Angelica Hamilton, she had no beau, no baby, and no house in Bloomingdale. Nor was her mother's newest baby—an infant Philip to replace the one she'd lost—proving to be any consolation. Perhaps the party was intended to cheer the girl, or even nudge her back to herself, through pleasure and the love and support of friends. Maybe her parents imagined that if she did the things that girls her age enjoyed—a daylong *fête*, with dancing and a dinner—she would return to her "normal" teenage self.

Angelica's Aunt Angelica did not voice any opinion of this parenting, but she pointedly criticized her sister's execution of the party. "The breakfast is fixed for nine o'clock, this is in the true good housewife style," she wrote to her son Phil. "The company must wear their night caps to arrive on time." The early hour was exacerbated by the fact that the Hamiltons' new house was nearly ten miles from New York, near the village of Harlem. Nor—"oh direful misfortune!"—had the Hamiltons invited or engaged a leader for the country dancing. Likely the real problem was that her sister had planned a party without consulting her.

The day of Angelica's *fête* was rainy, but the Hamiltons' new house was large, and there were piazzas along two sides for the guests to take air without getting rain on their party clothes. Inside, mirrors brought what light the gray day held into the many-sided rooms. In one room stood the piano Aunt Angelica had sent her namesake from London, along with advice to her mother to see to it that Angelica learned French.

Perhaps young Angelica played the piano for her guests. Perhaps she spoke a little French with Gouverneur Morris, who came to the party from his home just across the Harlem River, or with her sophisticated Aunt Angelica, who would have arrived late even if the breakfast had not been so early. Perhaps she sang with her father, as she had done as child. Perhaps she danced. Perhaps it was only the spring rain that made the day seem so bittersweet.

The day following his daughter's party, Alexander received a curt letter from the vice president. Two days after that, John Barker Church and Nathaniel Pendleton called upon Aaron Burr to speak on Alexander Hamilton's behalf: "It is not to be denied that my animadversions on the political principles character and views of Col. Burr have been extremely severe," Alexander Hamilton was willing to concede. But he would not disavow his statements without proof that he was mistaken. John knew from experience what Aaron Burr would say to that.

Predictably, no resolution was reached.

On the Fourth of July, the gentlemen all dined together with the Society of the Cincinnati. Jack Trumbull was there also, just home from Europe. "Burr, contrary to his wont, was silent, gloomy, sour," the painter of faces noted of his friends. "Hamilton entered with glee into all the gaiety of a convivial party, and even sung an old military song."

After the reunion, Alexander went home and wrote a letter to his sleeping wife.

In the morning, he gave a document transferring all his debts, owing and paying, to his brother-in-law for one dollar, and John Barker Church gave him the dueling pistols. Four years had passed since one had shot a hole through Aaron Burr's coat; two had passed since one had shot a hole into Alexander Hamilton's son.

All John could do now was make sure that Nathaniel Pendleton understood how to activate the hair-trigger mechanism by pushing the trigger forward to engage it. With the hair trigger, only a few ounces of pressure would be necessary to fire the gun, making it possible to shoot faster and more accurately.

When Alexander crossed the river, John did not cross with him.

For a quarter century, the two men had handled one another's business—shadow partners in trade, finance, politics, and family. One could stand for both.

If Angelica was not already suspicious, the first she heard of the duel was when a messenger arrived from William Bayard's house, two miles upriver, with the news that Alexander had been shot.

Angelica flew to Mr. Bayard's. She found her brother-in-law lying on blood-soaked linens conscious, but paralyzed. When Elizabeth arrived from Harlem, Angelica yielded the place nearest to Alexander. Needing something to do, she ordered pen and paper.

"I have the painful task to inform you that General Hamilton was this morning wounded by that wretch Burr, but we have every reason to hope that he will recover," she scrawled across the page to her brother Philip. Her handwriting—almost as fine as a man's when she wrote to dignitaries—was now ragged and sloping.

Angelica Church had been reporting political news since the war for American independence. For nearly three decades, she had written letters to her extensive network of friends—including the man now suffering within earshot of her borrowed desk. In that time, she had relayed news of assassins in General Washington's guard, updates on British naval movements at Newport, reports of the affairs of the French Army, thoughts on the Treaty of Paris that ended the American Revolution, rumors of the mysterious mental state of the king of England, intelligence on the beheadings in France, and information about the imprisonment of her dear friend Lafayette.

She had lost many friends to the cause of revolution. This July morning, however, the blood lost was so dear it might have been her own.

We have every reason to hope he will recover.

She had witnessed enough history, though, to know that writing a thing didn't make it true.

When Gouverneur Morris came the next day, he found Alexander alive, but speechless. Overcome by the scene, he retreated to the garden for air. Then he rejoined the bedside vigil until the end.

When Alexander was dead, the doctor opened the wound and found the ball lodged in vertebrae. Elizabeth was frantic.

Angelica wrote to the family, "My dear sister bears with saintlike fortitude this affliction."

The funeral procession began from the Churches' house at 25 Robinson Street, where crowds had been milling for hours already.

Finally, at noon, two Black servants dressed all in white—except for the black trim on their turbans—emerged, leading the general's gray horse, saddled but riderless. From each stirrup hung an empty boot. With the arrival of the horse, a band began to play. The crowd, curious to see if there was blood on the boots, pressed forward. But the drums and pipes and the shifting energy of the crowd startled the horse, which skittered sideways over the cobblestone.

The crowd sucked back again.

Distracted by the general's dancing horse, the crowd was slow to notice that the house doors had opened, and the coffin had been carried out. Belatedly, the regiment saluted the general himself. After that, the event hewed more closely to the plan. An artillery regiment led the march, followed by one of militia, and then by the Society of the Cincinnati. After these soldiers past and present came the general's coffin on a bier, the riderless gray horse, and the dead man's sons.

So far, it was a solemn event, decorum aided by pomp and ceremony. But that could change. The vice president had just shot and killed the leader of the opposite party. Not so long ago, Angelica had paraded Aaron Burr on her own arm after he and her husband had exchanged pistol shots. Now she called him "that wretch Burr." Still, Angelica understood that this marching masse must not become a mob.

At the tip of Manhattan Island, they passed Battery Park, and then Government House and the Bowling Green. Finally, Broadway brought them to Trinity Church. Even this church, now hung with black, was different. The Trinity Church they had known as girls had faced the river. Its much-larger replacement faced Wall Street.

They had promenaded on the church green as girls. As women, both sisters had buried a son in its churchyard, their lives tiding like that great river just beyond. Now, they would bury a man they both loved. But grief belonged to Elizabeth.

"Fail not my Beloved to let me daily know the state of your afflicted sister," her father had written to Angelica as soon as he heard. "My anxiety on her account rends my heart."

A platform had been erected in front of the church. Careful of his wooden leg, Gouverneur Morris climbed onto that stage with the Hamilton boys. When the time came, he stood to speak. Before him, New Yorkers were in a "consternation." In the open air, before so many people, his voice barely carried, but perhaps that was just as well.

"You know that he never courted your favour by adulation, or the sacrifice of his own judgement," Gouverneur told the crowd. "You have seen him contending against you, and saving your dearest interests, as it were, in spite of yourselves. And you now feel and enjoy the benefits resulting from the firm energy of his conduct."

It was a shoddy job, the orator thought: "I find that what I have said does not answer the general Expectation." But Gouverneur Morris had seen too much of the French Revolution to play to this audience: "How easy would it have been," he recalled, "to make them for a Moment absolutely mad!"

Instead, politics churned forward without any member of the family having much to do with them. The month of the presidential election, Philip Schuyler's many maladies finally got the better of him, and he died without knowing that Thomas Jefferson had sailed to victory with 92% of the electoral vote.

By December, Philip Schuyler's children had manumitted the enslaved members of The Pastures household who were young and healthy enough to qualify for release. Then, with no way to divide its value and in too great a need of money for sentimentality, The Pastures, like the Hamiltons' Grange, was put up for sale.

It was the end of an era, and the beginning of a new one:

With Philip Schuyler's death, two men Tone and Stephen, and two women, Pheobe and Silva, and Silva's three children, Tallyho, Tom, and Hanover, obtained their "full, free manumission, emancipation, and freedom, from the day of the date hereof, fully, freely, and absolutely."

CHAPTER 27

"The Country of Angelica"

Angelica Church's grief was debilitating. In the summer of 1805, she wrote to her son Philip lamenting that his bride, Anna-Matilda, "only knew me saddened and depressed." As to visiting the newlyweds on their Genesee homestead that year, she wrote that her "spirits were not equal to the undertaking."

Philip Church was relieved. He had made a concerted effort to dissuade his mother from venturing west to see the family's land tract on the Genesee the previous summer. Before he had received word that his Uncle Hamilton had died of a gunshot wound, Phil had written blithely to his mother to keep her and her opinions far away. "I believe it was one of the Roman Emperors who always had a person at his elbow to remind him that he was mortal. For my part I do not require that. The Fleas feelingly remind me what I am. Not all the writings in existence could so effectually convince me of the vanity of grandeur as a flea bite. The above observation alone may perhaps convince you how unpleasantly you would pass your time at this place. Besides, my dear Mother, if you want to reach Angelica, you could not go to Belvidere Farm unless you went on horseback, so bad is the road. Indeed, the road from Bath here is almost impassable."

Angelica's son had forgotten the distances to which she'd gone before, over land and sea, for the sake of the people she loved, undeterred by blackflies or mosquitoes, the fatigue of riding in a saddle, or by war, fear of shipwreck, or the complications of traveling with a newborn. "When my friends require my assistance there are few more willing than myself," she had boasted to Thomas Jefferson when she was younger. By the time she received her son's playful effort to keep her from meddling in his current endeavors, however, mortality had stunned her into stillness. Younger women had been calling Angelica "le Declín" for years, but she could hardly get much lower than she felt in 1805 and remain among the living. In the course of a few years, she had lost both of her parents, her siblings Peggy and Johnny, her brother-in-law Alexander, and—from the newest generation—her son Alexander, her nephew Philip, and, in a different way, her niece Angelica.

Angelica had known death all her life, and the turning of the century had ended the era of the living for many of her friends: Benjamin Franklin, Jeremiah Wadsworth, François-Jean de Beauvoir de Chastellux, Louis-Dominique Éthis de Corny, and her darling Baron von Steuben were all in the ground. Sarah Jay was dead. Martha Washington was dead. Other friends weren't dead, but just as gone: Lucy Knox, after ten miscarriages and perpetual financial strain, had turned bitter, and she and Henry Knox had moved to Maine. Caty Greene had likewise moved to South Carolina, hoping to scrape together a living farming rice. Thomas Jefferson, still the president, was no longer her friend. Aaron Burr had fled west. The Adamses, now retired home to Massachusetts, had come to loathe her late brother-in-law so intensely that even after his death they railed about his "Fornication Adultery Incest, Libelling and electioneering Intrigue," insinuating, among other things, that the friendship between the statesman and his sister-in-law—who had once won their friendship—went beyond the pale. And their son, John Quincy Adams, once a regular visitor at the house on London's Sackville Street, had represented the insurance company denying payment for the lost cargo of the brigantine *Aurora* in the case of *Church v. Hubbart*, that young lawyer's first (albeit unsuccessful) argument before the US Supreme Court.

On top of it all, Angelica seemed to have lost heart, as if the spirit of the war years, along with the audacity of her youth, had snagged upon the treacheries beneath the mirrored surface of righteous conviction. This new country, which she and her generation had brought into being, seemed to be slipping into a state of derangement, riven by partisanship and talk of secession. Its patriots were resorting to pistols to resolve their political differences, rather than through the political representation they had fought a war to obtain.

The shining ideas of Angelica's youth had been made real by the achievement of a free and independent United States and by the Constitution and the Bill of Rights. But the architects, so eager to innovate, had not yet thought of or agreed on everything. Now the flaws showed, and cracks were forming where the foundation wasn't firm. Thomas Jefferson had seen the interference of women in politics as corruption. John Adams had called it caprice. But the paradox was simple: Because women existed outside the democratic process, any political act a woman attempted—petitions for "favors," calling a president by something other than what the Congress had decided, advising her spouse—was inherently antidemocratic.

The correction that the country now implemented was to guard more vigorously against women committing political acts. In New Jersey, women who met the criteria of landownership were still voting in national elections, but the rising opposition railed that their doing so was voter fraud. Meanwhile, Massachusetts had that year reaffirmed that married women were not entitled to citizenship separate from their spouses. Women still wore Grecian-style gowns, thin muslin revealing their natural, minimally fettered form, but their sphere was being cinched ever more tightly: Soon, the corset would be back in style. Emblematic of the problem was the simple fact that the American president's consort was, very literally, his slave.

Some of Angelica's oldest friends understood exactly how she felt and what she needed.

"Why don't you follow the Blessed plan you Have Had to pay a visit to France?" urged her friend Lafayette, who had likewise known his share of grief.

True, many of their old friends were dead and France had changed under the heavy hand of Napoleon Bonaparte. But Angelica could avoid politics, ride through the Bois de Boulogne, contemplate art and fashion. She could visit Maria Cosway's new *Maison d'education* for young ladies in Lyon. If the censored plays were no good, at least she and Maria could play music together.

Certainly, France would welcome her back. "I was speaking of it the other day to Madame de Corny," the ex-marquis persisted. "We Agreed that Your objections to this Voyage were totally Groundless."

Marguerite de Corny had suffered, too. For years she had aided Americans in France, opening doors for Thomas Jefferson, Gouverneur Morris, Robert R. Livingston, and Angelica herself, advocating for a country she had never seen. She was rewarded for her past endeavors with charity from her friends and occasional letters from Angélique or the United States president.

She too was concerned about Angelica, and she always advocated for her friends. "You are so far beyond pettiness that I do not fear telling you about Madame Church," she wrote to Thomas Jefferson that spring of 1805. "Her health is failing; she has undergone such deep and repeated losses that my only wish is for her to get away for a while. Given her great sadness, I no longer fear that my extreme solitude would be a problem for her. I have finished with the world, but she has cause to lament. It would do her good to be here with me." But the president did not extend any condolences to his old friend.

Kind as these offers of friendship were, Angelica did not want to go to France, or anywhere. But time passed, and the pain ebbed, and her life went on like the river after the shudder and groan of the ice breaking up.

Her father's story had ended, and so had that of Alexander Hamilton. Her gambler husband was on the rocks, his luck spent and his fortune all but drained away, but Angelica had always plotted her own story. And hers had another chapter.

It wasn't France that called Angelica back to herself, or England, which still beckoned John. It was, once again, her own country. As she had brought her influence to bear in support of the many movements that had come before—for "freedom" from tyranny, for American independence, for the Articles of Confederation, for the Constitution, for the Jay Treaty, and even for the Louisiana Purchase—Angelica rose to meet the new moment, to lead and shape the next movement.

This time, it was a physical movement. Thomas Jefferson referred to the westward expansion of the United States as the "Empire of Liberty." He imagined this would be different from Napoleon Bonaparte's spreading empire. Where France was seeking military control and cultural hegemony in Europe, the American president imagined the spread of American governance would spread by peaceful diplomacy, replete with "the peace & friendship of the various Indian tribes." But he had more immediate political goals as well: "By enlarging the empire of liberty, we multiply it's auxiliaries, & provide new sources of renovation," the president wrote that year. "Should it's principles at any time, degenerate; in those portions of our country which gave them birth." This remark spoke directly to the fears New Englanders had of the Louisiana Purchase—that "multiplying auxiliaries" would diminish the political voices of northern states already shortchanged by the Constitution's three-fifths clause that awarded additional representation to states with large (nonvoting) enslaved populations. Of course, it was speculation at this point.

Indeed, land speculators had anticipated the president. For more than a decade prior to the Louisiana Purchase, buying up rights and claims had been a booming business. Whereas at the start of the war, most of the Province of New York had lain within the watersheds of Lake Champlain and the North River—now known more often as Hudson's River—by 1805, the state of New York reached the shores of Lake Erie, fully doubled in size. The Church family had joined in this fray by default—specifically, Robert Morris's default. John still preferred the sea to land when it came to fishing for opportunities, but his spoliation claims remained uncompensated, and until Congress saw fit to settle those claims against France that the country had assumed with the Louisiana Purchase, he lacked sufficient liquid capital to merchandise at any great scale. Thus, as the ambitious young nation turned its voracious gaze westward, the gambler followed suit. Land, it seemed, was the only game in play.

That summer, an expedition was mapping the new territory and whatever lay beyond it—as Henry Hudson had once explored the river up which Angelica had been born. If Meriwether Lewis and William Clark and their Corps of Discovery survived the coming winter, they would carry back stories of fantastic landscapes, unfamiliar peoples, and prolific game and resources—very like those relayed by the crew of the Dutch East India Company ship, the *Halve Maen*. Conquest would follow, then the transplantation of people, livestock, and culture, of apple trees and wheat, thistle and dandelions, of cattle and sheep, of church steeples and schoolhouses, jails and gallows, markets and banks. This new beginning might look like earlier beginnings—from the Dutch patroonships and each of the other "New World" colonies—from the violence to the lawlessness to the social reinvention.

Agents for the Church family had placed advertisements for "the Country of Angelica" in newspapers throughout New England. "For Settlement," the papers offered, "one Hundred Thousand Acres of Land . . . of an excellent quality, and the country, from the purity and abundance of the streams with which it is watered, is remarkably healthful." Better yet, the advertisement explained, this land lay within a wagon ride of three critical waterways: The Genesee flowed north to Lake Ontario, the Susquehanna drained to Philadelphia, and, twenty miles to the west, soon to be connected by road, the navigable Allegheny flowed south to Pittsburgh, into the Ohio River, and on, to the Mississippi. The "Country of Angelica," like the expanding United States, seemed to be pure potential, available for twenty percent down, and seven equal annual payments thereafter. Now, the "Empire of Freedom" was moving past the stage of paperwork, of deeds and treaties, and the matter of how "freedom" might be made manifest was coming into vogue.

Even in the haze of grief, Angelica was intrigued. She had seen Paris and London, New York and Philadelphia, Boston and Williamsburg (though not yet the immense construction site on the Potomac, where her old friend Pierre L'Enfant had sketched out wide avenues for the new capital city and Maria Cosway's architect-brother George Hadfield had drafted the plans for the Capitol building and the City Hall). The question of what American society would look like was playing out in both the design of individual buildings and their arrangement. Social architecture, the layout of human interactions, was close to the heart of a woman who understood that every social gathering was a microcosmic experiment wherein the individual participated in friendship, alliance, kinship, patriotism, community, and the society that was as much the making of a country as the acquisition of land or the making of laws.

Of course, Angelica was limited in her imagination by having grown up in the preexisting order. She was, like everyone, "moving through the labyrinth of [her] age," with only her past to inform her. Angelica was the descendant of patroons, the daughter of colonists, but she herself was a revolutionary. She wasn't drafting systems of governance, but just as critically she was drafting these bonds and relationships, manifesting scenes of happiness that were the basis for a nation.

The following summer, when Angelica Church was fifty, her spirit returned to her.

The journey to the Genesee—four hundred fifty miles with a newborn grandchild, in a caravan of wagons—would take weeks. But Angelica and her daughter-in-law agreed on one thing: It couldn't be as bad as crossing the Atlantic. (Since sailing from Ireland as a child, Anna-Matilda had hated crossing any water—even the ferry from New York to New Jersey terrified her.)

As to luggage, the Church family's westward expedition took with them months of provisions—lemons, tea, and casks of wine—along with material supplies: bed linens, and likely a bed to put them on. John brought his traveling bar. Angelica brought a full formal dinner service. They likely brought homemaking supplies for Phil and Anna-Matilda, and gifts for the Seneca who lived nearby.

As to the company, the Churches' eight-year-old son Richard may have been one of the adventurers. But their other children were otherwise occupied—and John and Angelica were not on speaking terms with their daughter Betsy, who had eloped with her beau the previous summer. As for staff, since 1800, the Churches had not reported any enslaved household members in their New York house, but they did not travel without drivers for the wagons and some defense in case of robbers on those long stretches of road. Surprisingly, the person who seemed to enjoy the idea of striking out for the so-called wilderness most was Angelica's chef. Years earlier, the Churches had hired the Frenchman when his penchant for singing revolutionary songs wasn't appreciated in the Windsor Castle kitchens. He had remained with the Churches ever since, at Sackville Street and Down Place, then in New York. Now, the travelers took pleasure in capturing fresh wild game and fish for the French chef to prepare.

To get to their patch of wilderness, they traveled up the North River to Albany, visiting all the friends and relatives who were still alive and well. At Rhinebeck, Angelica's brother Philip had a new wife. Janet Montgomery had a new house. And Cornelia Livingston's son was now married to Robert Livingston's daughter. From there, the caravan pressed north to Albany, where they had to cross the river. Angelica may have visited her uncles at Crailo and Claverack, and Peggy's widower, Stephen van Rensselaer, and his beautiful new wife, another Cornelia, at the still-grand Van Rensselaer manor house. The Pastures had been listed for sale that summer, so if they stayed there, it was for the last time and bittersweet. Their next visit after Albany was at Palatine, where Angelica's Aunt Geertruy and Uncle John Cochran now lived on a beautiful farm on rolling hills that misted over on summer mornings.

As the party progressed westward, the towns became smaller. There were taverns and inns along the stagecoach route that skirted the northern end of a series of narrow lakes, but these, like the road, dwindled and deteriorated the farther west they went. They were all but nonexistent once they traced one of the blue fingers southwest, to arrive at a place one British land speculator had named Bath, after the luxe spa-town Angelica had visited in England. Here began the newly cut road, still stump-studded, that would take them the final forty miles, over a divide, and into the valley of the Genesee River.

The Churches named their Genesee home Belvidere: a beautiful view.

After so much loss, they were looking forward. It was a new century, in a still-new country, of which a new generation was starting to take the reins. New ideas were being made—Philip already had ideas for a canal system. In the Seneca language, the name *Genesee* means "pleasant valley," but to those who spoke English and French, it resonated with the word *genesis*.

Of course, the Country of Angelica was no paradise, and the coming settlers—the Churches very much included—would perpetrate an array of sins that were anything but original. But paradise was never the point, as happiness was never the point. The point was the pursuit. Angelica had modeled idealized versions of that happiness—what Thomas Jefferson had called "those scenes for which alone my heart was made"—with the same studied attention as Maria Cosway had painted idealized allegories and John Trumbull had painted idealized histories. She was a conductor of relationships, a conduit, a river—fluid and fluent.

Angelica recommended leaving mature trees and natural lines. She recommended symmetry, buildings of substance and plainness. She was, once again, "country-mad." She wanted to build a riverside villa of her own that she would call Triana, after herself, Anna-Matilda, and her granddaughter, Angelica, and invoking the Petit Trianon, the onetime garden château where the late queen Marie-Antoinette escaped the formality of court life. As Americans began moving westward, they attempted again in each future town to form a more ideal place, carrying with them what they loved of the past—a piano, or the knowledge of French cooking, a cutting from a favorite apple tree—reinventing and refining the rest, trying to do a little better with each generation.

As for Angelica, she contributed what she could to the grand endeavor. Much of it was immeasurable. Peace has no victors. She was like the light in the room—the lux. So it was Josephine du Pont, whose family would also settle for a time on the Genesee, who summed Angelica up best one summer's end: "After having metamorphosed for a moment our forest, bringing transiently all the refinements of luxury, and agreeable company, Madame Church leaves us."

In fact, Angelica would live eight more years and through another war. Naval battles would be fought on Lake Ontario. Her son Jack, who would settle on that lake and had his father's North Sea love of ships, may have participated. The Seneca from Caneadea would offer to post a guard at Belvidere, where Anna-Matilda and her children lived alone—Phil Church was in England when the war broke out and could not return. Angelica would die in 1814, in New York, on a cold March night glittering with light snow, shortly after returning home from a journey.

For all she had done to help create a country with a government for the people and by the people, Angelica Church would never vote. Her daughters would never vote. Her granddaughters would never vote. She would never write or deliver a speech or sign a treaty or storm a barricade, although her daughter Betsy was likely the "E. Bunner" who wrote a history of Louisiana. Two of her children would choose not to live out their lives in the United States—Kitty would move her family to France, and Angelica's youngest son, Richard, would return to England with his father. In London, John Barker Church would die four years after his wife, with a scant £1,500 remaining of his past fortune. Left to his own resources, Phil Church, his mother's undeserving favorite, would come to lord over his small dominion with such haughtiness that the French families that settled in the miniature Paris called Angelica would abandon their plans and move on: A contingent of settlers would leave the Genesee River in New York and migrate westward to form Genesee County, in Michigan Territory. One month after his mother "completed her career" and was interred in the Livingston crypt at Trinity Church, Captain Church raised eyebrows: "The etiquette of mourning does not seem to torment him," remarked one woman who saw him, "strolling all over the streets of New York wearing blue buttons and a yellow waistcoat."

Of course, Phil would live out his life in the country of Angelica and never outshine his mother, no matter how much yellow he wore. Few of his generation would have their parents' chance at glory and fame, but they had their role to play. After all, it fell to them to preserve and tell their parents' stories, to craft all that had happened into history, to create the country's first origin stories. To his credit, where others culled women's words and relied upon familiar narratives of heroism and male greatness, Philip Church would keep not only the dueling pistols and the grand house overlooking the river, but all his mother's letters.

As for Angelica's own accomplishments, absent any measure for women's contributions, they are immeasurable, save for her indelible presence in the record, an impression too strong to fade with time.

ACKNOWLEDGMENTS

My first debt of gratitude is to Angelica, New York, the history-obsessed town that raised me and made this project possible. Specifically, I am grateful to the Angelica Free Library and Colonial Rooms, the Angelica Boosters, the Crooked Door, and our many local historians, past and present: Bob Dorsey, Rob Chamberlain, Rebecca Budinger-Mulhearn, Maria Farina, Charles Fleming, Doris Feldbauer, and others. I am especially thankful to Pam and Don Fredeen of Villa Belvidere, for welcoming me (and my scanners) into your home, and for the tremendous, multigenerational work you do safeguarding history.

To all the public and private historians, archivists, docents, and curators who tend the material history for the future so that it survives for reinterpretation by future thinkers. Especially helpful to this project were librarians and archivists at the Hagley Library, the Beinecke Library, the New-York Historical Society, the Hobart and William Smith Library, the Connecticut Historical Society, the Dolph Briscoe Center for American History, the University of Virginia Library, and, nearest and dearest to me, Clements Library at the University of Michigan.

For funding and support, I am indebted to the Institute for Research on Women and Gender at the University of Michigan and to the Ragdale Foundation, the Vermont Studio Center, and the Rockvale Writers' Colony, for providing essential time and space to think and write in the light of day, not just the predawn hours peripheral to teaching and parenting.

Thank you to my writing mentors—Brian Hall, David Dunaway, Diane Thiel, Gregory Martin, Jennifer Brice, Joy Harjo, Peter Balakian, and others—for putting me on the path. And to my nonfiction writing students at the University of New Mexico, Colgate University, Scripps College, and the University of Michigan, for stoking my faith in word-work. And to my colleagues at the once-great *Vela Magazine*, with whom I honed my intention of writing women into our collective sensemaking story. Individual thanks are due to my brilliant colleague Laura Sewell Matter, for moral, intellectual, and editorial advice; to my research assistant, Delaney Jorgensen, for going any distance; and to Amy Butcher, Dana Salvador, Kathleen Brendes, Olivia Long, Trish O'Connor, YJ Wang, and countless others, for their assistance at critical moments of this process. On the publishing end, thank you to my agent, Samantha Shea; my copyeditor, Kathleen Brendes; and especially to my editor, Alane Salierno Mason, who provided unsolicited support when this project was in the earliest stages, and I was badly in need of a navigational beacon.

Most importantly, I am thankful to my family, without whom this book would not exist: To my father and mother, Sam and Lucia, who tended the plants and animals and children and ghosts of past residents who populated our farm in Angelica, New York, with a free and wild love. To my in-laws, John and Glynda, who help us stay sane. To my extended family—Jill, Scoby, Lois and Avery, Audrey and Jamie, Lindsey and Amy, and Jennie and André—whose advice and support is precious to me. And finally, to my siblings, Stephanie and Clayton, and our summer-sister Laura; and to my partner, Steven, and our children, Avery, Winslow, and Robin: Thank you all for sharing the journey.

NOTES

Abbreviations

CTHS   Connecticut Historical Society
FA   Founders Archive
LOC   Library of Congress
MAHS   Massachusetts Historical Society
NYHS   New-York Historical Society
NYPL   New York Public Library
UVAL   University of Virginia Library
GLIAH   Gilder Lehrman Institute of American History

Chapter 1: Engeltje, 1755–1756

3 **"In hett Jaar 1755"**: Don Gerlach, *Philip Schuyler and the American Revolution in New York* (Lincoln: University of Nebraska Press, 1964), p. 18.

3 **Where Henry Hudson's**: Janny Venema, *Beverwijck* (Albany: State University of New York, 2003), p. 35; Oscar Williams, "Slavery in Albany, New York, 1624–1827," *Afro-Americans in New York Life and History* 34, no. 2 (2010), pp. 154–68.

5 **By local standards**: "Loudoun's Enquiry," Huntington Library; Peter Kalm, *Travels in North America*, vol. II, trans. Johann Reinhold Forster (London: T. Lowndes, 1771), p. 267.

6 **Waffles, crullers**: Peter G. Rose and Gysbert de Groot, *The Sensible Cook/De Verstandige Kock* (Syracuse, NY: Syracuse University Press, 1989).

7 **One colonial pamphleteer**: Cotton Mather, "Elizabeth in Her Holy Retirement" (Boston: B. Greene for Nicholas Boone, 1710).

7 **In his recent pamphlet**: Benjamin Franklin, *Observations Concerning the Increase of Mankind* (Tarrytown, NY: Repr., W. Abbatt, 1918).

7 **Catharina's mother-in-law, Cornelia**: Mary Gay Humphries, *Catherine Schuyler* (New York: Charles Scribner's Sons, 1897).

7 **In that year alone**: Reformed Dutch Church of Albany (NY), *Records, 1683–1809*, database by David Pane-Joyce (Year Books of the Holland Society of New York).

7 **They died of infections:** Charles L. Fisher et al., "Privies and Parasites: The Archaeology of Health Conditions in Albany, New York," *Historical Archaeology* 41 (2007).

7 **As for mothers:** "The Book of Burials of the Reformed Protestant Dutch Church of Albany," in *The Annals of Albany*, VI, ed. by Joel Munsell (Albany: J. Munsell, 1869).

7 **Guiding a woman's:** Thomas Chamberlayne et al., *The Compleat Midwife's Practice Enlarged* (London: R. Bentley, 1697).

8 **As for midwifery:** Catherine M. Scholten, *Childbearing in American Society: 1650–1850* (New York: New York University Press, 1985), pp. 16–17.

8 **But an experienced midwife:** Catherine M. Scholten, *Childbearing in American Society: 1650–1850* (New York: New York University Press, 1985), p. 26.

8 ***"In hett Jaar 1756":*** Schuyler Family Bible (Schuyler Mansion Historical Site).

8 **It was a book:** Janny Venema, *Kiliaen van Rensselaer: Designing a New World* (Albany, NY: SUNY Press, 2011).

9 **All that year:** Ron Chernow, *Washington* (New York: Penguin Books, 2011), p. 45.

Chapter 2: A Colonial Girl

10 **"the Quibbles":** *Military Affairs in North America, 1748–1765*, ed. Stanley Pargellis (London: D. Appleton-Century Company, 1936), p. 223.

11 **There was the sense:** Elizabeth M. Covart, "The American Revolution Comes to Albany, New York, 1756–1776," *Journal of the American Revolution* (2014).

11 **Soon the Schuylers:** Schuyler Mansion Tour. Ian Mumpton, Docent. 2019.

12 **A transatlantic voyage:** Stefan Bielinski, "Theodorus Frelinghuysen, Jr." *People of Colonial Albany* [database], New York State Museum.

12 **Planks and beams:** "Schuyler Mansion: A Historic Structure Report" (State of New York, 1977).

12 **The Schuylers' new house:** For more on early settlement of Albany, see Janny Venema, *Beverwijck* (Albany: State University of New York, 2003); for New Netherland, see Russell Shorto, *The Island at the Center of the World* (New York: Doubleday, 2004).

14 **At the end of July:** Susan L. May, "Catherine Schuyler: The Study of an Individual for the Understanding of an Era" (National Park Services, 1983).

14 **Fortunately, there were gifts:** "Schuyler Mansion: A Historic Structure Report" (State of New York, 1977).

15 **The sisters left:** Philip Schuyler, "Account Book for 5 March 1764," in Susan L. May, "Catherine Schuyler: The Study of an Individual for the Understanding of an Era" (National Park Services, 1983).

16 **The Schuylers stayed:** William Smith, Jr., "Letter to Philip Schuyler, 8 August 1764," NYPL.

16 **Days after the sisters:** [Advertisement], *New-York Gazette*, 11 April 1763.

16 **"The young ladies":** Robert James Livingston, "Letter to Philip Schuyler, 4 March 1765," NYPL.

17 **"More to keep us quiet":** Angelica Schuyler Church, "Letter to Anne MacVicar Grant, n.d.," in Anne MacVicar Grant, *Memoirs of an American Lady*, vol. 2 (New York: Dodd, Mead & Co., 1901).

Chapter 3: The Spirit of Riots, 1766

18 **In January 1766:** Beverly McAnear, "The Albany Stamp Act Riots," *William and Mary Quarterly* 4 (1947); "Albany, January 8th, 1766," *New-York Mercury*, no. 744 (27 January 1766), p. 2.

18 **Most of Albany's:** "Constitution of the Sons of Liberty of Albany" (New York State Museum, c. 1766).

18 **To Engeltje, enslavement:** Anne MacVicar Grant, *Memoirs of an American Lady* (New York: D. Appleton & Co., 1846), p. 35.

18 **When the mob:** Beverly McAnear, "The Albany Stamp Act Riots," *William and Mary Quarterly* 4 (1947); "Albany, January 8th, 1766," *New-York Mercury*, no. 744 (27 January 1766), p. 2.

19 **Instead of Philip Schuyler:** Ibid.

20 **Typically, Albany children:** Peter G. Rose and Gysbert de Groot, *The Sensible Cook (De Verstandige Kock, 1683): Dutch Foodways in the Old and the New World* (Syracuse, NY: Syracuse University Press, 1989).

20 **In late April:** Sung Bok Kim, *Landlord and Tenant in Colonial New York: Manorial Society, 1664–1775* (Chapel Hill: University of North Carolina Press, 1978).

20 **The crisis was:** Ibid.; Charles Carroll, *Journal of Charles Carroll of Carrollton* (Baltimore: Printed by John Murphy for the Maryland Historical Society, 1876).

21 **Philip Schuyler considered:** Don Gerlach, *Philip Schuyler and the American Revolution in New York, 1733–1777* (Lincoln: University of Nebraska Press, 1964), p. xvii.

21 **By March, evictions:** James Montresor and John Montresor, *The Montresor Journals*, G. D. Scull (New York, NYHS, 1881), p. 375; Sung Bok Kim, *Landlord and Tenant in Colonial New York: Manorial Society, 1664–1775* (Chapel Hill: University of North Carolina Press, 1978), pp. 381–96; Irving Mark, "Agrarian Revolt in Colonial New York, 1766," *American Journal of Economics and Sociology* 1, no. 2 (1942), pp. 111–42.

21 **The week of Pinkster:** A. J. Williams-Myers, *Long Hammering: Essays on the Forging of an African American presence in the Hudson River Valley* (Trenton, NJ: Africa World Press, 1994), pp. 87–97.

22 **Now he reported:** Thomas Gage, "Letter to Sec. of State Conway, 6 May 1766," Clements Library, University of Michigan.

22 **Years before the anti-rent:** Sung Bok Kim, *Landlord and Tenant in Colonial New York* (Chapel Hill: University of North Carolina Press, 1978), pp. 357, 394–400.

23 **General Gage immediately:** Ibid., pp. 399–400.

23 **By summer's end:** "The Following is a Copy of the Sentence Passed on Penderghast, Viz" (Hartford, CT, 1766), p. 3.

23 **Days after the "Leveller":** "New-York, August 18," *New-York Gazette*, no. 384 (18 August 1766), p. 3; James Montresor and John Montresor, *The Montresor Journals*, G. D. Scull (New York: NYHS, 1881), p. 385.

24 **Perhaps a steer:** Peter G. Rose and Gysbert de Groot, *The Sensible Cook (De Verstandige Kock, 1683): Dutch Foodways in the Old and the New World* (Syracuse, NY: Syracuse University Press, 1989).

24 **Far from harboring:** William Smith Jr., "Some Particulars Relative to the Life of the Late Sir [Henry] Moore [Baronet]," NYPL.

24 **Lady Catherine, like:** Edward Long, *The History of Jamaica* (London: T. Lowndes, 1774), p. 127.

24 **Governor Moore had been:** Vincent Brown, *Tacky's Revolt* (Cambridge: Harvard University Press, 2019), pp. 129–63.

24 **Instead, when he found:** James Montresor and John Montresor, *The Montresor Journals*, G. D. Scull (New York: NYHS, 1881), p. 351.

25 **When a "mob":** Ibid., p. 382.

25 **After the "Levellers'":** "New-York September 11" (Hartford, CT, 1766), p. 3.

26 **Lady Moore's adolescent:** Alexander Graydon and John S. Littell, *Memoirs of His Own Time: With Reminiscences of the Men and Events of the Revolution* (Philadelphia: Lindsay &

Blakiston, 1846), pp. 65–66; Janet Livingston Montgomery, John Ross Delafield, and David Schuyler, "Reminiscences," *Dutchess County Year Book* (1930).

26 **Lady Catherine also:** John Henry Moore, *Poetical Trifles* (Bath, UK: R. Cruttwell), 1778.

Chapter 4: The Bewilderment of Liberty: Or, a Political Education

28 **At two o'clock:** Henry Moore, "Letter to Philip Schuyler, 13 October 1766," NYPL.

29 **"They pleased everyone":** Anne MacVicar Grant, *Memoirs of an American Lady* (New York: D. Appleton & Co., 1846), p. 238.

29 **Governor Moore appointed:** Don Gerlach, *Philip Schuyler and the American Revolution in New York* (Lincoln: University of Nebraska Press, 1964), p. 174.

30 **The Schuylers' dinner guests:** Benson J. Lossing, *The Life and Times of Philip Schuyler*, vol. I (New York: Sheldon, 1872), pp. 222–23.

30 **"Men of Property":** Don Gerlach, *Philip Schuyler and the American Revolution in New York* (Lincoln: University of Nebraska Press, 1964), p. 231.

31 **Slavery in New York:** Shane White, "Slavery in New York State in the Early Republic," *Australasian Journal of American Studies* 14, no. 2 (1995), pp. 1–29.

31 **But for the labor:** Myra B. Young Armstead, *Memory and Enslavement: Schuyler House, Old Saratoga, and the Saratoga Patent in History, Historical Practice, and Historical Imagination* (National Park Service, US Department of the Interior, May 2023), pp. 47–50, 63; Anne MacVicar Grant, *Memoirs of an American Lady* (New York: D. Appleton & Co., 1846), pp. 114–16.

31 **Some great New York:** Janet Livingston Montgomery, John Ross Delafield, and David Schuyler, "Reminiscences," *Dutchess County Year Book* (1930).

33 **Then came Her Excellency:** Paul David Nelson, *William Tryon and the Course of Empire* (Chapel Hill: University of North Carolina Press, 1990), p. 8.

33 **The Tryons had not:** William Smith Jr., *Historical Memoirs of William Smith* (New York: Sabine, 1956), p. 136.

33 **New York's glamorous Janet:** Janet Livingston Montgomery, John Ross Delafield, and David Schuyler, "Reminiscences," *Dutchess County Year Book* (1930); William Tryon, *The Correspondence of William Tryon and Other Selected Papers*, William Stevens Powell 2 (North Carolina State Division of Archives and History, 1980); William Smith Jr., *Historical Memoirs of William Smith* (New York: Sabine, 1956), pp. 166–67; Katherine M. Babbitt, *Janet Montgomery: Hudson River Squire* (Monroe, NY: Library Research Associates, 1975), p. 1.

33 **Lady Gage was at once:** Janet Livingston Montgomery, John Ross Delafield, and David Schuyler, "Reminiscences," *Dutchess County Year Book* (1930).

34 **One Philadelphia newspaper:** "A Letter to Those Ladies, Whose Husbands Possess a Seat in Either House of Parliament," *Pennsylvania Gazette*, no. 2434 (16 August 1775), p. 1.

Chapter 5: The General's Daughter, 1775

39 **Angelica was newly nineteen:** New York Provincial Assembly, "Petition to His Majesty, George III," *Records of the Continental and Confederation Congresses and the Constitutional Convention*, National Archives.

39 **"On Tuesday night":** "Letter from Boston," *New-York Journal* (27 April 1775), p. 4.

40 **"Much as I love peace":** Philip Schuyler, "Letter to John Cruger, 29 April 1775," in *The Life and Times of Philip Schuyler*, ed. by Benson John Lossing (New York: Sheldon, 1775), p. 307.

40   **"It is now actually begun":** Ibid., p. 307.

41   **"Let me ask you":** George Washington, "Letter to Philip Schuyler, 24 December 1775," FA.

41   **"It would be seven":** Samuel A. Harrison and Oswald Tilghman, *Memoir of Lieut. Col. Tench Tilghman* (Albany, NY: J. Munsell, 1876), p. 96.

41   **When General Montgomery:** Janet Livingston Montgomery, John Ross Delafield, and David Schuyler, "Reminiscences," *Dutchess County Year Book* (1930); Louise Hunt and Janet Livingston Montgomery, *Biographical Notes Concerning General Richard Montgomery* (Poughkeepsie, NY: 1876).

42   **General Schuyler dispatched:** Samuel A. Harrison and Oswald Tilghman, *Memoir of Lieut. Col. Tench Tilghman* (Albany, NY: J. Munsell, 1876), pp. 89–90.

42   **One senior clan leader:** Isabel Thompson Kelsay, *Joseph Brant, 1743–1807: Man of Two Worlds* (Syracuse, NY: Syracuse University Press, 1984), pp. 150–55; Judith Gross, "Molly Brant: Textual Representations of Cultural Midwifery," *American Studies* 40 (1999), pp. 23–40; Samuel A. Harrison and Oswald Tilghman, *Memoir of Lieut. Col. Tench Tilghman* (Albany, NY: J. Munsell, 1876), p. 87.

43   **It was September:** Philip Schuyler, "Proclamation to Canadian Citizens," George Washington Papers, LOC.

43   **When Catharina Schuyler:** Susan Fenimore Cooper, "Mrs. Philip Schuyler: A Sketch," in *Worthy Women of Our First Century*, ed. by Sarah Butler Wister and Agnes Irwin (Philadelphia: J. B. Lippincott, 1877); Benjamin Franklin, "Letter to Philip Schuyler, 11 March 1776," FA; Catherine M. Scholten, *Childbearing in American Society: 1650–1850* (New York: New York University Press, 1985), p. 16.

44   **"There is such":** Richard Montgomery, "Letter to Robert R. Livingston, 5 October 1775," GLIAH.

44   **General Schuyler had written:** Philip Schuyler, "Letter to George Washington, 14 October 1775," FA.

44   **General Schuyler marched:** "General Schuyler's Account of His Expedition to Tryon County [3-part series]," *New-York Journal*, nos. 1728–1730 (15 February, 22 February, 29 February 1776).

44   **He had returned:** Philip Schuyler, "Letter to George Washington, 5–7 January 1775," FA; Reformed Dutch Church of Albany (NY), *Records, 1683–1809*, database by David Pane-Joyce (Year Books of the Holland Society of New York).

45   **These were the cannons:** Philip Schuyler, "Letter to George Washington, 5–7 January 1775," FA.

45   **General Schuyler's next letter:** Philip Schuyler, "Letter to George Washington, 13 January 1775," FA.

Chapter 6: Loyalties and Petty Treasons

46   **The week Angelica:** "Common Sense," *Connecticut Courant* (Hartford, CT), no. 578 (19 February 1776).

47   **Seventy-year-old Benjamin:** John Carroll, *The John Carroll Papers*, no. 1, ed. Thomas O'Brien Hanley (Notre Dame, IN: University of Notre Dame Press, 1976); Benjamin Franklin, "Letter to Josiah Quincy, 15 April 1776," FA.

47   **She dispatched summaries:** Angelica Schuyler, "Letter to Philip Schuyler, 4 July 1776," New York State Library Manuscripts and Special Collections.

48   **Angelica was fluent:** Angelica Schuyler, "Letter to Philip Schuyler, 4 July 1776," New York State Library Manuscripts and Special Collections.

48 **When they were girls:** Mary Gay Humphreys, *Catherine Schuyler* (New York: Charles Scribner's Sons, 1897), p. 95.

49 **Likewise, Polly Watts:** Philip Van Cortlandt. "Memoirs," in *The Van Cortlandt Family Papers*, ed. Jacob Judd (Tarrytown, NY: Sleepy Hollow Restorations, 1976), p. 31.

49 **So General Schuyler:** "General Schuyler's Account of His Expedition to Tryon County [3-part series]," New-York *Journal*, nos. 1728–1730 (15 February, 22 February, 29 February 1776).

49 **The public accused:** Philip Schuyler, "Letter to George Washington, 31 May 1776," FA.

49 **Opting not to pursue:** Philip Schuyler, "Letter to George Washington, 15 June 1776," FA.

49 **Holding a woman hostage:** Susan Griffith Colpoys [Johnson], *Adventures of a Lady in the War of Independence in America* (Workington, 1874); Mary Watts Johnson, "Letter to George Washington, 16 June 1776," FA.

50 **Angelica handled her furious:** Angelica Schuyler, "Letter to Philip Schuyler, 4 July 1776," New York State Library Manuscripts and Special Collections.

50 **She could still saddle:** William Smith, "Letter to Philip Schuyler, 9 July 1774," in *Historical Memoirs of William Smith*, ed. William H. W. Sabine (New York, 1956), p. 216.

50 **On July 4, 1776:** Angelica Schuyler, "Letter to Philip Schuyler, 4 July 1776," New York State Library Manuscripts and Special Collections.

51 **Treason, under English:** Susan Sage Heinzelman, "Women's Petty Treason: Feminism, Narrative, and the Law," *Journal of Narrative Technique* 20.2 (1990), pp. 89–106.

52 **With her white skin:** Myra B. Young Armstead, *Memory and Enslavement: Schuyler House, Old Saratoga, and the Saratoga Patent in History, Historical Practice, and Historical Imagination* (National Park Service, US Department of the Interior, May 2023); Anne MacVicar Grant, *Memoirs of an American Lady* (New York: D. Appleton & Co., 1846), p. 35.

53 **And Philip van Cortlandt:** Jacob Judd, *The Revolutionary War Memoir and Selected Correspondence of Philip Van Cortlandt* (Tarrytown, NY: Sleepy Hollow Restorations, 1976), p. 106.

54 **"Your amiable lady daughters":** Richard Varick, "Letter [draft] to Philip Schuyler, 24 November 1776," Richard Varick Papers, NYHS.

54 **"Marriages now are":** Janet Livingston Montgomery, "Letter to Perkins Magra, 25 May 1775," Clements Library, University of Michigan, Ann Arbor.

54 **Marriage was described:** Linda K. Kerber, *Women of the Republic: Intellect & Ideology in Revolutionary America* (Chapel Hill: Omohundro Institute of Early American History and Culture and University of North Carolina Press, 1980), pp. 119–36.

56 **One young officer:** John Trumbull, *Autobiography, Reminiscences and Letters of John Trumbull* (New York: Wiley and Putnam, 1841), p. 26.

57 **A few days later, Generals:** Ibid., p. 28.

Chapter 7: The Breach of the Fortress of Ticonderoga, 1777

58 **Promptly on arrival:** James Milligan, John Carter, and John Welles, "To the Public: The Commissioners Appointed," NYHS.

58 **General Schuyler welcomed:** Alexander Graydon and John S. Littell, *Memoirs of His Own Time: With Reminiscences of the Men and Events of the Revolution* (Philadelphia: Lindsay & Blakiston, 1846), pp. 143–44.

59 **To further prove:** William Duer, "Letter to Philip Schuyler, 4 September 1776," NYHS.

59 **He didn't just read:** "Subscribers," *Original poems on various subjects* (London: Cadell, 1775).

60 **When the auditors:** Horatio Gates, "Letter to John Carter, 4 October 1776," in *American Archives* 2, ed. Peter Force (Washington, DC: M. St. Clair Clarke and Peter Force, 1851).

60 **With equal arrogance:** John Carter, "Letter to Horatio Gates, 13 October 1776," in *American Archives* 2, ed. Peter Force (Washington, DC: M. St. Clair Clarke, 1851).

60 **Next, John Carter wrote:** John Carter, "Letter to Philip Schuyler, 28 October 1776," NYPL.

60 **The capture of the *Charming*:** *Journal of the Provincial Congress of the State of New York*, vol. 1 (Albany, 1842), p. 111.

61 **"The match":** Catharina V. R. Bonney, *A Legacy of Historical Gleanings* (Albany, NY: J. Munsell, 1875), p. 116.

61 **She ached:** Richard Varick, "Letter to Philip Schuyler, 29 March 1777," NYPL.

61 **From Fishkill:** *Connecticut Journal* (27 March 1777); *Massachusetts Spy* (3 April 1777); *Dunlap's Pennsylvania Packet* (29 April 1777).

62 **Meanwhile, observing:** Richard Varick, "Letter to Philip Schuyler, 26 April 1777," NYPL.

62 **In his unanswered letters:** Richard Varick, "Letters to Philip Schuyler," 16 April 1777, 21 April 1777, 26 April 1777, 12 May 1777, NYPL.

63 **"These unguarded expressions":** Ibid., 12 May 1777.

63 **What no one expected:** Enoch Poor, "Letter to Horatio Gates, 27 May 1777," FA.

63 **Horatio Gates, who had:** Horatio Gates, "Letter to George Washington, 2 June 1777," FA.

63 **A Seneca chief:** Philip Schuyler, "Letter to George Washington, 7 June 1777, Letterbook 3," NYPL.

64 **When he reached Fort Ticonderoga:** Philip Schuyler, "Letter to Gov. of Massachusetts, 14 June 1777," Letterbook 3, NYPL.

64 **On the morning of June:** William Smith, *Historical Memoirs of William Smith*, ed. William H. W. Sabine (New York, 1956), p. 164; [Joseph?] Trumbull, "Letter to His Wife, 30 June 1777 [quoted in a letter by descendant]," Philip Church Collection, Archives of Hobart and William Smith Colleges.

65 **Informing the Schuyler family:** John Carter, "Letter to Walter Livingston, 2 July 1777," NYHS.

65 **He wrote to the gentleman:** Philip Schuyler, "Letter to William Duer, 3 July 1777," in *The Life and Times of Philip Schuyler*, vol. II, ed. Benson John Lossing (New York: Sheldon Company, 1873).

65 **By July third:** William Smith, *Historical Memoirs of William Smith*, ed. William H. W. Sabine (New York, 1956), p. 171.

66 **"General Schuyler hourly":** John Carter, "Letter to James Milligan, 3 July 1777," NYHS.

66 **Philip Schuyler's old friend:** William Smith, *Historical Memoirs of William Smith*, ed. William H. W. Sabine (New York, 1956), p. 172.

66 **One year earlier:** John Trumbull, *Autobiography, Reminiscences and Letters of John Trumbull* (New York: Wiley and Putnam, 1841), pp. 31–32.

66 **Without specifying:** Richard Varick, "Letter to Philip Schuyler, 8 July 1777," Philip Schuyler Papers, NYPL.

Chapter 8: Join or Die

67 **The manager:** John Graham, "Letter to Philip Schuyler, July 6, 1777," Schuyler Papers, NYPL.

67 **Angelica's mother set off:** Henry Beekman Livingston, "Letter to Philip Schuyler, 30 July 1777," NYPL; Richard Varick, "Letter to Philip Schuyler, 14 July 1777," Philip Schuyler Papers, NYPL.

67 **People said Catharina Schuyler:** Catharine Cochrane, "Catharine Van Rensselaer/

Mrs. Philip Schuyler," in Katharine Schuyler Baxter, *Godchild of Washington* (New York: F. T. Neely, 1897), p. 395; *An Eyewitness Account of the American Revolution: The Journal of J. F. Wasmus*, trans. Helga Doblin, ed. Mary C. Lynn (Westport, CT: Greenwood Press, 1990), pp. 68–69.

68 **Some took scalps:** John Burgoyne, "General Burgoyne's Proclamation, 20 June 1777."

68 **Then a letter appeared:** Letter, *New-York Gazette and Weekly Mercury* (31 July 1777), p. 2.

68 **With each retelling:** Jeremy Engels and Greg Goodale, "'Our Battle Cry Will Be: Remember Jenny McCrea!' A Précis on the Rhetoric of Revenge," *American Quarterly* 61 (March 2009), pp. 93–112.

68 **Neither Janey McRea's:** Henry Beekman Livingston, "Letter to Philip Schuyler, 30 July 1777," NYPL.

68 **"She is a young housekeeper":** John Carter, "Letter to James Milligan, 7 August 1777," NYHS.

68 **William Smith recorded:** William Smith, *Historical Memoirs of William Smith*, ed. William H. W. Sabine (New York, 1956), p. 203.

69 **Some were calling:** John S. Pancake, *1777: The Year of the Hangman* (Tuscaloosa: University of Alabama Press, 1977).

70 **One visitor wrote:** Thomas Anburey, *Travels through the Interior Parts of America, by Thomas Anburey, Lieutenant in the Army of General Burgoyne*, vol. II (Boston: Houghton Mifflin, 1923), p. 41.

70 **Before the war began:** Don Gerlach, *Philip Schuyler and the American Revolution in New York* (Lincoln: University of Nebraska Press, 1964), p. 126.

70 **The residual animosity:** James Thacher, MD, *The American Revolution . . . Given in the Form of a Daily Journal* (Hartford, CT: Hurlbut, Kellogg & Co., 1861), p. 86.

Chapter 9: The Maiden Voyage of the *Angelica*

72 **The British soldiers had felled:** William Wood, "A View of the Country Round Boston, Taken from Beacon Hill [*ink and watercolor*]" (MASH Collections, c. 1775).

73 **From this vantage point, Angelica:** Samuel Adams Drake, *Historic Mansions and Highways Around Boston* (Boston: Little, Brown, 1899).

73 **During the siege, an artillery shell:** Samuel Breck, *Recollections of Samuel Breck* (Philadelphia: Porter & Coates, 1877), p. 18.

74 **Shortly after John:** Robert H. Patton, *Patriot Pirates: The Privateer War for Freedom and Fortune in the American Revolution* (New York: Pantheon Books, 2008), p. 27.

74 **Stories spread:** Ibid., p. 169.

74 **Butter, candles:** Lucy Knox, "Letter to Henry Knox, May 1777," GLIAH.

74 **Want of money:** Benjamin Franklin, Benjamin Harrison, and Robert Morris, "The Committee of Secret Correspondence to Silas Deane, 7 August 1776," FA.

74 **General Washington was more conflicted:** W. Laird Clowes et al., *The Royal Navy: A History from the Earliest Times to 1900*, vol. 4 (London: Sampson, Marston and Company, 1899), p. 3; Michael Crawford, "The Privateering Debate in Revolutionary America," *The Northern Mariner/le marin du nord* 21:3 (July 2011); Gardner Weld Allen, *Massachusetts Privateers of the Revolution* (Boston: The MASH, 1927).

75 **Many Boston women:** Sharon Block, "Rape without Women: Print Culture and the Politicization of Rape, 1765–1815," *Journal of American History* 89, no. 3 (2002), pp. 849–68.

76 **If anything delayed:** Lucy Knox, "Letter to Henry Knox, 23 August 1777," GLIAH.

76 **"When the price":** Lucy Knox, "Letter to Henry Knox, May 1777," GLIAH; Lucy Knox, "Letter to Henry Knox, 28 August 1777," in *The Revolutionary War Lives and Letters of*

Lucy and Henry Knox, ed. Phillip Hamilton (Baltimore: Johns Hopkins University Press, 2017), p. 122.

76 **"I can see":** Henry Knox, "Letter to Lucy Knox, 12 August 1777," GLIAH.

76 **First, Lucy Knox backed:** Sara T. Damiano, "Writing Women's History Through the Revolution: Family Finances, Letter Writing, and Conceptions of Marriage," *William and Mary Quarterly* 74, no. 4, Omohundro Institute of Early American History and Culture (2017), pp. 697–728; Lucy Knox, "Letter to Henry Knox, 25 October 1777," Clements Library, University of Michigan, Ann Arbor.

76 **That fall, the Carters:** Richard Elliott Winslow, *Wealth and Honor: Portsmouth During the Golden Age of Privateering, 1775–1815* (Portsmouth, NH: Portsmouth Marine Society, 1988), p. 35.

77 **The following week, a second:** William Heath, *Memoirs of Major-General William Heath* (New York: William Abbatt, 1901), p. 119.

77 **Locals who observed:** Hannah Winthrop, "Letter to Mercy Warren, 11 November 1777," in *Warren-Adams Letters* (Boston: MASH, 1917).

78 **These women were:** Louise Hall Tharp, *The Baroness and the General* (Boston: Little, Brown, 1962), p. 263.

78 **The revelry celebrating:** *Letters from America, 1776–1779,* trans. Ray W. Pettengill (Port Washington, NY: Kennikat Press 1924), p. 132.

78 **For another, although:** Friederike Riedesel, *Baroness von Riedesel and the American Revolution; Journal and Correspondence of a Tour of Duty, 1776–1783,* ed. Marvin L. Brown (Chapel Hill: Omohundro Institute of Early American History and Culture and University of North Carolina Press, 1965), p. 56.

78 **Her father had excused:** Ibid., p. 65.

78 **Her mother and Peggy:** John Lansing, "Letter to Philip Schuyler, 24 October 1777," in Susan L. May, "Catherine Schuyler: The Study of an Individual for the Understanding of an Era" (National Park Service, 1983).

79 **Called "Mrs. General":** Friederike Riedesel, *Baroness von Riedesel and the American Revolution; Journal and Correspondence of a Tour of Duty, 1776–1783* (Chapel Hill: Omohundro Institute of Early American History and Culture and University of North Carolina Press, 1965), pp. xxxii–lii.

79 **Prominent American women:** Anne Home Shippen Livingston, *Nancy Shippen, Her Journal Book,* ed. Ethel Armes (Philadelphia: J. B. Lippincott Company, 1935), pp. 116–17.

80 **Mrs. General admired:** Ibid., p. 70

80 **In January 1778, despite:** Richard Elliott Winslow, *Wealth and Honor: Portsmouth During the Golden Age of Privateering, 1775–1815* (Portsmouth, NH: Portsmouth Marine Society, 1988), p. 35.

80 **The fire started:** *Continental Journal* (Boston) 87 (22 January 1778).

82 **After the loss:** Henry Knox, "Letter to Lucy Knox, 13 July 1777," GLIAH.

82 **The so-called "Conway Affair":** William Alexander Stirling, "Letter to George Washington, 3 November 1777," FA.

82 **John Carter was delighted:** The Treasury Commissioners had had their own conflict with General Gates. See John Carter, "Letter to James Milligan, 7 August 1777," NYHS.

82 **"How strange":** John Carter, "Letter to Richard Varick, 11 March 1778," NYHS.

83 **Betsy had been recalled:** John Carter, "Letter to Richard Varick, 11 March 1778," NYHS.

83 **Even John was often:** John Carter, "Letter to Richard Varick, 11 March 1778," NYHS.

83 **"To all Gentlemen":** [Advertisement], *Norwich Packet,* 13 April 1778.

83 **Fresh off her stocks:** Thomas Greenleaf, "Letter to John Adams, 16 July 1778," MAHS;

Naval Documents of the American Revolution XIII (Washington, DC, Department of the US Navy, 2019), p. 56.

83 **Only after Philip was born:** "Baptisms," *The Records of Trinity Church, Boston, 1728–1830*, vol. lvi (Boston: The Colonial Society of Massachusetts, 1982), p. 578.

84 **As a gift:** Adam Babcock, "Letter to Archibald Langdon, 8 May 1778," Portsmouth Athenaeum, Portsmouth, NH.

84 **The Carters' enslaved:** Alexander Hamilton, "Letter to John Chaloner, 11 November 1784," FA.

84 **On the third of June:** Friederike Riedesel, *Baroness von Riedesel and the American Revolution; Journal and Correspondence of a Tour of Duty, 1776–1783* (Chapel Hill: University of North Carolina Press, 1965), pp. 71–72.

84 **Only John Carter:** John Langdon, "Letter to Josiah Bartlett, 20 June 1778," in *Naval Documents of the American Revolution* XIII (Washington, DC, Department of the US Navy, 2019), pp. 161, 297; *New-York Gazette and Weekly Mercury*, 1 June 1778.

84 **"Even the Carters":** Friederike Riedesel, *Baroness von Riedesel and the American Revolution; Journal and Correspondence of a Tour of Duty, 1776–1783* (Chapel Hill: University of North Carolina Press, 1965), pp. 71–72.

85 **Two weeks out:** Jeremiah Peirce, "Letter to Benjamin Franklin, 8 June 1779," FA; [Andromeda and Angelica], *Gentlemen's Magazine*, 1778, p. 330.

Chapter 10: Independency and Happiness, 1778–1779

86 **Their escort:** John Lansing, "Letter to Philip Schuyler, 10 June 1778," NYPL.

86 **Newly a mother:** Philip Schuyler, "Letter to Governor Clinton, 29 May 1778 (Letterbook 3)," Schuyler Papers, NYPL.

87 **Powerful British:** Thomas Hutchinson, "Strictures upon the Declaration of the Congress at Philadelphia," London, 1776.

88 **"The common Felicity":** William Smith, "Letter to Philip Schuyler, 28 July 1778," *Historical Memoirs of William Smith*, ed. William H. W. Sabine (New York, 1956).

88 **As for Janet Smith's:** Ibid.

88 **their acquaintance Tadeusz Kosciuszko:** Tadeusz Kosciuszko, "To The Public," *Continental Journal & Weekly Advertiser* (12 November 1778).

89 **"As Col. Kosciuszko":** John Carter, "From New-York Packet [Reprint]," *Boston Evening Post* (17 October 1778).

89 **Killing a man:** Stephen Banks, *A Polite Exchange of Bullets: The Duel and the English Gentleman, 1750–1850* (Woodbridge, UK: Boydell Press, 2010).

90 **Rather than risk charges:** Paul David Nelson, *General Horatio Gates* (Baton Rouge: Louisiana State University Press, 1976), pp. 196–97.

90 **This outburst:** John Cochran, "Letter to Philip Schuyler, 19 January 1779," Schuyler Papers, NYPL.

91 **He promised George Washington:** Philip Schuyler, "Letter to George Washington, 27 December 1778," FA.

92 **Philip Schuyler answered:** Philip Schuyler, "Letter to George Washington, 30 November 1778," FA.

92 **To "supercede":** Philip Schuyler, "Letter to George Washington, 1 March 1779," FA.

92 **From June to October:** George Washington, "Letter to John Sullivan, 31 May 1779," FA.

92 **The "extirpation":** Isabel Thompson Kelsay, *Joseph Brant, 1743–1807: A Man of Two Worlds* (Syracuse, NY: Syracuse University Press, 1984), pp. 254–67.

Chapter 11: A Change of Situation, 1780–1781

94 **"Whenever I meet":** Gilbert du Motier Lafayette, "Letter to John Cochran, 10 June 1779," in *Lafayette in the Age of the American Revolution: Selected Letters and Papers, 1776–1790*, eds. Stanley Idzerda and Linda Pike (Ithaca, NY: Cornell University Press, 1981).

95 **As for Boston:** Fitz-Henry Smith Jr., *The French at Boston During the Revolution* (Boston, 1913), pp. 35–37.

95 **When Samuel and Hannah:** Samuel Breck, *Recollections of Samuel Breck* (Philadelphia: Porter & Coates, 1877), pp. 25–26.

96 **Bostonians were:** Daniel Tillinghast, "Letter to George Washington, 28 June 1780," LOC.

96 **His store:** "Advertisement," *Independent Chronicle* (Boston), August 16, 1781.

96 **In his past:** "John Barker Church," *London Apprenticeship Abstracts, 1442–1850*, The London Archives.

97 **"The fields":** Jean-François-Louis de Clermont-Crèvecoeur, "Journal of the War in America During the Years 1780–1783," in *The American Campaigns of Rochambeau's Army*, ed. Howard C. Rice and Anne S. K. Brown (Princeton, NJ: Princeton University Press, 1972).

98 **Where the Continentals had little:** Samuel Adams Drake, *Old Landmarks and Historic Personages of Boston* (Cambridge, MA: Welch, Bigelow & Co., 1872), pp. 138–39.

98 **The French officers—men qualified:** Claude Blanchard, *The Journal of Claude Blanchard* (Albany, NY: J. Munsell, 1876).

98 **And the Abbé:** Claude Robin, *New Travels Through North America* (Boston: E. Battelle, 1784).

98 **Americans, one:** Ludwig von Closen, *Revolutionary Journal, 1780–1783* (Chapel Hill: University of North Carolina Press, 1958), p. 171.

98 **General Rochambeau, a thoughtful:** Claude Blanchard, *The Journal of Claude Blanchard* (Albany, NY: J. Munsell, 1876), p. 122.

99 **One commissary:** Ibid., p. 65.

99 **"Their singing":** Ibid., p. 62.

99 **American women, one Frenchman observed:** [Abbé] Robin, *New Travels Through North America* (Boston: E. Battelle, 1784), pp. 24–25.

100 **Angelica tried to explain:** François-Jean de Beauvoir de Chastellux, *Travels in North America* (London: Robinson, 1787), pp. 153–54.

100 **"During my stay":** Claude Blanchard, *The Journal of Claude Blanchard* (Albany, NY: Munsell, 1876), p. 50.

102 **"A European army":** Lee B. Kennett, *The French Forces in America, 1780–1783* (Westport, CT: Greenwood Press, 1977), p. 65.

102 **Soon, the Carters:** John Carter, "Letter to Jeremiah Wadsworth, 22 June 1782," and "2 April 1781," Wadsworth Papers, CTHS.

102 **Wadsworth & Carter was counting:** Benoît-Joseph [Intendant General] Tarle, "Letter to 'John Carter,' 9 December 1780," Wadsworth Papers, CTHS.

103 **"Send on":** John Carter, "Letter to Jeremiah Wadsworth, 18 November 1780," Wadsworth Papers, CTHS.

104 **Unlike her older:** Philip Schuyler, "Letter to Alexander Hamilton, 8 April 1780," LOC.

104 **"I am the happiest:"** Elizabeth Hamilton, "Letter to Margarita Schuyler, 21 January 1781," LOC.

104 **One French officer, "Lewis" Fleury:** François-Louis Fleury, "Letter to Alexander Hamilton, 20 October 1780," FA.

104 **Even Betsy's:** Elizabeth Hamilton, "Letter to Margarita Schuyler, 21 January 1781," LOC.

105 **Caty Greene, the wife:** Janet A. Stegeman and John F. Stegeman, *Caty: A Biography of Catharine Littlefield Greene* (Athens: The University of Georgia Press, 1777).

106 **No ball given:** "Ball at Newport, 1781," *New York Times* (17 August 1879).

106 **When he derided:** Alexander Hamilton, "Letter to Philip Schuyler, 18 February 1781," FA.

107 **"Long before":** Philip Schuyler, "Letter to Alexander Hamilton, 25 February 1781," FA.

107 **Their mutual friend:** François-Louis Fleury, "Letter to Alexander Hamilton, 20 October 1780," FA.

107 **On the twenty-fifth anniversary:** Reformed Dutch Church of Albany (NY), *Records, 1683–1809*, database by David Pane-Joyce (Year Books of the Holland Society of New York).

108 **"I felicitate you":** John Carter, "Letter to Jeremiah Wadsworth, 11 March 1781," Wadsworth Papers, CTHS.

Chapter 12: Home Front

109 **"I have been":** John Carter, "Letter to Alexander Hamilton, 18 May 1781," The Papers of Alexander Hamilton, LOC.

109 **He had been bled:** Philip Schuyler, "Letter to Alexander Hamilton, 30 May 1781," FA; Ethan Allen, "Letter to Philip Schuyler, 15 May 1781," FA.

110 **"This damn'd":** John Carter, "Letter to Jeremiah Wadsworth, 20 June 1781," CTHS.

110 **At least his exertions:** Alexander Hamilton, "Letter to Elizabeth Hamilton, 10 July 1781," FA.

110 **In an ordinary:** John McKinstry, "Letter to Philip Schuyler, 5 August 1781," Schuyler Papers, NYPL.

110 **Then, during dinner:** "Poughkeepsie, 13 August 1781," Connecticut *Intelligencer* (New London, CT, 1781), p. 2.

111 **Captain John Walden Mayers:** Mary Beacock Fryer, *Loyalist Spy: The Experiences of Captain John Walden Meyers During the American Revolution* (Brockville, ON: Besancourt, 1974), pp. 1–2.

111 **"Wench":** Benson John Lossing, *The Life and Times of Philip Schuyler* (New York: Sheldon Company, 1872).

111 **"Come on":** Philip Schuyler, "Letter to George Washington, 9 August 1781," FA.

111 **The raiding party:** Mary Beacock Fryer, *Loyalist Spy: The Experiences of Captain John Walden Meyers During the American Revolution* (Brockville, ON: Besancourt, 1974), pp. 131–34.

112 **Philip Schuyler wrote immediately:** Don Gerlach, *Proud Patriot: Philip Schuyler and the War of Independence* (Syracuse, NY: Syracuse University Press, 1987), p. 459.

112 **When the chaos was over:** "Poughkeepsie, 13 August 1781," Connecticut *Intelligencer* (New London, CT, 1781), p. 2.

113 **From Virginia, where the French:** Alexander Hamilton, "Letter to Elizabeth Hamilton, 12 October 1781," FA.

113 **From the Carolinas:** Nathanael Greene, "Letter to George Washington, 2 November 1781," FA.

113 **Alexander rode north:** Ron Chernow, *Alexander Hamilton* (New York: Penguin, 2005), p. 165.

113 **By mid-November:** William Heath, "Letter to Philip Schuyler, 21 November 1781," Schuyler Papers, NYPL.

113 **If Angelica and Peggy:** Ron Chernow, *Alexander Hamilton* (New York: Penguin, 2005), p. 165.

114 **A few weeks later, Alexander:** Alexander Hamilton, "Letter to Louis-Marie Noailles, December 1781," FA.

Chapter 13: Esprit de Corps

115 **From the windows:** Anne Wharton, *Martha Washington* (New York: Scribner's, 1907), pp. 140–41.

116 **Caty Greene was there:** George Washington, "Letter to Nathanael Greene, 15 December 1781," FA.

116 **The warm light:** Anne Wharton, *Martha Washington* (New York: Scribner's, 1907), p. 138.

116 **"Our success":** George Washington, "Letter to Philip Schuyler, 18 November 1781," FA.

117 **"It is an old":** George Washington, "Letter to James McHenry, 11 December 1781," FA.

117 **"People flatter":** Robert Morris, *The Papers of Robert Morris, 1781–1784*, eds. Ferguson and Catanzariti, vol. 3 (Pittsburgh: University of Pittsburgh Press, 1988); Elizabeth M. Nuxoll, "The Bank of North America and Robert Morris's Management of the Nation's First Fiscal Crisis," *Business and Economic History* 13 (1984), pp. 159–70.

117 **Nor could many:** Farley Grubb. *The Continental Dollar: How the American Revolution Was Financed with Paper Money* (Chicago: University of Chicago Press, 2023), pp. 148, 175.

118 **The proposed Bank:** "Bank of North America," *The Freeman's Journal, or the North-American Intelligencer*, 6 June 1781.

118 **Alexander Hamilton had already shared:** Alexander Hamilton, "Letter to Robert Morris, 30 April 1781," FA.

118 **But ideas meant:** John Carter, "Letter to Jeremiah Wadsworth, 11 August 1781," Wadsworth Papers, CTHS.

118 **Motivations aside:** Fritz Redlich, "The Business Leader in Theory and Reality," *The American Journal of Economics* 8 (1949).

119 **"Tis by introducing":** Alexander Hamilton, "Letter to Robert Morris, 30 April 1781," FA.

119 **"Mrs. Carter and Miss Schuyler":** George Washington, "Letter to Philip Schuyler, 8 January 1782," FA.

119 **General Washington was writing:** George Washington, *General Washington's Letters to the Marquis de Chastellux* (Charleston, SC: Sebring, 1825), p. 14.

Chapter 14: The Long Road from Yorktown, 1781–1783

121 **"We are still":** Hans Axel von Fersen, *Diary and Correspondence of Count Axel Fersen* (New York: Collier, 1902).

121 **"You cannot think":** Margarita Schuyler, "Letter to Catherine Schuyler, 5 June 1782," NYPL.

121 **John called the naval:** John Carter, "Letter to Benjamin Smith, 18 June 1782," CTHS.

122 **An early summer:** John Carter, "Letter to Elisha Abbe, 21 June 1782," CTHS.

122 **see Mary Byrd about hay:** Ami Pflugrad-Jackisch, "'What Am I but an American?': Mary Willing Byrd and Westover Plantation during the American Revolution," in *Women in the American Revolution: Gender, Politics, and the Domestic World*, ed. Barbara B. Oberg (Charlottesville: University of Virginia Press, 2019), pp. 171–91.

123 **"The children":** Claude Blanchard, *The Journal of Claude Blanchard* (Albany, NY: Munsell, 1876), p. 162.

123 **With input:** François-Jean de Beauvoir de Chastellux, *Travels in North America*, vol. 2 (London: Robinson, 1787), pp. 176–92.

125 **"What am I":** Mary Willing Byrd, "Letter to Thomas Jefferson, 28 February 1781," FA.

125 **"I consulted":** Ibid.

125 **Thomas Jefferson wrote back:** Thomas Jefferson, "Letter to Mary Byrd, 1 March 1781," FA.

126 **The sisters' Westover:** John Carter, "Letter to Jeremiah Wadsworth, 22 June 1782," CTHS.

126 **"Should we":** Ibid.

126 **Wadsworth & Carter had earned:** John Carter, "Letter to Jeremiah Wadsworth, 5 June 1782," CTHS.

127 **After agreeing:** Ibid.

127 **The first few:** Ibid.

127 **"The drought":** Hans Axel von Fersen, *Diary and Correspondence of Count Axel Fersen* (New York: Collier, 1902).

127 **For the trip:** John Carter, "Letter to John Chaloner, 10 June 1782," CTHS.

128 **"Mrs. Carter is a fine":** James McHenry, "Letter to Alexander Hamilton, 11 August 1782," FA.

128 **The French blamed:** James McHenry, "Letter to Alexander Hamilton, 11 August 1782," FA; Claude Blanchard, *The Journal of Claude Blanchard* (Albany, NY: Munsell, 1876), p. 170.

128 **When fever:** Philip Schuyler, "Letter to Angelica 'Carter,' 20 September 1782," UVAL.

129 **When John received letters:** Az Dunham, "Letter to Peter Colt, 18 Sept 1782," Wadsworth Papers, CTHS.

129 **"Few persons":** John Chaloner, "Letter to Wadsworth & Carter, 10 September 1782," Wadsworth Papers, CTHS.

129 **The morning he arrived:** John Carter, "Letter to Jeremiah Wadsworth, 23 September 1782," Wadsworth Papers, CTHS.

129 **His friend Walter:** Walter Livingston et al., "Letter to Robert Morris, 1781–1784," in *The Papers of Robert Morris* (Pittsburgh: University of Pittsburgh Press, 1988).

130 **By reputation, Robert Morris:** Elizabeth M. Nuxoll, "The Bank of North America and Robert Morris's Management of the Nation's First Fiscal Crisis," *Business and Economic History* 13 (1984), pp. 159–70.

130 **"Money I have none":** Robert Morris, "Diary Entry for 18 September 1782," in *The Papers of Robert Morris,* ed. John Catanzariti (Pittsburgh: University of Pittsburgh Press, 1988).

130 **"We have lately":** Ibid.

131 **As John fretted:** John Carter, "Letter to Jeremiah Wadsworth, 29 September 1782," Wadsworth Papers, CTHS.

131 **"Mrs. Carter is weak":** Philip Schuyler, "Letter to Elizabeth Hamilton, 2 December 1782," Schuyler Papers, NYPL.

132 **Their new privateer:** John Carter, "Letter to Jeremiah Wadsworth, 5 June 1783," CTHS; Philip Chadwick Foster Smith, *The Empress of China* (Philadelphia: Philadelphia Maritime Museum, 1984).

132 **When this news:** John Carter, "Letter to Jeremiah Wadsworth, 23 March 1783," CTHS.

132 **First, John sold:** John Carter, "Letter to Jeremiah Wadsworth, 4 June 1783," CTHS;

Philip Chadwick Foster Smith, *The Empress of China* (Philadelphia: Philadelphia Maritime Museum, 1984).

132 **"I doubt not":** John Carter, "Letter to Jeremiah Wadsworth, 5 June 1783," CTHS.

132 **As for Ben, Angelica:** Alexander Hamilton, "Letter to John Chaloner, 11 November 1784," and John Chaloner, "Letter to Alexander Hamilton, 25 November 1784," FA.

133 **On the eve of the Washingtons' arrival:** Philip Schuyler, "Letter to Stephen van Rensselaer, 13 July 1783," NYPL.

133 **"Must she":** Angelica Church, "Letter to Elizabeth Hamilton, 11 December 1794," LOC.

Chapter 15: *Siècle des Lumières*/The Age of Enlightenment, 1783

137 **In the summer of 1783:** Benjamin Franklin, "Meteorological Imaginations and Conjectures," *Memoirs of the Literary and Philosophical Society of Manchester* 2 (Manchester, UK, 1785).

137 **Even after eight:** Angelica Church, "Letter to Elizabeth Hamilton, 9 July 1796," LOC.

138 **To Benjamin Franklin, they:** Philip Schuyler, "Letter to Benjamin Franklin, 1 July 1783," FA.

138 **Summoned from his post:** Philip Schuyler, "Letter to John Jay, 1 July 1783," FA.

138 **Angelica needed no letters:** Gilbert du Motier Lafayette, "Letter to Jeremiah Wadsworth, 28 September 1783," in *Lafayette in the Age of the American Revolution*, ed. Stanley Idzerda and Linda Pike (Ithaca, NY: Cornell University Press, 1981).

139 **Art, theater, education:** Angelica Church, "Letter to Thomas Jefferson, 27 April 1802," LOC.

139 **At dinners, gentlemen:** Caroline Weber, *Queen of Fashion: What Marie Antoinette Wore to the Revolution* (New York: Henry Holt, 2006).

140 **At seventy-seven:** Angelica Schuyler, "Letter to Elizabeth Hamilton, 29 January 1784," LOC.

140 **The Jays also:** Ibid.

140 **Sarah, her husband:** Sarah Livingston Jay and John Jay, *Selected Letters of John Jay and Sarah Livingston Jay*, ed. Landa Freeman, Louise North, and Janet Wedge (London: McFarland & Co., 2005).

142 **"The humiliation":** Gilbert du Motier Lafayette, "Letter, 21 October 1783," in *Lafayette in the Age of the American Revolution*, ed. Stanley Idzerda and Linda Pike (Ithaca, NY: Cornell University Press, 1981), pp. 158–60.

142 **The marquis summoned:** Ibid.

142 **To the amazement:** Ibid.

142 **"Had our Revolution":** Gilbert du Motier Lafayette, "Letter to Jeremiah Wadsworth, 7 March 1784," in *Lafayette in the Age of the American Revolution*, ed. Stanley Idzerda and Linda Pike (Ithaca, NY: Cornell University Press, 1981), pp. 200–201.

142 **"Perhaps you had better":** John Jay, "Letter to Sarah Livingston Jay, 26 October 1783," in *Selected Papers of John Jay*, vol. 3, ed. Elizabeth M. Nuxoll (Charlottesville: University of Virginia Press, 2013).

143 **This was no longer:** "List of Bankrupts from the London *Gazette*" 55 (London, 1784).

143 **Either Temple Franklin:** Sarah Livingston Jay, "Letter to John Jay, 6 November 1783," in *Selected Letters of John Jay and Sarah Livingston Jay*, ed. Landa Freeman et al. (London: McFarland & Co, 2005).

144 **Sarah was uncomfortable:** Ibid.

144 **Three years earlier, after:** Sarah Livingston Jay, "Letter to Susannah French

Livingston, 28 August 1780," in *Selected Letters of John Jay and Sarah Livingston Jay*, ed. Landa Freeman et al. (London: McFarland & Co., 2005).

144 **The thirteenth and final:** Sarah Livingston Jay, "Letter to Kitty Livingston, 16 July 1783," in *Selected Letters of John Jay and Sarah Livingston Jay*, ed. Landa Freeman et al. (London: McFarland & Co., 2005).

144 **John Jay sent:** John Jay, "Letter to Sarah Livingston Jay, 23 November 1783," in *The Selected Papers of John Jay*, vol. 3, ed. Elizabeth M. Nuxoll (Charlottesville: University of Virginia Press, 2013).

144 **At La Muette:** Sarah Livingston Jay, "Letter to John Jay, 27 November 1783," in Ibid.

145 **In a letter in which:** Sarah Livingston Jay, "Letter to John Jay, 11 December 1783," FA.

145 **"I granted her":** Sarah Livingston Jay, "Letter to John Jay, 7 December 1783," FA.

145 **Days after Abbe:** Sarah Livingston Jay, "Letter to John Jay, 11 December 1783," FA.

145 **In Paris, there were:** Gilbert du Motier Lafayette, "Letter to Henry Knox, 8 January 1784," GLIAH.

145 **Angelica wrote home:** Angelica Church, "Letter to Elizabeth Hamilton, 27 January 1784," LOC.

146 **The United States was now independent:** Dael A. Norwood, "The Constitutional Consequences of Commercial Crisis: The Role of Trade Reconsidered in the 'Critical Period'," *Early American Studies* 18 (2020), pp. 490–524.

146 **Silk was the first:** Gilbert du Motier Lafayette, "Letter to Charles-Alexandre de Calonne, 31 January 1784," in *Lafayette in the Age of the American Revolution*, ed. Stanley Idzerda and Linda Pike (Ithaca, NY: Cornell University Press, 1981).

Chapter 16: Social Fabric

148 **This had happened:** John Russel, *A Second Journal of John Russel, Esq; Consul-General in Barbary* (Royal-Exchange, UK: Henry Whitridge, 1745); John H. Appleby, "Joshua Reynolds's Portrait of John Barker," *Metropolitan Museum Journal* 41 (2006), pp. 133–39.

148 **Had she known:** William Finch Crisp, *Chronological Retrospect of the History of Yarmouth* (Great Yarmouth, UK: 1877), p. 38.

148 **John's father:** *London Apprenticeship Abstracts*, 1442–1850, UK National Archives; R. Campbell, *The London Tradesman: Being an Historical Account of All the Trades, Professions, Arts, Both Liberal and Mechanic now Practised in the Cities of London and Westminster* (1747), p. 282.

149 **Typically, merchant:** Adam Smith, *An Inquiry into the Nature and Causes of the Wealth of Nations* (London: W. Strahan et al., 1776), p. 221.

149 **The mantua-maker:** R. Campbell, *The London Tradesman: Being an Historical Account of All the Trades, Professions, Arts, Both Liberal and Mechanic* (1747), pp. 227, 206.

149 **Trading in cloth:** Ursula Priestley, "The Fabric of Stuffs: The Norwich Textile Industry, c. 1650–1750," *Textile History* 16 (1985).

149 **Likewise, cloth:** D. Simonton et al., *Luxury and Gender in European Towns, 1700–1914* (Oxfordshire, UK: Routledge, 2015).

149 **Once, sumptuary:** Ursula Priestley, "The Fabric of Stuffs: The Norwich Textile Industry, c. 1650–1750," *Textile History* 16 (1985).

150 **The textile industry:** Jonathan Eacott, "Making an Imperial Compromise: The Calico Acts, the Atlantic Colonies, and the Structure of the British Empire," *William and Mary Quarterly* 69 (2012), pp. 731–62.

150 **In subsequent years:** Kariann Akemi Yokota, *Unbecoming British: How Revolutionary America Became a Postcolonial Nation* (Oxford: Oxford University Press, 2011).

150 **Matilda Church was particularly:** Charles John Palmer, *The Perlustration of Great Yarmouth*, vol. 2 (Great Yarmouth, UK: G. Nall, 1872), p. 321.

151 **Their great-grandmother:** Gilbert Geis and Ivan Bunn, *A Trial of Witches* (New York: Routledge, 1997), pp. 67–70, 218.

151 **Their Puritan father:** Ibid., pp. 4, 7.

151 **And an egg:** Charles John Palmer, *The Perlustration of Great Yarmouth*, vol. 2 (Great Yarmouth, UK: G. Nall, 1872), p. 322.

151 **Despite never marrying:** "Yarmouth, 14 February," *Norfolk Chronicle*, 16 February 1805, p. 3.

Chapter 17: A Separate Peace, 1784–1785

153 **Ten times the size:** Jerry White, *A Great and Monstrous Thing* (Cambridge: Harvard University Press, 2013).

153 **Angelica's rowhouse:** *Survey of London: Volumes 29 and 30, St James Westminster,* ed. FHW Sheppard (London, 1960). British History Online.

154 **Then her old friend John:** John Trumbull, *Autobiography, Reminiscences and Letters of John Trumbull* (New York: Wiley and Putnam, 1841), pp. 22, 69; John Trumbull, "Letter to Philip Schuyler, 19 February 1780," NYPL; John Carter, "Letter to Jeremiah Wadsworth, 11 February 1783," CTHS.

155 **The painting of Phil:** Benjamin West, *Prince Octavius*, c. 1782, The Royal Collection Trust, <https://www.rct.uk/collection/401410/prince-octavius-1779-83>; John Trumbull, *Philip Church*, c. 1784.

155 **As for Angelica, Jack:** Élisabeth Vigée Le Brun, *Marie-Antoinette with a Rose*, 1783, Palace of Versailles; John Trumbull, *Angelica Church with Her Child and Servant*, c. 1784, Private Collection.

156 **The first portrait:** Mary D. Sheriff, *The Exceptional Woman: Elisabeth Vigée-Lebrun and the Cultural Politics of Art* (Chicago: University of Chicago Press, 1996), pp. 143–66.

156 **John boasted:** John Barker Church, "Letter to Alexander Hamilton, 15 June 1784," LOC.

156 **Instead, Elizabeth Church:** Gouverneur Morris, "21 March 1792," in *The Diaries of Gouverneur Morris: Digital Edition*, eds. Melanie Randolph Miller and Hendrina Krol (Charlottesville: University of Virginia Press/Rotunda, 2015).

157 **John seemed happier:** John Barker Church, "Letter to Jeremiah Wadsworth, 22 August 1785," Wadsworth Papers, CTHS.

158 **Soon, Phil would:** Henry Churchill Maxwell Lyte, *A History of Eton College, 1440–1875* (London: Macmillan, 1911).

158 **Then, in the *Morning*:** "Advertisements and Notices [Down Place]," *Morning Post* (19 October 1785).

158 **"Jack is grown":** John Barker Church, "Letter to Alexander Hamilton, 5 April 1786," FA.

159 **"I would write you":** Angelica Church, "Letter to Elizabeth Hamilton, 4 March 1786," in *The Intimate Life of Alexander Hamilton*, ed. Allan McLane Hamilton (1786).

159 **Angelica gave birth to her third:** "Richard Church," 7 August 1786, St. Michael, Bray, Berkshire Baptisms Index.

Chapter 18: A "Charming Coterie," 1786–1887

161 **Two autumns earlier:** Abigail Adams, "Letter to Elizabeth Cranch, 3 December 1784," MASH.

161 **Now and then, the Adamses:** Abigail Adams II, "Letter to John Quincy Adams, 26 August 1785" and "5 December 1785"; Abigail Adams, "Letter to John Quincy Adams, 6 September 1785," MASH.

161 **Richard Cosway was a prominent painter:** Stephen Lloyd et al., *Richard and Maria Cosway: Regency Artists of Taste and Fashion* (Edinburgh: Scottish National Portrait Gallery, 1995), p. 45.

161 **"She Colls me":** Maria Cosway, "Letter to Thomas Jefferson, 25 December 1787," FA.

161 **One London wit:** Adam Eaker, "Coxcombs and Macaronis: Fashion, Gender, and the Canon of Art History" (2023); Horace Walpole, "The Letters of Horace Walpole," vols. 15-16 (Oxford: Clarendon Press, 1903), v. 15-16, p. 431; v. 13-14, pp. 359, 445.

162 **"Staring in men's":** Samuel Johnson and James Boswell, *Dr. Johnson's Table Talk* (London: C. Dilly, 1798).

162 **Nabby Adams described:** Abigail Adams Smith, "Letter to John Quincy Adams, 30 January 1786," MASH.

162 **On their heels:** Thomas Jefferson, "Letter to Maria Cosway, 12 October 1786," FA.

163 **In Paris, Jack:** William Howard Adams, *The Paris Years of Thomas Jefferson* (New Haven, CT: Yale University Press, 1997), pp. 91, 222-27.

163 **In the light-filled:** Thomas Jefferson, "Letter to Maria Cosway, 12 October 1786," FA.

163 **Jack Trumbull would tactfully:** John Trumbull, *Autobiography, Reminiscences and Letters of John Trumbull* (New York: Wiley and Putnam, 1841), pp. 117-18.

164 **"It is an excess":** Maria Cosway, "Letter to Thomas Jefferson, 30 October 1786," FA.

164 **A month later:** Maria Cosway, "Letter to Thomas Jefferson, 17 November 1786," FA.

164 **"I am always":** Thomas Jefferson, "Letter to Maria Cosway, 24 December 1786," FA.

164 **Her baby Richard:** "Richard Church," 30 March 1787, St. Michael, Bray, Berkshire Burial Index.

165 **A mother of four:** Abigail Adams, "Letter to Thomas Jefferson, 6 July 1787," FA.

165 **Maria Cosway also:** Abigail Adams Smith, "Letter to John Quincy Adams, 30 January 1786," MASH.

166 **"If I had had confidence":** Thomas Jefferson, "Letter to Marguerite de Palerne de Corny, 30 June 1787," FA.

166 **Now it was Marguerite:** Marguerite de Palerne de Corny, "Letter to Thomas Jefferson, 9 July 1787," FA.

166 **Abigail Adams favored:** Abigail Adams, "Letter to Thomas Jefferson, 10 September 1787," FA.

167 **Even Jack Trumbull:** John Trumbull, *Autobiography, Reminiscences and Letters of John Trumbull* (New York: Wiley and Putnam, 1841), p. 5.

169 **"Have you seen yet":** Maria Cosway, "Letter to Thomas Jefferson, 25 December 1787," FA.

169 **"I never saw her before":** Thomas Jefferson, "Letter to Maria Cosway, 14 January 1788," in *My Head and My Heart: A Little History of Thomas Jefferson and Maria Cosway*, ed. Helen Duprey Bullock (New York: G. P. Putnam's Sons, 1945).

Chapter 19: Constitutional Convention, Paris, 1788

171 **"The internal Situation":** Gilbert du Motier Lafayette, "Letter to George Washington, 1 January 1788," FA.

171 **Only in the finest:** Charles Lefeuve, *Histoire de Paris, Rue par Rue, Maison par Maison* (Paris: Reinwald, 1875).

173 **"I have seen too little":** Thomas Jefferson, "Letter to Maria Cosway, 31 January 1788," FA.

173 **Angelica's Paris shopping:** Thomas Jefferson, "Letter to André Limozin, 31 December 1787," FA.

173 **"I give you free":** Maria Cosway, "Letter to Thomas Jefferson, 25 December 1787," FA.

173 **"It was not my fault":** Thomas Jefferson, "Letter to Maria Cosway, 31 January 1788," FA.

174 **He would recall:** Jan Lewis, "Those Scenes for Which Alone My Heart was Made: Affection and Politics in the Age of Jefferson and Hamilton," in *An Emotional History of the United States*, eds. Stearns and Lewis (New York, 1998), pp. 52–65; Thomas Jefferson, "Letter to Angelica Church, 7 June 1793," FA.

175 **The Marquis de Lafayette reported:** Gilbert du Motier Lafayette, "Letter to Henry Knox, 4 February 1788," GLIAH.

175 **Thomas Jefferson was the least:** Thomas Jefferson, "Letter to John Adams, 13 November 1787," FA.

175 **Anonymous no longer:** Robert Lamb, *Thomas Paine and the Idea of Human Rights* (Cambridge: Cambridge University Press, 2015), pp. 38–39.

175 **The corsetmaker:** Thomas Jefferson, "Letter to Thomas Paine, 23 December 1788," FA; Don C. Seitz, "Thomas Paine: Bridge Builder," *Virginia Quarterly Review* 3 (1927), pp. 571–84.

176 **"Ingratitude":** Thomas Paine, "Dissertatons on Government; the Affairs of the Bank; and Paper Money," in *The Writings of Thomas Paine*, vol. II, ed. Moncure Daniel Conway (New York: AMS Press, 1967), pp. 132–87.

176 **From this vantage point, his:** Gilbert du Motier Lafayette, "Letter to George Washington, 1 January 1788," FA.

176 **Angelica Church's opinions:** Alexander Hamilton, "Letter to Angelica Church, 22 January [1800]," FA.

176 **If Angelica held back:** Alexander Hamilton, John Jay and James Madison, *The Federalist*, Thomas Jefferson Library Collection, LOC Rare Book Room.

176 **"French ladies miscalculate":** Thomas Jefferson, "Letter to Angelica Church, 21 September 1788," Angelica Schuyler Church Collection, UVAL.

176 **Such limitations:** Thomas Jefferson, *Notes on the State of Virginia* (Boston: Lilly and Wait, 1832).

177 **Since coming to Paris:** Brian Steele, "Thomas Jefferson's Gender Frontier," *Journal of American History* 95, no.1 (New York: Oxford University Press, June 2008), pp. 21–22.

177 **Jack and Angelica had carried:** Abigail Adams, "Letter to Thomas Jefferson, 5 December 1787," FA.

178 **Thomas Jefferson loathed:** Thomas Jefferson, "Letter to George Washington, 4 December 1788," FA.

178 **Angelica knew better:** Angelica Church, "Letter to Thomas Jefferson, 21 July 1788," UVAL.

178 **And the diplomat:** Thomas Jefferson, "Letter to Angelica Church, 17 August 1788," FA.

178 **In Luzarches:** John Trumbull, "Letter to Thomas Jefferson, 18 February 1788," FA.

Chapter 20: Summer in New York, 1789

180 **The voyage from the British Isles:** [Shipping News], *Gazette of the United States*, 9 May 1789; [Shipping News], *Daily Advertiser*, 11 May 1789.

180 **Given the equinox:** Thomas Jefferson, "Letter to Angelica Church, 17 August 1788," UVAL.

180 **Instead, Angelica made the trip:** William Maclay, *The Journal of William Maclay* (New York: A. & C. Boni, 1927), p. 41.

181 **To his inauguration:** *The New-York Weekly Museum*, 2 May 1789; "Advertisement," *Daily Advertiser*, vol. V, no. 1310 (2 May 1789), p. 2.

182 **"Col. Beckwith":** Angelica Church, "Letter to Elizabeth Hamilton, 25 April 1788," LOC.

183 **New York's ladies:** Rufus W. Griswold, "The Republican Court; or American Society in the Days of Washington" (New York: D. Appleton, 1856), p. 155; J. P. Brissot de Warville, *New Travels in the United States of America* (London: J. S. Jordan, 1792), p. 157.

183 **For all the spectacle:** Susanna Reid, "Letter to Catherine Rutherfurd, 13 July 1789," in *Family Records and Events: Compiled Principally from the Original Manuscripts in the Rutherfurd Collection*, ed. Livingston Rutherfurd (New York: De Vinne Press, 1894).

184 **At the ball:** John Adams, "Letter to William Tudor, 9 May 1789," MASH.

184 **Thomas Jefferson had initially:** Thomas Jefferson, "Letter to Abigail Adams, 30 August 1787," FA.

184 **More recently:** Thomas Jefferson, "Letter to Angelica Church, 15 February 1789," Angelica Schuyler Church Collection, Alderman Library, University of Virginia.

184 **In code:** John Jay, "Letter to Thomas Jefferson, 25 November 1788," FA.

185 **"If France had wished":** John Armstrong, "Letter to Horatio Gates," in Rufus W. Griswold, "The Republican Court" (New York: D. Appleton, 1856), p. 93.

185 **Besides, the French ball:** Ibid., p. 157.

185 **A subsequent coded:** James Madison, "Letter to Thomas Jefferson, 27 May 1789," FA.

186 **Even their father:** Philip Schuyler, "Letter to Alexander Hamilton, 20 May 1789," FA; Alexander Hamilton, "Letter to Elizabeth Hamilton 28 May 1789]," FA.

187 **She was a favorite:** Friedrich de Steuben, "Letter to Angelica Church, 7 November 1789," trans. Peggy Gowen, Yale University Library, 1789.

187 **This "saucy" banter:** Erick Trickey, "The Prussian Nobleman Who Helped Save the American Revolution," *Smithsonian Magazine* (2017); William Benemann, *Male-Male Intimacy in Early America* (New York: Harrington Park Press, 2006).

187 **When the senator:** Philip Schuyler, "Letter to Catherine Schuyler, 29 July 1789," Schuyler Papers, NYPL.

187 **After a week's visit:** Philip Schuyler, "Letter to Catherine Schuyler, 9 August 1789," Bromeley Papers.

188 **The French minister recorded:** Eleanor Elie de Moustier, "Conversation with Comte de Moustier, 13 September 1789 [translation]," FA.

188 **The key to this:** Ibid.

189 **Thirteen days later:** "Versailles, July 16, 1789," *Daily Gazette* (New York, 1789).

189 **Via the pilot:** Angelica Church, "Letter to Alexander Hamilton, [7 November 1789]," LOC.

190 **To soothe her:** Friedrich de Steuben, "Letter to Angelica Church, 7 November 1789," trans. Peggy Gowen, Yale University Library, 1789.

190 **To Alexander she:** Angelica Church, "Letter to Alexander Hamilton, [7 November 1789]," LOC.

190 ***Mais cruelle!":*** Friedrich de Steuben, "Letter to Angelica Church, 7 November 1789," trans. Peggy Gowen, Yale University Library, 1789.

190 **Her sister Elizabeth sent:** Elizabeth Hamilton, "Letter to Angelica Church, 8 November 1789." UVAL.

Chapter 21: Head Full of Politicks, 1790–1792

191 **"I am impatient":** Angelica Church, "Letter to Alexander Hamilton, [Spring 1790]," FA.

191 **She promised the secretary:** Angelica Church, "Letter to Alexander Hamilton, 4 February 1790," FA.

191 **America had forgotten:** Angelica Church, "Letter to Alexander Hamilton, [Spring 1790]," FA.

191 **The storming of the Bastille may have been:** Thomas Jefferson, "Letter to John Jay, 19 July 1789," FA.

192 **When the committee:** Thomas Jefferson, "Letter to John Jay, 19 July 1789," FA.

192 **At Versailles, King Louis:** François Furstenberg, *When the United States Spoke French: Five Refugees Who Shaped a Nation* (New York: Penguin Press, 2014), p. 84.

193 **The Marquis Lafayette would have:** Thomas Jefferson, "Letter to Thomas Paine, 17 July 1789," FA.

193 **She returned to learn:** *The History of Parliament* (1986).

193 **Angelica had confided:** Angelica Church, "Letter to Alexander Hamilton, 2 October 1787," LOC.

193 **In response, the radical:** Charles Pigott, *The Whig Club* (London: W. Priest, 1794), p. 134.

193 **Even King George:** George III, "Letter to William Pitt, 24 June 1787," in *The Later Correspondence of George III* (Cambridge: Cambridge University Press, 1962).

194 **"You are happy":** Angelica Church, "Letter to Alexander Hamilton, 4 February 1790," LOC.

194 **Angelica likely assumed:** Gouverneur Morris, "6 September 1789," in *A Diary of the French Revolution,* ed. Beatrix Cary Davenport (Freeport, NY: Books for Libraries Press, 1971). Alternatively: *The Diaries of Gouverneur Morris: Digital Edition,* eds. Melanie Randolph Miller and Hendrina Krol (Charlottesville: University of Virginia Press/Rotunda, 2015).

194 **Irreverent, loose:** William Howard Adams, *Gouverneur Morris: An Independent Life* (New Haven, CT: Yale University Press, 2003), p. 127.

195 **At dinner, he managed:** Gouverneur Morris, "2, 4, 5, and 15 April 1790," *The Diaries of Gouverneur Morris: Digital Edition,* eds. Melanie Randolph Miller and Hendrina Krol (Charlottesville: University of Virginia Press/Rotunda, 2015).

195 **Mrs. Church said vaguely:** Ibid., "15 and 17 April 1790."

195 **There was speculation:** Ibid., "24 and 28–29 April 1790"; Jan Bondeson, *The London Monster: Terror on the Streets in 1790* (Stroud, UK: Tempus, 2005).

196 **Gouverneur Morris witnessed:** Ibid., "5 March 1790."

196 **One Loyalist refugee:** Ibid., "22 April 1790."

197 **Alas for Angelica:** Philip Schuyler, "Letter to Catharina Schuyler, 19 June 1790," Schuyler Papers, NYPL.

197 **She may have known, or guessed:** William Howard Adams, *Gouverneur Morris: An Independent Life* (New Haven, CT: Yale University Press, 2003), p. 231.

198 **"Are they men?":** Ibid., p. 161.

198 **A decade earlier, when drafting:** *Journals of the Provincial Convention . . . of the State of New York* I (Albany, NY, 1842), p. 887.

199 **She was designing:** In G. C. Williamson, *Richard Cosway, R.A.* (London: G. Bell and Sons, 1905), p. 45.

199 **"Here Friendship":** Gouverneur Morris, "28 May 1790," *The Diaries of Gouverneur Morris: Digital Edition,* eds. Melanie Randolph Miller and Hendrina Krol (Charlottesville: University of Virginia Press/Rotunda, 2015).

200 **Londoners quipped:** Hester Lynch Thrale, *Thraliana*, ed. Katharine Balderston, vol. II (Oxford: Clarendon Press, 1942), p. 875.

200 **In June, the so-called:** Ibid., p. 770.

200 **If Angelica went:** Philip Schuyler, "Letter to Angelica Church, 20 October 1790," Yale University Library; Marguerite de Palerne de Corny, "Letter to Thomas Jefferson, July 1790," FA.

200 **William Short, the American:** William Short, "Letter to Gouverneur Morris, 27 July 1790." In *The Diaries of Gouverneur Morris: Digital Edition*, eds. Melanie Randolph Miller and Hendrina Krol (Charlottesville: University of Virginia Press/Rotunda, 2015).

201 **After receiving the oath:** Serge Bokobza, "Liberty Versus Equality: The Marquis de La Fayette and France," *The French Review* (2009).

201 **"A Frenchman loves":** Gouverneur Morris, "Letter to William Short, 10 August 1790," in Ibid.

201 **Gouverneur Morris also had:** George Washington, "Letter to Gouverneur Morris, 13 October 1789," FA.

202 **Likewise, President:** George Washington, "Letter to Angelica Church, 6 February 1791," FA.

202 **Alexander seconded:** Alexander Hamilton, "Letter to Angelica Church, 31 January 1791," FA.

202 **"I wish Mr. Church":** Thomas Jefferson, "Letter to Angelica Church, 23 June 1790," FA.

203 **"You hurt my":** Alexander Hamilton, "Letter to Angelica Church [2 October 1791]," FA.

203 **In her 1792 New Year:** Angelica Church, "Letter to Elizabeth Hamilton, 3 January 1792," LOC.

203 **In February 1792:** [Births], *Gazetteer and New Daily Advertiser*, 17 February 1792.

203 **Directly across Piccadilly:** Alexander Church, baptized 10 April 1792, Westminster, London. England Births & Baptisms 1538-1975.

Chapter 22: The House on Sackville Street, 1793–1796

204 **One of the first to arrive:** François Furstenberg, *When the United States Spoke French* (New York: Penguin Press, 2014), pp. 35-37.

204 **Next to arrive:** "News." *Evening Mail*, August 31-September 2, 1791.

205 **Recently famous:** "Rapport sur L'Instruction Publique," Charles-Maurice de Talleyrand-Perigord, 1791.

205 **Whereas the younger:** Angelica Church, "Letter to Elizabeth Hamilton, 4 February 1794," LOC.

205 **One social reformer:** François Furstenberg, *When the United States Spoke French* (New York: Penguin Press, 2014), pp. 2-3.

205 **Frédéric de Liancourt had:** Frances Burney, *The Diary and Letters of Madame D'Arblay* (London: Frederick Warne and Co., 1892), p. 29.

205 **A former dancer:** Charles Pigott, *The Whig Club* (London: W. Priest, 1794), pp. 124-25; Rees Gronow, *The Reminiscences and Recollections of Captain Gronow* (John C. Nimmo, 1900), pp. 289-90.

206 **"The French are mad":** Angelica Church, "Letter to Elizabeth Hamilton, 1 January 1793," LOC.

206 **John Barker Church joined:** "Advertisement," *Morning Post and Daily Advertiser* (London), Monday, June 13, 1791.

206 **Down Place was listed:** "Advertisement," *Oracle*, 27 September 1792.

207 **By Angelica's next:** Angelica Church, "Letter to Elizabeth Hamilton, 1 January 1794" [ASC misdated this letter as 1793].

207 **She reopened:** Angelica Church, "Letter to Thomas Jefferson, 17 February 1793," FA.

207 **When the British ordered:** Angelica Church, "Letter to Samuel and Hannah Breck, 4 February 1794," NYPL; Angelica Church, "Letter to Elizabeth Hamilton, 4 February 1794," LOC.

208 **"The kindness":** Charles-Maurice de Talleyrand, "Letter to Angelica Church, 11 May 1794," trans. by the author, UVAL.

208 **Delighted to hear:** Angelica Church, "Letter to Elizabeth Hamilton, 30 July 1794," LOC.

208 **Letter by letter:** François Furstenberg, *When the United States Spoke French: Five Refugees Who Shaped a Nation* (New York: Penguin Press, 2014), pp. 186–95.

209 **She urged her sisters:** Angelica Church, "Letter to Elizabeth Hamilton, 4 February 1794," LOC.

209 **Soon, Peggy:** Caroline Moorehead, *Dancing to the Precipice: The Life of Lucie de la Tour du Pin* (New York: HarperCollins, 2009), pp. 201–2, 206.

209 **"If I remain":** Quoted in "Talleyrand," *The Atlantic* (July 1892).

209 **"Expatriation":** Quoted in François Furstenberg, *When the United States Spoke French: Five Refugees Who Shaped a Nation* (New York: Penguin Press, 2014), p. 122.

209 **"I wish they would":** Angelica Church, "Letter to Elizabeth Hamilton, 27 February 1794," NYHS.

210 **To Thomas Jefferson, Angelica:** Angelica Church, "Letter to Thomas Jefferson, 19 August 1793," LOC.

210 **General Lafayette, whose good:** Paul S. Spaulding, *Lafayette: Prisoner of State* (Columbia: University of South Carolina Press, 2010), p. 6.

210 **When Angelica heard:** Angelica Church, "Letter to Thomas Jefferson, 19 August 1793," FA.

211 **Secretary Jefferson responded:** Thomas Jefferson, "Letter to Angelica Church, 27 November 1793," FA.

211 **"The less we meddle":** Gouverneur Morris, "Letter to Thomas Pinckney, 13 September 1792," in *The Diaries of Gouverneur Morris: Digital Edition*, eds. Melanie Randolph Miller and Hendrina Krol (Charlottesville: University of Virginia Press/Rotunda, 2015).

211 **As for the British:** Paul S. Spaulding, *Lafayette: Prisoner of State* (Columbia: University of South Carolina Press, 2010), pp. 38–40.

211 **In the spring of 1794:** Erich Bollmann, "Letter to Angelica Church, 9 July 1794," UVAL.

212 **At Brünn:** Ibid.; Paul S. Spaulding, *Lafayette: Prisoner of State* (Columbia: University of South Carolina Press, 2010), pp. 84–124.

212 **When he arrived and told:** Alexander Hamilton, "Letter to George Washington, 19 January 1796," FA.

213 **"I took leave":** Philip Schuyler, "Letter to Angelica Church, 12 May 1794," UVAL.

213 **Even Charles-Maurice de Talleyrand:** Charles-Maurice de Talleyrand, "Letter to Angelica Church, 11 May 1794," trans. by the author, UVAL.

213 **Angelica reported of their arrival:** Angelica Church, "Letter to Elizabeth Hamilton, 30 July 1794," LOC.

213 **John Jay also reported:** John Jay, "Letter to Alexander Hamilton, 18 July 1794," FA.

213 **John Jay engaged:** Angelica Church, "Letter to Elizabeth Hamilton, 11 December 1794," NYHS; "Mortuary Notice," *Massachusetts Mercury* IV, no. 35 (28 October 1794), p. 3.

214 **"My Task is done":** John Jay, "Letter to Alexander Hamilton, 19 November 1794," FA.

214 **"I wrote you last":** Alexander Hamilton, "Letter to Angelica Church, 25 June 1796," FA.

215 **Angelica replied via:** Angelica Church, "Letter to Elizabeth Hamilton, 9 July 1796," LOC.

Chapter 23: The *Fair American*: 1796–1799

219 **"There is something independent":** Angelica Church, "Letter to John Bradstreet Schuyler, 1792," NYHS.

219 **An auction preview:** Advertisements and Notices. *Daily Advertiser*, 26 September 1796 (London).

219 **Charles James Fox, who owed:** Charles James Fox, "Letter to John Barker Church, 17 September 1796," in *The Perlustration of Great Yarmouth*, ed. Charles J. Palmer (Great Yarmouth, UK: G. Nall, 1872).

219 **"Mrs. Church intends":** John Quincy Adams, "Letter to Abigail Adams, 20 February 1796," FA.

220 **"If friendship is":** Angelica Church, "Letter to Alexander Hamilton [19 February 1796]," FA.

220 **Alexander replied:** Alexander Hamilton, "Letter to Angelica Church. 19 June 1796," FA.

220 **"I cannot now":** Angelica Church, "Letter to Elizabeth Hamilton, 7 August 1796," LOC.

220 **Only two years earlier:** Henriette Lucie Dillon La Tour du Pin Gouvernet, *Memoirs of Madame de La Tour du Pin* (New York: McCall, 1971); Oscar Williams, "Slavery in Albany, New York, 1624–1827," *Afro-Americans in New York Life and History* 34, no. 2 (2010), pp. 154–68.

220 **Angelica wrote: "The:** Angelica Church, "Letter to Alexander Hamilton, 20 January 1797," LOC.

221 **Six weeks into:** [New York], *Diary and Mercantile Adviser*, 22 May 1797.

221 **"Dear Madam":** Thomas Jefferson, "Letter to Angelica Church, 24 May 1797," UVAL.

222 **One young lady:** Harriet Trumbull Silliman and Maria Trumbull Hudson, *A Season in New York* (Pittsburgh: University of Pittsburgh Press, 1969).

223 **They arrived from Europe:** *A Minute Detail of the Attempt to Assassinate his Royal Higness the Duke of Cumberland* (London: J. J. Stockdale, 1810); Margaret Manigault, "Letter to Josephine du Pont, 3 August 1800," Hagley Library (Wilmington, DE) and in Betty-Bright P. Low, "Of Muslins and Merveilleuses: Excerpts from the Letters of Josephine du Pont and Margaret Manigault," *Winterthur Portfolio* 9 (1974).

223 **To supplement:** Alexander Hamilton, "Account with John Barker Church [15 June 1797]," FA.

223 **As for Ben, there had been:** Alexander Hamilton, "Letter to John Chaloner, 11 November 1784," FA.

223 **"When I can":** Angelica Church, "Letter to Elizabeth Hamilton, 9 July 1796," LOC.

223 **At first, Angelica:** Philip Schuyler, "Letter to Angelica Church, 12 May 1794," UVAL.

224 **Then a public letter:** James Thomson Callender, "To Alexander Hamilton, Esquire," *Greenleaf's New York Journal* (July 15, 1797), p. 1.

224 **"I am this Instant":** John Barker Church, "Letter to Alexander Hamilton, 13 July 1797," FA.

224 **With his brother:** David Gelston, "Account of an Interview between Alexander Hamilton and James Monroe, 11 July 1797," FA.

225 **"My real crime":** Alexander Hamilton, "Reynolds Pamphlet," 1797, FA.

225 **"Tranquillize your":** Angelica Church, "Letter to Elizabeth Hamilton, [1797]," New York State Library.

225 **Cornelia Schuyler, who has:** Massachusetts State Vital Records, 7 October 1797; *Memoir of the Life of Eliza S. M. Quincy* (Boston: J. Wilson, 1861).

225 **Rensselaer Schuyler, on the other hand:** Philip Schuyler, "Letter to Angelica Church, 7 December 1797," University of Virginia.

225 **Peggy van Rensselaer owed:** John Barker Church, "Letter to Stephen van Rensselaer, 28 August 1797," NYHS.

225 **Robert Morris hoped:** Ryan K. Smith, *Robert Morris's Folly: The Architectural and Financial Failures of an American Founder* (New Haven, CT: Yale University Press, 2014); Barbara A. Chernow, "Robert Morris: Genesee Land Speculator," *New York History* 58, no. 2 (April 1977), pp. 194–220; Robert Morris, "Letter to Alexander Hamilton, 23 May 1797," FA.

225 **When Philip Schuyler:** Philip Schuyler, "Letter to John Barker Church, 13 June 1796," University of Virginia.

226 **"If he were":** Robert Morris, "Letter to Alexander Hamilton, 1 November 1797," FA.

226 **John kept his cards:** Ryan K. Smith, *Robert Morris's Folly* (New Haven, CT: Yale University Press, 2014).

226 **"My good Mrs. Church":** Marguerite de Corny, "Letter to Thomas Jefferson, 19 May 1801," FA.

226 **All one critic:** Walter Rutherfurd, "Letter to John Rutherfurd, 4 January 1798," in *Family Records and Events*, ed. Livingston Rutherfurd (New York: De Vinne Press, 1894).

227 **So he partnered:** *Delafield v. Colden*, 1828. Reports of Cases Argued and Determined in the Court of Chancery.

227 **"A negro boy":** James Hardie, *Account of the Malignant Fever, Lately Prevalent in the City of New-York* (1799).

228 **"His time hangs":** Alexander Hamilton, "Letter to Oliver Wolcott, Jr., [2 June 1798]," FA.

228 **Another ship:** *Delafield v. Colden*, 1828. Reports of Cases Argued and Determined in the Court of Chancery, p. 140.

228 **John and Alexander had known:** Nancy Isenberg, *Fallen Founder: The Life of Aaron Burr* (New York: Viking, 2007).

229 **Then, at a dinner:** *Political Correspondence and Public Papers of Aaron Burr*, ed. Mary-Jo Kline and Joanne Wood Ryan (Princeton, NJ: Princeton University Press, 1983), pp. 407–10.

229 **As the challenged:** Merrill Lindsay, "Pistols Shed Light on Famed Duel," *Smithsonian Magazine* (March 1976).

230 **John's pistol ball:** "[John B. Church; Col. Burr; Mr. Hammond]," *Daily Advertiser* (New York) XIV, no. 4545, September 4, 1799, p. 2; *Spectator* (New York) II, no. 203 (September 4, 1799), p. 3.

230 **As Thomas Jefferson had put it:** Thomas Jefferson, "Letter to Angelica Church, 24 May 1797," UVAL.

231 **Alexander Hamilton and Thomas Jefferson:** Jan Lewis, "Those Scenes for Which Alone My Heart was Made: Affection and Politics in the Age of Jefferson and Hamilton," in *An Emotional History of the United States*, eds. Stearns and Lewis (New York, 1998),

231 **"Your letter":** Thomas Jefferson, "Letter to Angelica Church, 7 June 1793," FA.

231 **Secretary of the Treasury Alexander Hamilton:** Alexander Hamilton, "Letter to Angelica Church, 27 December 1793," FA.

231 **"Do you know her?":** Josephine du Pont, "Letter to Margaret Manigault, 22 February 1800," Hagley Library (Wilmington, DE) and in Betty-Bright P. Low, "Of Muslins and Merveilleuses: Excerpts from the Letters of Josephine du Pont and Margaret Manigault," *Winterthur Portfolio* 9 (1974).

231 **Not yet thirty:** "Josephine du Pont, "Letter to Margaret Manigault, 18 May 1800," in Ibid.

232 **"What I like":** "Josephine du Pont, "Letter to Margaret Manigault, 30 November 1800," in Ibid.

232 **Despite her poor English:** Ibid.

Chapter 24: Mother/Country

233 **When Angelica's firstborn son:** "For the *Bee*," *Bee* (New London, CT), 8 May 1799.

233 **Angelica had dined:** Angelica Church, "Letter to Elizabeth Hamilton, n.d. [1799]," Hamilton Papers, LOC.

234 **Throughout the 1790s:** Rosemarie Zagarri, *Revolutionary Backlash* (Philadelphia: University of Pennsylvania Press, 2008).

234 **Without a vote:** Linda Kerber, "The Republican Mother: Women and the Enlightenment—An American Perspective," *American Quarterly* 28 (1976); Linda Kerber, *Women of the Republic: Intellect & Ideology in Revolutionary America* (Chapel Hill: Omohundro Institute of Early American History and Culture and University of North Carolina Press, 1980), pp. 269–88.

235 **General Hamilton's "favorable":** Alexander Hamilton, "Letter to James McHenry, 28 July 1798," FA.

235 **Sixteen-year-old Phil:** Ron Chernow, *Hamilton* (New York: Penguin, 2004), p. 651.

235 **Only George Washington:** George Washington, "Letter to Angelica Church, 4 December 1798," Angelica Church Papers, UVAL.

236 **"The conjuror":** Peter August Jay, "Letter to Anne Jay, 14 February 1799," Columbia University Library, New York.

237 **"I am as worried":** Josephine du Pont, "Letter to Margaret Manigault, 23 October 1800," in Betty-Bright P. Low.

237 **"I know too":** [Chevalier de] Colbert-Maulévrier, "Letter to Alexander Hamilton, 7 May 1800," LOC in French, trans. in *The Intimate Life of Alexander Hamilton* (1800).

237 **They had also heard:** Robert C. Alberts, *The Golden Voyage: The Life and Times of William Bingham* (Boston: Houghton Mifflin, 1969), pp. 371–77.

237 **Josephine du Pont confided:** Josephine du Pont, "Letter to Margaret Manigault, 26 April 1800," Hagley Library (Wilmington, DE), and in Betty-Bright P. Low.

238 **Mourning ensued:** Josephine du Pont, "Letter to Margaret Manigault, 20 December 1800," Hagley Library, and in Betty-Bright P. Low.

238 **Kitty Church was elated:** Catharine Church, "Letter to Thomas Jefferson, 23 February 1801," FA.

238 **President Jefferson and Vice President Burr:** Thomas Jefferson, "Letter to Catharine Church, 27 March 1801," FA.

239 **Of her siblings:** Alexander Hamilton, "Letter to Elizabeth Hamilton, 10 March 1801," FA.

239 **"Viewing all that":** Alexander Hamilton, "Letter to Elizabeth Hamilton, 16 March 1801," FA.

239 **Two months after the election:** "Reports of Cases Argued and Adjudged in the Supreme Court of the United States, February 1804–February 1805" (United States Supreme Court, William Cranch, Chief Judge, 1806).

240 **"Philip Hamilton":** Elizabeth De Hart Bleecker, "Diary," NYPL.

241 **By express, she wrote:** Angelica Church, "Letter to Rensselaer Schuyler, 24 November 1801," NYPL.

241 **Philip Schuyler wrote to advise:** Philip Schuyler, "Letter to Elizabeth Hamilton, 19 February 1802," LOC.

241 **Angelica Church wrote to President:** Angelica Church, "Letter to Thomas Jefferson, 27 April 1802," LOC.

242 **Angelica was among those:** This presumption is based on Angelica Church's and especially Kitty Cruger's future friendship with Pierre Toussaint. Hannah Farnham Lee, *Memoir of Pierre Toussaint, Born a Slave in St. Domingo* (Crosby, Nichols, and Co., 1854), pp. 60–66.

243 **The first two United States:** *Heads of Families at the First Census of the United States Taken in the Year 1790,* US Bureau of the Census, 1907; "Return of the Whole Number of Persons within the Several Districts of the United States," U.S. House of Representatives, 1800.

244 **Alexander wrote to his wife:** Alexander Hamilton, "Letter to Elizabeth Hamilton, 13 March 1803," FA.

Chapter 25: Purchase, 1802–1804

245 **From a distance, he had idolized:** Don Gerlach, *Proud Patriot: Philip Schuyler and the War of Independence* (Syracuse, NY: Syracuse University Press, 1987), p. 518.

246 **Phil rode west:** Barbara A. Chernow, "Robert Morris: Genesee Land Speculator," *New York History* 58, no. 2 (April 1977), pp. 194–220.

246 **After purchasing:** "Philip Church's Career," *New York Times,* June 23, 1895.

247 **By the time he returned:** Victor du Pont, "Letter to Josephine du Pont, 12 January 1806," Hagley Library, Wilmington, DE.

247 **"Your knowledge":** Robert R. Livingston, "Letter to Angelica Church, 27 February 1802," NYHS.

248 **"Alas what pain":** Ibid.

248 **"Let me hear":** Ibid.

249 **When Victor and Josephine:** Catharine Church, "Letter to Thomas Jefferson, 9 February 1802," FA.

249 **Shocked by this development:** Thomas Jefferson, "Letter to Robert R. Livingston, 18 April 1802," FA.

250 **"I wish you":** Thomas Jefferson, "Letter to Pierre Samuel du Pont de Nemours, 25 April 1802," FA.

250 **"If it is surely war":** Pierre Samuel du Pont de Nemours, "Letter to Thomas Jefferson, 12 May 1802," FA.

251 **Of course, Charles-Maurice:** Angelica Church, "Letter to Philip Church, 7 June 1804," NYHS.

251 **Developing the land:** Philip Church, "Letter to John Barker Church, 26 June 1804," Belvidere.

251 **He had hoped to build:** Philip Church, "Letter to Philip Schuyler, 26 June 1804," NYPL.

252 **"I [went] to":** Josephine du Pont, "Letter to Margaret Manigault, 12 December 1803," Hagley Library, Wilmington, DE.

252 **"Jerome Buonaparte":** Angelica Church, "Letter to Philip Church, 7 June 1804," NYHS.

252 **"Bonaparte dips":** Ibid.

Chapter 26: Hair Triggers, 1804

253 **"Born, as I":** Thomas Jefferson, "Letter to Marguerite de Corny, 23 April 1802," FA.

254 **"The animosity":** Philip Schuyler, "Letter to Elizabeth Hamilton, 16 April 1804," LOC.

254 **One handbill:** Charles D. Cooper, *Evening Post*, 25 April 1804.

254 **Alexander Hamilton feared:** "Speech at a Meeting of Federalists in Albany," 10 February 1804, FA.

254 **John wrote to the newspapers:** *Morning Chronicle* (New York), 26 April 1804.

255 **Now nineteen:** James Kent, *Memoirs and Letters of James Kent* (Boston: Little, Brown, 1898), p. 143.

255 **Her parents disapproved:** Aaron Burr, "Letter to Theodosia Burr Alston, 28 March 1804," in *Memoirs of Aaron Burr*, ed. Matthew L. Davis (New York: Harper & Bros, 1836).

255 **"The breakfast":** Angelica Church, "Letter to Philip Church, 14 June 1804," NYHS.

256 **The day following:** "Statement on Impending Duel with Aaron Burr," [28 June-10 July 1804], FA.

256 **On the Fourth of July:** John Trumbull, *Autobiography, Reminiscences and Letters of John Trumbull* (New York: Wiley and Putnam, 1841), p. 244.

257 **All John could do:** Merrill Lindsay, "Pistols Shed Light on Famed Duel," *Smithsonian Magazine* (1976); *Evening Post* (New York), 19 July 1804.

257 **"I have the painful":** Angelica Church, "Letter to Philip Jeremiah Schuyler, 11 July 1784." NYPL.

258 **When Gouverneur:** Gouverneur Morris, "12 July 1804," in *The Diaries of Gouverneur Morris: Digital Edition*, eds. Melanie Randolph Miller and Hendrina Krol (Charlottesville: University of Virginia Press/Rotunda, 2015).

258 **Angelica wrote to the family:** Angelica Church, "Letter to Philip Jeremiah Schuyler, 11 July 1784." NYPL.

258 **The funeral procession:** "The Funeral," *Evening Post* (New York), 14 July 1804.

259 **"Fail not my":** Philip Schuyler, "Letter to Angelica Church."

259 **A platform:** Gouverneur Morris, "14 July 1804," in *The Diaries of Gouverneur Morris: Digital Edition*, eds. Melanie Randolph Miller and Hendrina Krol (Charlottesville: University of Virginia Press/Rotunda, 2015).

260 **By December:** *Albany County Book of Manumissions*, p. 34.

Chapter 27: "The Country of Angelica"

261 **Angelica Church's grief:** Angelica Church, "Letter to Philip Church, 18 August 1805," NYHS.

261 **As to visiting:** Angelica Church, "Letter to Philip Church, 30 August 1805," NYHS.

261 **Philip Church was relieved:** Philip Church, "Letter to Angelica Church, 25 July 1804," Private Collection.

262 **"When my friends":** Angelica Church, "Letter to Thomas Jefferson, 17 February 1793," LOC.

262 **The Adamses, now retired:** John Adams, "Letter to Benjamin Rush, 25 February 1808," FA.

262 **And their son, John Quincy:** *Church v. Hubbart*, in *Reports of Cases Argued and Adjudged in the Supreme Court of the United States, February 1804 and February 1805* (United States Supreme Court, 1806), pp. 187-236.

263 **She could visit Maria:** Carol Burnell, *Divided Affections: The Extraordinary Life of Maria Cosway* (UK: Column House, 2007), p. 350.

263 **"Why don't you":** Gilbert du Motier Lafayette, "Letter to Angelica Church, 14 May 1805," UVAL.

264 **"You are so far beyond":** Marguerite de Corny to Thomas Jefferson, 25 April 1805," translated, FA.

264 **Thomas Jefferson referred:** Thomas Jefferson, "Letter to Benjamin Chambers, 28 December 1805," FA.

266 **Agents for the Church family:** Joseph McClure, "Letter to John Barker Church, 22 October 1804," Belvidere Collection.

266 **"For Settlement":** "Advertisement," *The Sun*, 8 April 1805.

266 **She had seen Paris:** Michael Richman, "George Hadfield: His Contribution to the Greek Revival in America," in *Journal of the Society of Architectural Historians* 33:3 (October 1974), pp. 225–43.

267 **She was, like everyone:** Don Gerlach, *Proud Patriot: Philip Schuyler and the War of Independence* (Syracuse, NY: Syracuse University Press, 1987), p. xiii.

267 **As for staff:** Irene A. Beale, *Genesee Valley Women 1743–1985* (Geneseo, NY: Chestnut Hill Press, 1985).

269 **Angelica recommended:** Angelica Church, "Letter to Philip Church, n.d.," NYHS.

269 **She was, once again:** Thomas Jefferson, "Letter to Angelica Church, 27 July 1788," FA.

269 **So it was Josephine:** Josephine du Pont, *Our Transplantation to America*, 1826, Hagley Library, Wilmington, DE.

269 **The Seneca from Caneadea:** Angelica Church Hart, "Speech Given to the Daughters of the American Revolution," 1905; "Philip Church's Career," *New York Times*, 23 June 1895.

269 **Angelica would die:** Elizabeth Sadler, "Letter to Josephine du Pont, 5 March 1814," Hagley Library, Wilmington, DE.

270 **She would never write:** E. Bunner, *History of Louisiana* (New York: Harper & Bros., 1842).

270 **In London, John Barker Church:** David R. Fisher, *The House of Commons 1790–1820*, ed. R. Thorne (London: Boydell & Brewer, 1986), p. 442.

270 **One month after his mother:** Margaret Manigault, "Letter to Josephine du Pont, 19 March 1814"; Josephine du Pont, "Letter to Margaret Manigault, 24 May 1814," Hagley Library, Wilmington, DE.

INDEX